War in the Persian Gulf Biographies

From Operation Desert Storm to Operation Iraqi Freedom

War in the Persian Gulf Biographies

From Operation Desert Storm to Operation Iraqi Freedom

LAURIE COLLIER
HILLSTROM

Julie Carnagie,
Project Editor

U·X·L
An imprint of Thomson Gale,
a part of The Thomson Corporation

THOMSON
GALE

Detroit • New York • San Francisco • San Diego • New Haven, Conn. • Waterville, Maine • London • Munich

THOMSON
GALE

War in the Persian Gulf Biographies: From Operation Desert Storm to Operation Iraqi Freedom

Laurie Collier Hillstrom

Project Editor
Julie L. Carnagie

Permissions
Margaret Chamerberlain

Imaging and Multimedia
Lezlie Light, Mike Logusz, Kelly A. Quin, Leitha Etheridge-Sims

Product Design
Pamela Galbreath

Composition
Evi Seoud

Manufacturing
Rita Wimberley

Library of Congress Control Number: 2004005308

Printed in the United States of America
10 9 8 7 6 5 4 3 2 1

ISBN 0-7876-6564-9

This title is also available as an e-book. ISBN 0-7876-9347-2
Contact your Gale sales representative for ordering information.

Contents

Reader's Guide

War in the Persian Gulf Biographies: From Operation Desert Storm to Operation Iraqi Freedom presents profiles of thirty men and women who participated in or were affected by the U.S.-led wars against Iraq that took place in 1991 and 2003. The volume includes a diverse mix of personalities from the United States, Iraq, and other countries that played key roles in the conflicts. *Biographies* features politicians, diplomats, military leaders, soldiers, journalists, and others involved in the wars.

Detailed biographies of major figures from the 1991 Persian Gulf War (such as George H. W. Bush, Saddam Hussein, Tariq Aziz, and H. Norman Schwarzkopf) and the 2003 Iraq War (such as George W. Bush, Donald Rumsfeld, and Tony Blair) are included. But *War in the Persian Gulf Biographies: From Operation Desert Storm to Operation Iraqi Freedom* also provides biographical information on lesser-known, but nonetheless important and fascinating, men and women from both conflicts. Examples include April Glaspie, the U.S. ambassador to Iraq who was accused of encouraging Saddam Hussein to invade Kuwait in 1990; Peter Arnett, the controversial journalist who broadcast the first air strikes of the 1991 war live from a Baghdad hotel; Michael Donnelly, an American fighter pilot who became a champion of veterans suffering from Gulf War syndrome; Jessica Lynch, a U.S. soldier who was captured during the 2003 Iraq War and later rescued by U.S. Special Operations forces; Mohammed Said al-Sahhaf, the Iraqi information minister known for using colorful insults and denying the presence of U.S. troops in Baghdad in 2003; and Ahmad Chalabi, an Iraqi opposition leader who became a member of the Iraq Governing Council following the fall of Saddam Hussein in April 2003.

Format

War in the Persian Gulf Biographies: From Operation Desert Storm to Operation Iraqi Freedom also features informative sidebars that contain brief biographies and interesting facts about the issues and events discussed in the main body of the text. More than sixty black-and-white photographs illustrate the work. In addition, *War in the Persian Gulf Biographies: From Operation Desert Storm to Operation Iraqi Freedom* contains a timeline of key events, a glossary, a "People to Know" section, sources for further reading, and a subject index.

War in the Persian Gulf Reference Library: From Operation Desert Storm to Operation Iraqi Freedom

War in the Persian Gulf Biographies: From Operation Desert Storm to Operation Iraqi Freedom is only one component of a three-volume War in the Persian Gulf Reference Library: From Operation Desert Storm to Operation Iraqi Freedom. The other two titles in this multivolume set are:

- *War in the Persian Gulf Almanac: From Operation Desert Storm to Operation Iraqi Freedom* presents a comprehensive overview of the 1991 and 2003 U.S.-led wars against Iraq. The volume's twelve chapters are arranged chronologically and cover all aspects of the two conflicts, from Iraq's 1990 invasion of Kuwait through the fall of Baghdad to U.S. forces in 2003. The *Almanac* begins by describing the history of the Middle East and Saddam Hussein's rise to power in Iraq and concludes by examining the complex issues involved in the transition to a democratic Iraqi government. More than sixty black-and-white photographs and maps help illustrate the text. Numerous sidebars highlight interesting individuals and facts. *War in the Persian Gulf Almanac: From Operation Desert Storm to Operation Iraqi Freedom* also includes a timeline of important events, a glossary, a "People to Know" section, research and activity ideas, sources for further reading, and an index.

- *War in the Persian Gulf Primary Sources: From Operation Desert Storm to Operation Iraqi Freedom* presents twelve full or excerpted documents related to the 1991 and 2003 U.S.-led wars against Iraq. These documents range from notable speeches that mark important points in the conflicts to personal diaries and letters that reflect the experiences of ordinary soldiers and civilians. The excerpts are arranged chronologically, beginning with Iraqi leader Saddam Hussein's decision to invade Kuwait in 1990 and ending with an Iraqi citizen's 2003 Internet diary describing conditions in Baghdad under U.S. occupation. Each excerpt has a glossary that runs alongside the reprinted document to identify unfamiliar terms and ideas contained within the material. *War in the Persian Gulf Primary Sources: From Operation Desert Storm to Operation Iraqi Freedom* also includes photographs, sidebars, a timeline of key events, a glossary, a "People to Know" section, and an index.

- A cumulative index of all three titles in War in the Persian Gulf Reference Library: From Operation Desert Storm to Operation Iraqi Freedom is also available.

Advisors

A note of appreciation is extended to the *War in the Persian Gulf Biographies: From Operation Desert Storm to Operation Iraqi Freedom* advisors who provided invaluable suggestions when the work was in its formative stages:

Erik D. France
Librarian
University of Liggett Upper School
Grosse Pointe Woods, Michigan

Ann West LaPrise
Junior High/Elementary Librarian
Huron School District
New Boston, Michigan

Angela Leeper
Educational Consultant
Wake Forest, North Carolina

Comments and Suggestions

We welcome your comments on *War in the Persian Gulf Biographies: From Operation Desert Storm to Operation Iraqi Freedom* and suggestions for other topics in history to consider. Please write: Editors, *War in the Persian Gulf Biographies: From Operation Desert Storm to Operation Iraqi Freedom,* U•X•L, 27500 Drake Road, Farmington Hills, MI 48331-3535; call toll-free 800-877-4253; fax to 248-699-8097; or send e-mail via http://www.gale.com.

Timeline of Events

1922	British High Commissioner Sir Percy Cox establishes the borders of Iraq and Kuwait.
1927	British explorers make the largest oil strike in the world to date at Kirkuk in northern Iraq.
1932	Iraq gains its independence from British colonial rule.
1937	Saddam Hussein is born in a village near Tikrit, Iraq.
1952	Hussein ibn Talal becomes the king of Jordan.
1961	Kuwait gains its independence from British colonial rule.
1968	The Baath Party takes control of the government of Iraq.
1977	Jabir al-Ahmad al-Jabir Sabah becomes emir (ruler) of Kuwait.
1979	Saddam Hussein becomes president of Iraq.
1979	The government of nearby Iran is overthrown by Islamic fundamentalists under the Ayatollah Khomeini.
1980	Iraq declares war against Iran.

1982 King Fahd becomes the ruler of Saudi Arabia.

1983 Iraq uses chemical weapons for the first time during the Iran-Iraq War.

1986 Yitzhak Shamir becomes prime minister of Israel.

1988 The Iran-Iraq War ends.

1988 Iraq uses chemical weapons against the Kurdish people of northern Iraq.

July 17, 1990 Hussein threatens to use force against Kuwait.

July 24, 1990 Tens of thousands of Iraqi troops begin gathering along the Kuwaiti border.

July 25, 1990 Hussein meets with April Glaspie, the U.S. ambassador to Iraq.

July 31, 1990 Iraqi and Kuwaiti officials meet in Jedda, Saudi Arabia, to discuss Iraq's concerns about border issues and oil prices.

August 2, 1990 Iraq invades Kuwait.

August 2, 1990 The United Nations (UN) Security Council passes Resolution 660, condemning Iraq's invasion of Kuwait.

August 6, 1990 The UN Security Council passes Resolution 661, imposing economic sanctions on Iraq.

August 6, 1990 Saudi Arabia agrees to allow American and other foreign troops into the country.

August 7, 1990 U.S. President George H. W. Bush begins sending American troops to Saudi Arabia for Operation Desert Shield.

August 8, 1990 Hussein announces the annexation of Kuwait by Iraq.

August 10, 1990 The UN Security Council passes Resolution 662, condemning Iraq's annexation of Kuwait.

August 15, 1990 Hussein makes peace with Iran by agreeing to all conditions of the 1988 cease-fire that ended the Iran-Iraq War.

August 18, 1990 Iraq announces that it plans to hold Westerners who had been in Iraq and Kuwait at the time of the invasion and use them as "human shields" at military targets.

September 1, 1990 Iraq begins releasing some Western women and children it had been holding hostage since the invasion.

September 9, 1990 U.S. President George H. W. Bush meets with Soviet President Mikhail Gorbachev at the Helsinki Summit; the two leaders reach agreement on a plan to deal with Iraq.

November 1, 1990 More than one million refugees have fled from Iraq and Kuwait since the invasion.

November 8, 1990 Bush announces the deployment of an additional two hundred thousand American troops to the Persian Gulf.

November 29, 1990 The UN Security Council passes Resolution 678, which establishes a deadline of January 15, 1991, for Iraq to withdraw from Kuwait and authorizes members to use force if Iraq fails to comply.

December 6, 1990 Iraq releases remaining Western hostages.

January 9, 1991 U.S. Secretary of State James Baker meets with Iraqi Foreign Minister Tariq Aziz in Geneva, Switzerland, but they fail to reach an agreement to avoid war.

January 12, 1991 The U.S. Congress authorizes the president to use force to liberate Kuwait.

January 15, 1991 Iraqi forces fail to withdraw from Kuwait by the UN deadline.

January 16, 1991 President Bush makes a televised speech announcing the start of the Persian Gulf War.

January 17, 1991 A U.S.-led coalition launches an air war against Iraq to begin Operation Desert Storm.

January 17, 1991 Journalist Peter Arnett broadcasts live reports of the bombing from Baghdad on the cable news channel (CNN).

January 18, 1991 Iraq begins firing Scud missiles at Israel.

January 20, 1991 U.S. patriot missiles successfully intercept Iraqi Scud missiles aimed at Dharan, Saudi Arabia.

January 20, 1991 U.S. Navy officer and prisoner of war Jeffrey Zaun is forced to appear on Iraqi television and make statements against the war.

January 21, 1991 CBS News correspondent Bob Simon and his three-man crew are taken prisoner by Iraqi soldiers just inside the border of Kuwait.

January 22, 1991 Iraqi soldiers begin setting fire to Kuwait's oil production facilities.

January 23, 1991 U.S. Army General Colin Powell announces that the coalition has achieved air superiority.

January 25, 1991 Iraqi forces release millions of gallons of oil into the Persian Gulf.

January 30, 1991 Iraqi forces capture the Saudi Arabian border town of Khafji.

January 31, 1991 Saudi Arabian troops backed by U.S. Marines reclaim Khafji after an intense battle.

February 13, 1991 U.S. laser-guided bombs destroy a bunker in Baghdad, killing more than one hundred Iraqi civilians.

February 15, 1991 Iraq offers to withdraw from Kuwait but coalition leaders find Iraq's conditions unacceptable and reject the offer.

February 18, 1991 Soviet President Gorbachev announces a new plan to end the war, but Bush rejects it because it does not meet all of the UN Security Council resolutions.

February 22, 1991 Bush sets a deadline of the following day for Iraqi troops to withdraw from Kuwait or face a ground war.

February 24, 1991 The U.S.-led coalition launches a ground war against Iraq.

February 26, 1991 An Iraqi Scud missile hits a U.S. Army camp in Dharan, Saudi Arabia, killing twenty-eight American soldiers.

February 27, 1991 Kuwait City is liberated by coalition forces.

February 27, 1991 U.S. General H. Norman Schwarzkopf describes coalition military strategy in Operation Desert

Storm in a televised press briefing.

February 27, 1991 U.S. Army flight surgeon Rhonda Cornum is captured by Iraqi forces after her search-and-rescue helicopter is shot down.

February 28, 1991 Bush declares victory over Iraq and orders a cease-fire.

February 28, 1991 U.S. Army Captain Samuel G. Putnam III describes his experiences during the ground war in a letter to his wife.

March 2, 1991 Shiite Muslims in southern Iraq and Kurds in northern Iraq stage rebellions against Hussein's rule; Hussein violently crushes the attempts to overthrow his government.

March 3, 1991 Iraq agrees to all allied terms for a permanent cease-fire.

March 14, 1991 Sheik Jaber al-Ahmad al-Sabah, the emir of Kuwait, returns to his country.

April 3, 1991 The United Nations passes Resolution 687, formally ending the Persian Gulf War.

April 15, 1991 The United Nations conducts the first international weapons inspections in Iraq.

November 1991 The last oil-well fires are extinguished in Kuwait.

1992 The United States establishes a "no-fly zone" in southern Iraq to protect the country's Shiite minority from an attack by the Iraqi air force.

1992 Ahmad Chalabi founds the Iraqi National Congress, a coalition of Iraqi opposition groups.

1993 Iraq refuses to cooperate with UN weapons inspectors, and the United States responds by firing cruise missiles at a suspected chemical weapons plant near Baghdad.

1993 Iraqi operatives attempt to assassinate former U.S. President Bush during his visit to Kuwait; the United States retaliates by destroying Iraqi intelligence headquarters with cruise missiles.

January 1993 Bill Clinton is inaugurated the fortieth president of the United States.

1994 Iraq moves troops toward the Kuwait border, but pulls back when the United States sends aircraft carriers to the Persian Gulf.

1995 The UN Security Council Resolution 986 allows Iraq to sell limited amounts of oil in international markets and use the proceeds to buy food.

1995 The Iraqi National Congress launches an unsuccessful coup against Hussein.

1995 Jacques Chirac becomes president of France.

1996 Iraqi troops capture Erbil, the capital of the Kurdish-controlled region of northern Iraq. The United States responds by expanding the "no-fly zone" to northern Iraq.

1997 The U.S. House of Representatives launches an investigation into the possible causes of the mysterious collection of ailments among Gulf War veterans known as Gulf War syndrome.

1997 Tony Blair becomes prime minister of Great Britain.

1998 Iraq stops cooperating with UN weapons inspectors, and inspectors leave Iraq.

1998 U.S. and British forces launch Operation Desert Fox, a bombing campaign aimed at destroying suspected weapons of mass destruction in Iraq.

1998 Retired U.S. Air Force fighter pilot Michael Donnelly publishes *Falcon's Cry: A Memoir,* about his experiences in the Persian Gulf War and his struggles with Gulf War syndrome.

1999 King Hussein of Jordan dies of cancer.

January 2001 George W. Bush is inaugurated the forty-first president of the United States.

September 11, 2001 The terrorist group Al Qaeda hijacks four commercial airliners and crashes two into the World Trade Center in New York City, one into the Pentagon near Washington, D.C., and a fourth thwarted attempt into an empty Pennsylvania field, killing more than three thousand people.

January 29, 2002 U.S. President George W. Bush makes his "axis of evil" speech, officially expanding the fight against terrorism to include nations that shelter terrorists or provide weapons, training, or financial support for their activities. Among the countries that he accuses of supporting terrorists are Iraq, Iran, and North Korea.

August 15, 2002 Brent Scowcroft, who served as U.S. national security advisor during the 1991 Persian Gulf War, publishes his editorial "Don't Attack Saddam," expressing his opposition to another war in Iraq.

September 12, 2002 Bush challenges the United Nations to enforce its resolutions against Iraq that ended the 1991 Persian Gulf War.

September 16, 2002 Iraq says it will allow UN inspections to resume "without conditions."

October 11, 2002 The U.S. Congress authorizes the use of military force against Iraq.

November 8, 2002 The UN Security Council passes Resolution 1441, which authorizes a new round of weapons inspections in Iraq and promises "serious consequences" if Hussein fails to comply.

November 18, 2002 Iraq allows UN weapons inspectors to return to the country after a four-year absence.

January 28, 2003 In his second State of the Union address, Bush cites British intelligence reports claiming that Iraq tried to acquire uranium from Africa to build nuclear weapons.

February 5, 2003 U.S. Secretary of State Colin Powell presents evidence of Iraqi weapons programs to the United Nations.

February 14, 2003 Head UN weapons inspector Hans Blix challenges Powell's evidence and praises Iraq's cooperation with inspections.

February 15, 2003 Large-scale antiwar protests take place in dozens of cities around the world.

February 24, 2003 The United States introduces a new UN resolution authorizing the use of military force to disarm Iraq, but France threatens to veto the resolution.

March 17, 2003 Bush withdraws the proposed UN resolution and gives Hussein and his two sons forty-eight hours to leave Iraq or face a U.S.-led invasion.

March 19, 2003 The United States launches air strikes against targets in Iraq to begin the 2003 Iraq War.

March 20, 2003 U.S. and British ground forces begin advancing into Iraq.

March 21, 2003 Coalition forces launch the "shock and awe" bombing campaign.

March 23, 2003 Members of the U.S. Army's 507th Maintenance Company are ambushed in the city of Nasiriyah.

March 23, 2003 Private First Class Jessica Lynch is among the American soldiers taken prisoner by Iraq.

April 1, 2003 U.S. Special Forces rescue Private Jessica Lynch from an Iraqi hospital in Nasiriyah.

April 4, 2003 U.S. forces capture Saddam International Airport outside Baghdad.

April 5, 2003 U.S. tanks roll through the streets of Baghdad for the first time.

April 7, 2003 British forces take control of the city of Basra in southern Iraq.

April 8, 2003 Iraqi Information Minister Mohammed Said al-Sahhaf makes his final broadcast, declaring that there were no American tanks near Baghdad.

April 9, 2003 A statue of Hussein is toppled in central Baghdad's Firdos Square, symbolizing the fall of the Iraqi regime; looting and violence erupts in the city.

April 14, 2003 The Pentagon declares that major combat operations in Iraq have ended.

April 15, 2003 The first meeting to plan Iraq's future is held in the ancient city of Ur.

May 1, 2003 Bush makes his historic speech aboard the aircraft carrier USS *Abraham Lincoln,* announcing that major combat operations in Iraq are over and that the Iraqi people have been freed from Hussein's rule.

May 12, 2003 American diplomat L. Paul Bremer III arrives in Baghdad to head the Coalition Provisional Authority, the U.S.-led civil administration in charge of Iraq's reconstruction.

May 22, 2003 The UN Security Council passes Resolution 1483, formally recognizing the United States and Great Britain as "occupying powers" in Iraq.

July 6, 2003 Former U.S. Diplomat Joseph Wilson accuses the Bush administration of exaggerating the threat posed by Iraq's alleged weapons programs.

July 13, 2003 The Iraq Governing Council is formed as the first interim government of the new Iraq; it consists of twenty-five prominent Iraqis from diverse ethnic and religious backgrounds.

July 22, 2003 Hussein's two sons, Uday and Qusay, are killed in a firefight with U.S. troops in Mosul.

August 7, 2003 A car bomb explodes outside the Jordanian embassy in Baghdad, marking the first terrorist attack following the fall of Saddam Hussein.

August 19, 2003 A truck bomb explodes outside the UN headquarters in Baghdad, killing twenty-three people, including Sergio Vieira de Mello, the UN Special Representative to Iraq.

August 31, 2003 The number of U.S. troops killed in Iraq following the end of major combat operations surpasses the number killed during the war.

September 7, 2003 Bush asks the U.S. Congress to approve his request for $87 billion to pay for ongoing military and rebuilding efforts in Afghanistan and Iraq.

November 27, 2003 On Thanksgiving, Bush makes a surprise visit to U.S. military forces in Baghdad.

December 13, 2003 Former Iraqi leader Saddam Hussein is captured by U.S. forces.

Words to Know

A

Al Qaeda: A radical Islamic terrorist group responsible for the September 11, 2001, terrorist attacks against the United States.

Arab League: An alliance of twenty Arab nations and the Palestine Liberation Organization that promotes political, military, and economic cooperation in the Arab world.

Arabs: People of North Africa and the Middle East who speak the Arabic language.

B

Baath Party: A radical political movement founded in the 1940s with the goal of uniting the Arab world and creating one powerful Arab state.

C

Civilians: People not involved in fighting a war, including women and children.

Coalition: A temporary alliance of countries working toward a common goal.

Coalition Provisional Authority: The U.S.-run civil agency in charge of Iraq's 2003 postwar reconstruction.

Cold War: A period of political tension and military rivalry between the United States and the Soviet Union that began in the 1940s and ended with the collapse of the Soviet Union in 1989.

E

Economic sanctions: Trade restrictions intended to punish a country for breaking international law.

F

Fedayeen: A group of Iraqi paramilitary fighters that was intensely loyal to Iraqi President Saddam Hussein.

G

Geneva Conventions: A set of rules developed in Geneva, Switzerland, between 1864 and 1949 that are intended to guarantee the humane treatment of enemy soldiers and prisoners and the protection of civilians during wartime.

I

Insurgency: Organized resistance against an established government or occupying force.

Iran: A non-Arab nation in the Middle East that came under control of Shiite Muslim fundamentalists in 1979 and fought against Iraq during the Iran-Iraq War (1980–88).

Iraq Governing Council (IGC): The first transitional government in Iraq following the 2003 fall of Iraqi President Saddam Hussein; its membership included twenty-five prominent Iraqis whose political, ethnic, and religious backgrounds reflected the diversity of Iraq's population.

Israel: A Middle Eastern state created by the United Nations in 1948 as a homeland for all Jewish people. It is now the scene of major conflicts between the Israeli people and the Palestinians.

K

Kurds: A group of non-Arab Muslim people of northern Iraq who opposed Iraqi President Saddam Hussein's government.

M

Muslims: People who practice the religion of Islam.

O

Organization of Oil Exporting Countries (OPEC): An organization formed in the 1960s by the world's major oil-producing nations to coordinate policies and ensure stable oil prices in world markets.

Ottomans: A group of non-Arab Turkish invaders who conquered much of the Middle East around 1500 and ruled over a vast empire until 1920.

P

Palestine Liberation Organization (PLO): A political organization representing displaced Palestinians. The main goals of the PLO include reclaiming lost territory from Israel and establishing an independent Palestinian state.

Palestinians: An Arab people whose ancestors lived in the region that is now covered by the Jewish state of Israel. The creation of Israel in 1948 displaced hundreds of thousands of Palestinians and contributed to later conflicts in the Middle East.

R

Reconstruction: The process of rebuilding a country's infrastructure, government, and economy following a war.

Republican Guard: An elite, 100,000-man force that was the best-trained and best-equipped part of Iraq's army.

S

Shiite: A branch of the Islamic religion practiced by 15 percent of the world's Muslims, but 60 percent of Iraq's population.

Sunni: A branch of the Islamic religion practiced by 85 percent of the world's Muslims, but only 20 percent of Iraq's population.

T

Taliban: A radical Islamic group that took over the government of Afghanistan in 1996. The Taliban sheltered Osama bin Laden and Al Qaeda, the terrorists behind the attacks against the United States on September 11, 2001.

U

United Nations Security Council: The division of the United Nations charged with maintaining international peace and security. It consists of five permanent member nations (the United States, Russia, Great Britain, France, and China) and ten elected members that serve two-year terms.

People to Know

A

Madeleine Albright (1937–): U.S. ambassador to the United Nations (1993–97) and U.S. secretary of state (1997–2000) under President Bill Clinton.

Tariq Aziz (1936–): Iraqi foreign minister and lead negotiator during the 1991 Persian Gulf War who was captured by coalition forces during the 2003 Iraq War.

B

James Baker (1930–): U.S. secretary of state during the 1991 Persian Gulf War.

Ahmed Hassan al-Bakr (1914–1982): Older cousin of Saddam Hussein and Baath Party leader who served as the president of Iraq from 1968 to 1979.

Osama bin Laden (1957–): Saudi-born Muslim cleric who formed the Al Qaeda terrorist group and organized the September 11, 2001, attacks against the United States.

Tony Blair (1953–): Prime minister of Great Britain during the 2003 Iraq War.

L. Paul Bremer III (1941–): American diplomat and head of the Coalition Provisional Authority, the group charged with Iraq's reconstruction.

George H. W. Bush (1924–): President of the United States (1989–93) during the 1991 Persian Gulf War.

George W. Bush (1946–): President of the United States (2003–) during the 2003 Iraq War; son of former President George H. W. Bush.

C

Dick Cheney (1941–): Served as U.S. secretary of defense during the 1991 Persian Gulf War and vice president during the 2003 Iraq War.

Jacques Chirac (1932–): President of France who led international opposition to the 2003 Iraq War.

Bill Clinton (1946–) President of the United States from 1993 to 2001.

Sir Percy Cox (1864–1937): British government official who established the modern borders of Iraq, Saudi Arabia, and Kuwait in 1921.

H

Saddam Hussein (1937–): President of Iraq (1979–2003) during the 1991 Persian Gulf War who was removed from power during the 2003 Iraq War.

K

Ayatollah Khomeini (1900–1989): Islamic religious leader and outspoken opponent of Saddam Hussein who ruled Iran during the Iran-Iraq War (1980–88).

M

Ali Hassan al-Majid (1941–): Iraqi army general known as "Chemical Ali" for allegedly ordering the use of chemical weapons against the Kurdish people of northern Iraq. He was captured following the 2003 Iraq War.

P

Colin Powell (1937–): U.S. military general and chairman of the Joint Chiefs of Staff during the 1991 Persian Gulf War; also served as secretary of state during the 2003 Iraq War.

Q

Abdul Karim Qassem (1914–1963): Military ruler of Iraq from 1958 to 1963, when he was assassinated by members of the Baath Party.

R

Donald Rumsfeld (1932–): U.S. secretary of defense who played a leading role in deciding military strategy for the 2003 Iraq War.

S

Jabir al-Ahmad al-Sabah (1926–): Emir (ruler) of Kuwait during the 1991 Persian Gulf War.

Mohammed Said al-Sahhaf (1940–): Iraqi information minister during the 2003 Iraq War. He became known as "Baghdad Bob" and "Comical Ali" due to his defiant and overly optimistic statements to the media.

H. Norman Schwarzkopf (1934–): U.S. Army general and commander of allied forces during Operation Desert Storm.

T

Margaret Thatcher (1925–): Prime Minister of Great Britain during the 1990 Iraqi invasion of Kuwait.

Christiane Amanpour

Born 1958
London, England

War correspondent who first came to public attention during the Persian Gulf War

As the London-based chief international correspondent for CNN, Christiane Amanpour is one of the best-known and most-respected journalists in the world. She first came to public attention during the 1991 Persian Gulf War, when she reported on all aspects of the conflict from inside Iraq and Saudi Arabia. Amanpour went on to even greater fame after the war, largely on the strength of her award-winning coverage of the ethnic strife in the former Yugoslavian republic of Bosnia.

"I remember I wanted to have a reason to be in the middle of things, with all the movers and shakers. I wanted to be a foreign correspondent."

Christiane Amanpour in People *magazine.*

Chooses a career in journalism

Christiane Amanpour was born in London, England, in 1958. She was the eldest daughter of Mohamed Amanpour, an Iranian airline executive, and his wife Patricia, a British citizen. The Amanpour family moved to Tehran, the capital of the Middle Eastern nation of Iran, when Christiane was a baby. She enjoyed a privileged upbringing in which she learned to speak Farsi (the main language spoken in the non-Arab nation of Iran), French, and English. Even as a child, Amanpour showed hints of the fearless nature that later

Christiane Amanpour.
AP/Wide World Photos.
Reproduced by permission.

1

helped make her reputation as a war correspondent. "When I was five, I clambered onto a table to retrieve a balloon that had gotten stuck on the ceiling and pulled the entire chandelier down," she recalled in *Vogue* magazine.

At the age of eleven Amanpour was sent away to Holy Cross Convent School in England. She was homesick and miserable throughout her five years at the school. At sixteen she transferred to New Hall, the oldest girls' Catholic school in England. She dreamed of someday becoming a surgeon, but eventually realized that her grades were not good enough to get into medical school. She decided to pursue a career in journalism by chance. One of her sisters had been accepted to a London journalism school but changed her mind about attending. When the school refused to reimburse the tuition, Amanpour talked the admissions department into letting her attend in her sister's place.

Around this time, Iran underwent a revolution that forced Amanpour's family to leave Tehran. For many years Iran had been controlled by Mohammed Reza Pahlavi, the shah of Iran. The shah had been installed as the country's ruler by Western nations (the noncommunist countries of Western Europe and North America) following World War II (1939–45). Though the shah received support from Western governments, his government was unpopular in Iran. In 1979 it was overthrown by a group of Islamic fundamentalists (a movement stressing strict following of the basic principles of Islam) led by a Shiite Muslim religious leader named Ayatollah Ruhollah Khomeini. Khomeini established a new government based on strict Islamic principles and tried to eliminate all Western influence from the country.

Amanpour's family settled safely in London, but it was a difficult time because they lost all of their property and most of their money. Still, the experience reinforced Amanpour's determination to become a journalist and cover conflicts around the world. "My father lost everything. We had to start over," she told *People* magazine. "But I remember I wanted to have a reason to be in the middle of things, with all the movers and shakers. I wanted to be a foreign correspondent." In 1980 Amanpour's grandmother paid the tuition for her to attend the University of Rhode Island. She graduated with honors in 1983 with a bachelor's degree in journalism.

Becomes a reporter for CNN

Upon graduation Amanpour took a job with the Cable News Network (CNN), a relatively new television network that was dedicated to providing continuous twenty-four-hour news coverage. At that time, few people thought that the concept of twenty-four-hour news would succeed or believed that CNN could compete with the major TV networks. But Amanpour viewed the new network as a great opportunity to get a start in journalism.

Though she arrived at CNN's headquarters in Atlanta, Georgia, with only a bicycle and a few dollars, she soon impressed everyone with her hard work and ambition. Amanpour's duties were limited to answering phones, running errands, and typing scripts as she learned the news business. She even came into the office on weekends to practice writing scripts. In 1984 she paid her own way to the Democratic National Convention in exchange for a CNN press pass. Since the network was shorthanded, they ended up using her to cover the convention.

By 1986 Amanpour was promoted to producer-correspondent in CNN's New York bureau. In 1989 communist governments began falling from power in several countries in Eastern Europe. (Communism is a system of government where the nation's leaders are selected by a single political party that controls all aspects of society. Private ownership of property is eliminated and government directs all economic production. The goods produced and accumulated wealth are, in theory, shared relatively equally by all. All religious practices are banned.) Eager to cover such a major international news story, Amanpour accepted a position at CNN's offices in Frankfort, Germany. Immediately after she arrived the people of Romania launched a revolution to overthrow the country's longtime dictator Nicolae Ceausescu. Amanpour went to Bucharest, Romania, to cover the fall of the government and the effects of the revolution.

Makes a name for herself covering the Persian Gulf War

In August 1990 the Middle Eastern nation of Iraq invaded its smaller neighbor, Kuwait. Iraqi leader **Saddam Hussein** (see entry) argued that Iraq had a historical claim to Kuwait's ter-

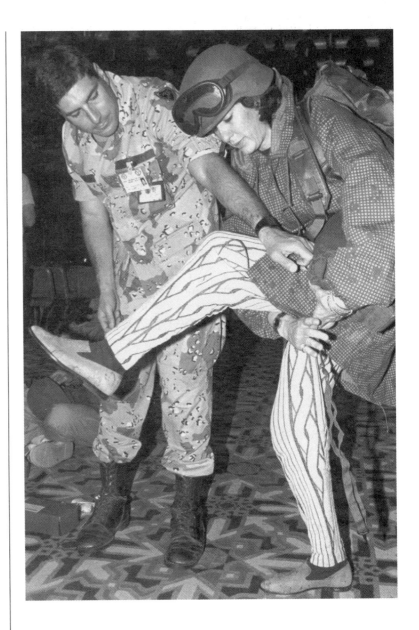

Reporter Christiane Amanpour being fitted for the Defense Department's civilian combat reporting pool before being sent to cover the Persian Gulf War. *Photograph by Bob Daugherty. AP/Wide World Photos. Reproduced by permission.*

ritory. He also wanted to control Kuwait's oil reserves and to gain access to Kuwait's port on the Persian Gulf. Countries around the world condemned the invasion and demanded that Iraqi leader Saddam Hussein immediately withdraw his troops from Kuwait. Many of these countries then began sending military forces to the Persian Gulf region as part of a U.S.-led coalition against Iraq. The United States sent more than four hundred thousand troops to the Persian Gulf over the next six months.

By this time Amanpour had demonstrated such a talent for reporting international conflicts that CNN agreed to send her to the Persian Gulf. She covered the invasion of Kuwait and the coalition military buildup in Saudi Arabia. She earned praise for her courage as well as her remarkable ability to deliver unscripted live reports of the action. In fact, she and her all-woman crew became known as the "three holy newsbabes."

In November 1990 the United Nations Security Council established a deadline of January 15, 1991, for Iraq to withdraw from Kuwait or face war. When Hussein failed to meet the deadline, the U.S.-led coalition launched a series of air strikes against military targets in Iraq. The air war went on for nearly six weeks and caused major damage to Iraq's military capability. Amanpour went to Baghdad to report on coalition bombing of the Iraqi capital.

On February 24 the coalition launched a dramatic ground assault to push the Iraqi forces out of Kuwait. Amanpour was there to cover the advance of American ground forces, which succeeded in liberating Kuwait from Iraqi occupation after only four days of fighting. After the war ended, Kurdish rebels in northern Iraq rose up against Hussein's government. Amanpour remained in Iraq to report on this rebellion, which was soon crushed by the Iraqi military. Hundreds of thousands of Kurds fled from the country to refugee camps in Turkey, and Amanpour also covered the Kurdish refugee crisis.

Wins awards for reporting the conflict in Bosnia

Amanpour's impressive coverage of the Persian Gulf War made her a household name among television news viewers around the world. In 1991 she used her clout to convince CNN to cover a rapidly escalating conflict between Serbs and Muslims in Bosnia, a republic of the former Yugoslavia. Yugoslavia was once made up of six republics—Serbia, Croatia, Bosnia-Herzegovina, Macedonia, Slovenia, and Montenegro. The people of Yugoslavia came from many different ethnic groups, and their strong feelings of ethnic loyalty led to many internal conflicts over the years. Yugoslavia began to come apart in 1991, when Slovenia declared its independence and the other republics followed in turn.

Arthur Kent: The Persian Gulf War's "Scud Stud"

Journalist Arthur Kent was born in 1954 in Medicine Hat, Alberta, Canada. The son of a newspaper editor, he began working as a reporter for the *Calgary Herald* in 1972. He soon switched to broadcast journalism, however, and worked his way through college as a reporter for CJOH-TV in Ottawa. Upon graduating in 1976, he became the Canadian Broadcasting Corporation's youngest news correspondent.

During the mid-1980s Kent spent several years covering the war in Afghanistan that pitted Afghan rebel groups against troops from the Soviet Union. Kent's coverage of this conflict came to the attention of Tom Brokaw, the anchor of *NBC News* in the United States. Brokaw arranged for Kent to be offered a job as a correspondent for NBC in 1988. Over the next two years Kent won Emmy Awards for his coverage of the overthrow of dictator Nicolae Ceausescu in Romania and of the student protests in Tiananmen Square in Beijing, China.

In January 1991 NBC sent Kent to Saudi Arabia to cover the Persian Gulf War.

He was based in Dhahran, a city on the Persian Gulf that contained a major U.S. military base. Iraq fired a total of eighty-six Soviet-built Scud missiles during the war, forty-six at Saudi Arabia and the rest at Israel. Although many of the Scuds were intercepted by U.S. Patriot defense missiles, one hit a U.S. Army Reserve camp in Dhahran, killing twenty-eight American soldiers and wounding eighty more.

Kent reported on the Scud attacks against Saudi Arabia from the roof of the Dhahran International Hotel. His clean-cut good looks, perfect hair, dashing leather bomber jacket, and courageous reporting captivated millions of female television viewers around the world. He became an overnight sensation, and was known by the nickname "Scud Stud."

Throughout his seven weeks in Saudi Arabia, Kent received hundreds of faxes, letters, and packages from his admirers. His fan mail included poetry and marriage proposals. He was surprised and a little bit concerned about his sudden rise to stardom. "Two years ago I was a tramp on the

Bosnia became the site of terrible violence during this time. Ethnic Serbs, with the support of former Yugoslav President Slobodan Milosevic, began a systematic campaign of arrests, torture, and murder to eliminate the Muslims who formed the ethnic majority in Bosnia. Serb troops forced Muslims from their land and destroyed their property. The campaign to eliminate the Muslims from Bosnia became known as "ethnic cleansing."

fringes of NBC," Kent told Maria Wilhelm in *People*. "Now here I am, with 40 people backing me up, the subject of quite extraordinary and undue attention.... I'll pay for it down the line. Even within our own happy little community, there will be a backlash."

When the war ended, NBC tried to take advantage of Kent's popularity. He spent a week as a substitute cohost of the *Today Show*, but viewers and critics found him disappointingly dull in the role. The network then tried him out as a correspondent for its *Dateline* news magazine, but Kent clashed with the show's producers because he wanted to cover hard news stories. "They're doing lousy, sensational programs," he told Marjorie Rosen in *People*.

In August 1992 Kent was fired by NBC. The network said that his large ego made him impossible to work with. But Kent claimed that the problems stemmed from his demands to cover tough foreign assignments. He sued NBC for wrongful dismissal, and two years later he received an apology and large financial settlement from the network.

Kent was hired by CNN as a correspondent in 1996, but he lasted less than a year before being fired again. He then took some time off to write a book, *Risk and Redemption: Surviving the Network News Wars*. In addition to an autobiographical account of his own rocky career, the book provides a critical look at the declining standards of TV news.

In 1998 Kent returned to Iraq to produce the award-winning documentary *A Wedding in Basra* for PBS. In 2001 he went back to Afghanistan to produce another PBS documentary, *Afghanistan: Captives of the Warlords*, that also won several awards. The leather jacket he made famous during the Persian Gulf War later became part of an exhibit at the Newseum media museum near Washington, D.C.

Sources: "Arthur Kent." Newsmakers 1997. Reproduced in Biography Resource Center. Farmington Hills, MI: Gale Group, 2003; "Heroes of the War: Arthur Kent." People, Summer 1991; Kobel, Peter. "Whatever Happened to Arthur Kent?" Entertainment Weekly, January 23, 1998; Rosen, Marjorie. "Kent's State—He's Gone." People, September 7, 1992; Wilhelm, Maria. "With Fan Clubs Lifting Off Like Patriot Missiles, NBC's Arthur of Arabia Is the New Rising Star in the Gulf." People, February 18, 1991.

Amanpour's instincts told her that this conflict would be her generation's war. She convinced CNN to cover it before the American media showed much interest. "Other correspondents before me had World War II or Vietnam," she explained in *People*. "Well, this is my Vietnam." Many people credit Amanpour's passion for bringing the Bosnian crisis to the world's attention. She argued that a country that was recognized by the United Nations was being destroyed by its neighbors in violation of international law. She felt that the world community should be made aware of the situation and take action to stop it. Over the next several years Amanpour became strongly identified with the Bosnian conflict.

Amanpour faced significant danger during her time in Bosnia. In fact, she often gave reports while wearing a helmet and flak jacket, which is similar to a bulletproof vest. In 1992 her camera operator, Margaret Moth, was shot in the face by a Serbian sniper. Moth survived, but she required extensive surgery to rebuild her jaw. "What happened to Margaret made me realize how vulnerable we all are," Amanpour told *People*. "But it never made me have second thoughts about doing my job."

Another time, Amanpour was covering the war from Sarajevo when her hotel was bombed. "I heard this awful whistling noise," she recalled in *People*. "It was a howitzer mortar shell, apparently mis-aimed. It landed in a room two doors down from mine—but it didn't explode. Otherwise, it would have been over for me." Despite the danger, Amanpour turned down several offers of network anchor positions in order to remain on the front lines of the conflict.

Amanpour was occasionally criticized for showing bias in her coverage of the Bosnian conflict. Believing that her coverage favored the Muslims, Serb forces sometimes spit on her or made threatening motions as if they were cutting her throat. Amanpour rejected the idea that she showed favoritism in her coverage, and said that she only reported what she saw. At the same time, however, she admitted in the *New York Times* that "there are some situations one simply cannot be neutral about, because when you are neutral you are an accomplice. Objectivity doesn't mean treating all sides equally. It means giving each side a hearing." Amanpour earned more than a dozen prestigious awards for her work in Bosnia, including an Emmy Award in the News and Documentary category, a George Foster Peabody Award, a George Polk Memorial Award, and a Courage in Journalism Award.

Named CNN's chief international correspondent

By the mid-1990s Amanpour was widely viewed as one of the most prominent war correspondents of her generation. Her reputation for fearlessly reporting from the world's hot spots led to the slogan "Where there's war, there's Amanpour." She also was known for her husky, exotic voice and precise manner of speaking in a British accent. Over the years, Amanpour gained so much power that she no longer received assignments, but instead made her own decisions about what to cover. In addition to her work in Bosnia, Amanpour reported on conflicts in Somalia, Haiti, Rwanda, and Afghanistan.

Amanpour's reputation helped her get exclusive interviews with a number of world leaders over the years. She was the last journalist to interview King Hussein of Jordan before his death in 1999, for example, and the first to interview the country's new ruler, King Abdullah. She also interviewed former Russian leader Mikhail Gorbachev that year, on the tenth anniversary of the fall of communism. In 2002 she interviewed **Yasir Arafat** (see entry), leader of the Palestine Liberation Organization, while his headquarters was being blockaded by the Israeli army.

Amanpour was pursued by all the major television networks when her contract with CNN expired in 1994. She chose to remain with CNN and became the network's chief international correspondent. In 1996 she signed an unprecedented deal in which CNN maintained first rights to her services for breaking news stories, but she also was allowed to contribute five or six reports a year to the CBS news program "60 Minutes." The deal made her one of the highest paid people in the TV news business.

In 1998 Amanpour married James Rubin, who worked as a U.S. State Department spokesman and was a close advisor to Secretary of State Madeleine Albright. In 2000 she gave birth to a son, Darius John Rubin. Although she was determined to continue her career after starting a family, she did begin taking greater precautions to ensure her safety.

Where to Learn More

"Anchors and Reporters: Christiane Amanpour." *CNN.com.* Available online at http://edition.cnn.com/CNN/anchors_reporters/amanpour.christiane.html (accessed March 23, 2004).

Arias, Ron. "CNN's Woman at Front." *People,* December 20, 1993.

"Christiane Amanpour." *Biography Today.* Detroit, MI: Omnigraphics, 2002.

"Christiane Amanpour." *Newsmakers 1997*. Reproduced in Biography Resource Center. Farmington Hills, MI: Gale Group, 2003.

Jolis, Alan. "Eyewitness: From Sarajevo to Somalia, CNN's Christiane Amanpour Covers the World"s Prime Trouble Spots." *Vogue,* March 1994.

Yasir Arafat

Born October 29, 1929
Cairo, Egypt

Palestine Liberation Organization leader
who supported Iraq during the 1991
Persian Gulf War

Yasir Arafat, the longtime leader of the Palestine Liberation Organization (PLO), is one of the most controversial political figures in the world. Supporters view him as a hero in the struggle to create an independent Palestinian state and a statesman in the efforts to forge a lasting peace in the Middle East. But critics view him as a terrorist who is determined to destroy the Jewish state of Israel.

When Iraq invaded Kuwait in 1990, Arafat and the PLO supported Iraq's actions. As a proponent of Palestinian statehood and a bitter enemy of Israel, Iraqi leader Saddam Hussein was a popular figure among the Palestinians. But Arafat's decision to support Iraq turned out to be a diplomatic disaster for the PLO. It cost the PLO a great deal of world sympathy as well as financial support from the wealthy Arab nations of the Persian Gulf region.

Supports the rights of the Palestinians

Yasir Arafat was born Mohammed Abdel-Raouf Arafat al-Qudwa al-Husseini on October 29, 1929, in Cairo, Egypt.

"We can only be in the camp hostile to Israel and its imperialist allies, who have mobilized all their sophisticated war machine not to come to anybody's aid but to protect their own interests."

Yasir Arafat in Arafat and the Palestine Liberation Organization.

Yasir Arafat. *Photograph by Ron Sachs. Getty Images. Reproduced by permission.*

11

He acquired the nickname Yasser, which means "easygoing," while he was in high school. Arafat's parents were Palestinians. They were descended from an Arab people that had lived in the region of the Middle East known as Palestine, located between the Jordan River and the Mediterranean Sea, since ancient times.

During Arafat's youth, Palestine was controlled by British authorities. The British were supposed to supervise the formation of a Jewish homeland (an area set aside to be a state for a people of a particular racial, cultural, or national origin) in the region. But the British moved slowly due to opposition to the plan from the surrounding Arab nations, which opposed Jewish immigration to the region. Thousands of European Jews made their way to Palestine anyway, but they were met with hostility from Arabs. Before long, the Arabs and Jews were fighting against each other and against the British authorities for control of Palestine.

Arafat spent his youth in Cairo and Jerusalem, a historic city in the heart of Palestine. During his teen years he became involved in a Palestinian nationalist group, which supported the idea of turning Palestine into an Arab state. In 1947, the year that Arafat graduated from high school, the United Nations (UN) passed a resolution that divided Palestine into Arab and Jewish sectors. This plan was put into effect the following year over the strong objections of the surrounding Arab states. Immediately afterward, leaders of the Jewish part of Palestine announced the creation of an independent state called Israel, which would provide a homeland for the world's Jews.

The newly created state of Israel covered two-thirds of Palestine (the remaining one-third consisted of the West Bank in Jordan and the Gaza Strip in Egypt). When Israel took over this territory, about five hundred thousand Palestinians fled and became refugees in neighboring countries. The creation of Israel and displacement of the Palestinians angered many Arabs. In fact, five Arab countries—Egypt, Syria, Jordan, Lebanon, and Iraq—went to war against Israel shortly after it was formed. The Arab-Israeli War lasted for nine months before Israel defeated the Arab armies in early 1949.

Becomes chairman of the Palestine Liberation Organization (PLO)

Upon the creation of Israel, Arafat went back to Cairo, where he studied engineering at Cairo University. He founded a Palestinian student union that grew rapidly over the next several years. By the late 1950s Arafat's student group became one of the main parts of the Palestinian nationalist movement called Fatah. Fatah activists argued that the Palestinians should try to regain their own country through their own efforts, rather than by working with Arab nations. In 1965 Fatah launched an armed struggle against Israel using tactics of guerilla warfare (an unconventional fighting style that uses methods like ambushes, booby traps, and sniper attacks). In the meantime, the Arab countries of the Middle East created their own group to deal with the question of Palestinian statehood, called the Palestine Liberation Organization (PLO).

In 1967 the tension between Israel and its Arab neighbors once again erupted into war. Israel quickly prevailed in this conflict, which became known as the Six-Day War. Israeli forces crushed the combined armies of Egypt, Syria, and Jordan, and took control over the remainder of ancient Palestine as well as large areas of enemy territory. Israel captured the Sinai Peninsula and Gaza Strip from Egypt, the strategic Golan Heights from Syria, and the West Bank from Jordan. Israel's military occupation of these Arab territories displaced thousands more Palestinians and forced thousands of others to live under Israeli military rule.

The Arab countries' humiliating defeat in the Six-Day War attracted many new followers to the Fatah movement. In 1969 Fatah merged with the PLO and Arafat was elected chairman of the combined organization, which retained the PLO name. The PLO established guerilla camps in Jordan and Lebanon and stepped up its attacks against Israel. One of the most publicized attacks came at the 1972 Olympic Games in Munich, Germany, when Palestinian terrorists kidnapped and murdered eleven Israeli athletes.

Moves away from his terrorist image

In 1974 the United States government took an active role in seeking a negotiated settlement of the conflict between Israel and the Palestinians. The PLO participated in the negotiations with the goal of creating an independent Palestinian state in the West Bank and Gaza Strip, the areas of historic Palestine that Israel had occupied since 1967. Arafat represented the PLO before the United Nations. In a famous gesture, he showed up carrying symbols of both war and peace. "I have come bearing an olive branch and a freedom fighter's gun," he explained. "Do not let the olive branch fall from my hand."

The 1974 negotiations broke down when the PLO failed to make it clear that their desired Palestinian state could exist alongside Israel. The PLO had long refused to recognize Israel's right to exist, and its terrorist activities were aimed at destroying the Jewish state. As a result, Israel refused to deal with the PLO. In 1975 the U.S. government proclaimed that it would no longer negotiate with the PLO until the group recognized Israel's right to exist.

The violent clashes between Palestinians and Israelis over the occupied territories continued into the 1980s. In 1982 Israel invaded Lebanon in order to destroy PLO guerilla camps there. The Israeli army managed to trap Arafat and his forces in Beirut, but U.S. leaders negotiated to evacuate the PLO from the Lebanese capital. In 1987 Palestinians living in the West Bank and Gaza launched a series of uprisings against Israeli occupation of these lands. The uprisings, which included mass demonstrations as well as violence against Israeli troops and civilians, became known as the Intifada, which means "throwing off" in Arabic. The Israeli government reacted strongly against the Intifada uprisings. Israeli troops were sent into the occupied territories and authorized to use force to put down the rebellions.

Israel's hard-line response to the Intifada aroused new sympathy for the Palestinians around the world. International news broadcasts showed Palestinian boys being killed for throwing rocks at heavily armed Israeli soldiers. Arafat emerged as a statesman during this time by leading the PLO toward a political rather than military solution. In 1988 he stunned many people by accepting a UN resolution that called upon the Palestinians to renounce terrorism and recognize Israel's right to exist. It appeared likely that the U.S. government would recognize the PLO and allow Arafat to take part in Middle East peace talks.

Supports Iraq during the Persian Gulf War

But the world's view of Arafat and the PLO changed dramatically in 1990. On August 2, 1990, Iraqi leader **Saddam Hussein** (see entry) had ordered his military forces to invade the neighboring country of Kuwait. Hussein argued that Iraq had a historical claim to Kuwait's territory. He also wanted to control Kuwait's oil reserves and to gain access to Kuwait's port on the Persian Gulf. Countries around the world condemned the invasion and demanded that Hussein withdraw his troops from Kuwait immediately. Many of these countries began sending military forces to Saudi Arabia as part of a U.S.-led coalition against Iraq. Arafat, on the other hand, expressed his support for Iraq's actions. International television news broadcasts showed the PLO leader in the Iraqi capital of Baghdad, grinning and embracing Hussein.

A few days after the Iraqi invasion of Kuwait, representatives of the Arab nations held an emergency meeting. They voted 12 to 3 in favor of a resolution condemning Iraq's actions. The twelve countries that voted in favor of the resolution sent military troops and equipment to assist the U.S.-led coalition. The PLO joined Jordan and Libya as the only parts of the Arab world that supported Iraq.

Many observers found it strange that Arafat and the PLO would support Iraq's invasion of Kuwait. After all, Kuwait provided millions of dollars of financial assistance to the PLO and was home to a large population of Palestinians. Others pointed out that Iraq's military takeover and occupation of another country was similar to what Arafat had dedicated his life to fighting against, Israel's takeover and occupation of Palestinian territory.

But Hussein had long been a popular figure among Palestinians. He was a strong supporter of Palestinian statehood and a bitter enemy of Israel. During the months leading up to the Persian Gulf War, Hussein repeatedly tried to link Iraq's withdrawal from Kuwait with Israel's withdrawal from the occupied territories. This stance made Hussein even more popular among the Palestinians.

The final factor in Arafat's decision to support Iraq was that the United States rushed to defend Kuwait and Saudi Arabia. Arafat resented the close ties between the United States and Israel, and he felt that American leaders were only

Palestinian leader Yasir Arafat meets with Iraqi President Saddam Hussein (right). Arafat supported Hussein during the Persian Gulf War. ©*Francoise de Mulder/Corbis. Reproduced by permission.*

trying to protect their oil interests in the Persian Gulf. "We can only be in the camp hostile to Israel and its imperialist allies, who have mobilized all their sophisticated war machine not to come to anybody's aid but to protect their own interests," he told the PLO news agency WAFA, as quoted in *Arafat and the Palestine Liberation Organization.*

After six months of negotiations failed to find a peaceful resolution to the crisis, the U.S.-led coalition launched a series of air strikes at Iraq on January 17, 1991. The air strikes lasted for six weeks and destroyed much of Iraq's military capability. On February 24, coalition forces launched a dramatic ground assault to push Hussein's army out of Kuwait. The ground war met with little Iraqi resistance and succeeded in liberating Kuwait after only four days of fighting.

Following Iraq's lopsided defeat in the Persian Gulf War, it became clear that Arafat's decision to support Hussein was a diplomatic disaster for the PLO. Although the decision was popular among Palestinians, it drew a firestorm of criticism from around the world. The wealthy Arab states of the Persian Gulf were furious and withdrew their financial support from the PLO. In addition, thousands of Palestinians who lived and worked in these countries were forced to leave. During the war, when Iraq fired Scud missiles at cities in Israel, international news reports showed Palestinians in the occupied territories cheering and waving Iraqi flags. The Palestinians thus lost any sympathy they had gained during the Intifada. By the time the war ended, many experts claimed that Arafat's support of Iraq had undone many of the PLO's gains of the previous ten years.

Continues efforts to establish a Palestinian State

In the fall of 1991 representatives of Israel and its Arab neighbors gathered for peace talks in Madrid, Spain. Although the PLO was not formally invited to participate, Arafat helped choose the Palestinian delegation that attended the talks. The peace talks failed to produce an agreement, partly because of the uncompromising positions taken by the Israeli government. When Yitzhak Rabin became the new prime minister of Israel the following year, the two sides tried again.

In 1993 Arafat met with Rabin for secret negotiations in Oslo, Norway. They signed the Oslo Accord, which established Palestinian self-rule in the West Bank and Gaza Strip and mapped out future extensions of Palestinian independence. In 1994 Arafat went to Gaza to establish the first Palestinian government in the occupied territories. Later that year he shared the Nobel Peace Prize with Rabin and Israeli Foreign Minister Shimon Peres.

Arafat reacted with shock and grief when Rabin was assassinated by a Jewish extremist in 1995. "I lost my partner," Arafat said in *Time* magazine. "The man paid with his life for the peace of the brave." The following year, Arafat was elected president of the Palestinian Authority (the government of the occupied territories). When new Israeli Prime Minister Benjamin Netanyahu removed Israeli military forces from the occupied territories, Arafat removed the part of the Palestinian constitution that called for the destruction of Israel. The peace process broke down a short time later, however, when Israel began building Jewish settlements in Jerusalem. The Palestinians responded with a new round of violent attacks.

In 2000 Arafat and Israeli Prime Minister Ehud Barak met with U.S. President Bill Clinton in Camp David, Maryland. Arafat announced that the PLO planned to declare an independent Palestinian state by the end of the year regardless of the status of the peace talks with Israel. But Arafat postponed the declaration several times in an effort to facilitate negotiations. The peace talks broke down when violent clashes erupted between Israeli security forces and Palestinians in the occupied territories. Although Arafat asked the Palestinians to end violent attacks against Israelis, his words had little effect. In January 2001 Barak suspended the peace talks.

In July 2001 Ariel Sharon became prime minister of Israel. Sharon was an outspoken opponent of Arafat who had called the PLO leader a terrorist and a murderer. Palestinian extremists reacted to the election of Sharon with more attacks, including a series of suicide bombings against Israeli civilians. In December 2001 Sharon ordered Israeli troops to place Arafat under house arrest in his presidential compound in Ramallah. In September 2002 the Israeli army placed the compound under military siege (surrounded it and bombarded it with explosives) in retaliation for Palestinian suicide bombings. Israel lifted the siege after ten days in response to international pressure, but it left Arafat's compound in ruins.

By this time Arafat was facing increasing pressure from younger members of the PLO to reform the organization. Israeli officials refused to work with Arafat, and a growing number of Palestinians believed that there could be no further advancement in the peace process as long as Arafat was in charge. His opponents demanded that Arafat appoint a prime minister to govern the West Bank and Gaza. In early 2003 Arafat accepted the choice of Mahmoud Abbas as prime minister of the Palestinian Authority. Arafat remained president, but many of his duties were transferred to Abbas.

Arafat's shaky hold over the PLO helped convince him to remain silent when the United States went to war to remove Iraqi leader Saddam Hussein from power in 2003. Once this war ended, U.S. leaders seemed poised to make a major push toward resolving the Israeli-Palestinian conflict.

In fact, President **George W. Bush** (see entry) unveiled a "road map" for peace in the Middle East that included forming an independent Palestinian state by 2005. Some experts believe that American leaders need to settle the issue of Palestinian statehood, which fuels Arab anger toward the United States, in order to improve their chances of establishing a democratic government in Iraq.

But the peace process stalled once again in the fall of 2003. Some frustrated Israeli leaders blamed Arafat for failing to stop a series of violent attacks by Palestinian opposition groups. In fact, the Israeli government threatened to kill or exile Arafat in order to "remove this obstacle" to peace. Although the Bush administration stopped short of supporting Arafat, it did take steps to prevent Israel from harming him.

Where to Learn More

"Arafat Under Siege, Again." *Economist,* September 28, 2002.

Gaouette, Nicole. "Arafat Deal Paves Way for Peace Plan." *Christian Science Monitor,* April 25, 2003.

Gowers, Andrew, and Tony Walker. *Behind the Myth: Yasser Arafat and the Palestinian Revolution.* New York: Olive Branch Press, 1992.

Hart, Alan. *Arafat: Terrorist or Peacemaker.* London: Sidgwick and Jackson, 1984.

Kiernan, Thomas. *Arafat: The Man and the Myth.* New York: Norton, 1976.

MacLeod, Scott. "Interview with Arafat." *Time* Magazine, November 20, 1995.

Reische, Diana. *Arafat and the Palestine Liberation Organization.* New York: Franklin Watts, 1991.

Rubenstein, Danny. *The Mystery of Arafat.* South Royalton, VT: Steerforth Press, 1995.

Stetloff, Rebecca. *Arafat.* New York: Chelsea House, 1988.

"Triumphant from the Rubble." *Global Agenda,* September 30, 2002.

"Yasser Arafat." *Encyclopedia of World Biography,* 1998. Reproduced in *Biography Resource Center.* Farmington Hills, MI: Gale Group, 2003.

"Yasser Arafat." *Newsmakers 1997.* Reproduced in *Biography Resource Center.* Farmington Hills, MI: Gale Group, 2003.

Peter Arnett

Born November 13, 1934
Riverton, New Zealand

Controversial journalist who broadcast the first coalition air strikes of the 1991 Persian Gulf War live from a Baghdad hotel

J ournalist Peter Arnett has reported on more than a dozen wars during his long career. But he is probably best known for his dramatic live coverage of the first U.S. air strikes against Baghdad, Iraq, during the 1991 Persian Gulf War. Arnett and his colleagues Bernard Shaw and John Holliman, who became known as the "Boys of Baghdad," faced great personal risk in order to broadcast the start of the war live from their hotel room. Their reports on the first U.S. bombing raids aired on the Cable News Network (CNN) a full half-hour before American military leaders officially announced that the war had begun.

Arnett remained in Iraq throughout the 1991 war and provided controversial reports about the conflict's effect on the Iraqi people. He resumed his controversial role during the 2003 Iraq War, when he returned to Baghdad to report on the U.S.-led invasion. After criticizing the American war plan in an interview that appeared on Iraqi television, Arnett was fired from his job.

"I knew that interviewing Saddam Hussein in the middle of this war was going to be controversial."

Peter Arnett in Live from the Battlefield: From Vietnam to Baghdad—35 Years in the World's War Zones.

Peter Arnett. *Photograph by Charles Tasnadi. ©AP/Wide World Photos. Reproduced by permission.*

Adventurous young man becomes a journalist

Peter Gregg Arnett was born in Riverton, New Zealand, on November 13, 1934, the second of three sons born to Eric Lionel Arnett and Jane (Gregg) Arnett. Arnett spent his childhood in Bluff, a small town on the southern coast of New Zealand that had once been a home port for many whaling ships. Although few whales remained by the time Arnett was a boy, he often saw seals and penguins along the shore.

Arnett's parents placed a high value on education, so they sent their sons away to an exclusive private boarding school, the Waitaki Boys High School. Arnett earned his high school diploma, but he was expelled from the school for breaking its rules against dating before he completed his college-preparatory classes.

In the early 1950s Arnett embarked on a career as a journalist. He started out working as a local reporter for newspapers in New Zealand, including the *Southland Times* in Invercargill and the *Standard* in Wellington. "I covered my share of cat shows, backyard brush fires, minor sports events and lots of anniversaries and committee meetings of the most obscure organizations," he recalled in his memoir *Live from the Battlefield.*

In 1958 the adventurous young man traveled to Southeast Asia as a tourist. Arnett enjoyed the atmosphere so much that he ended up staying for several years. He found a job as an associate editor for *Bangkok World,* an English-language newspaper in Thailand. In 1961 he became a Southeast Asia correspondent for the Associated Press (AP), a wire service that sells stories to newspapers and magazines across the United States.

Wins Pulitzer Prize for Vietnam War coverage

In 1962 Arnett accepted an assignment to cover the Vietnam War. This conflict pitted the Communist nation of North Vietnam and its secret allies, South Vietnamese Communists known as the Viet Cong, against the U.S.-supported nation of South Vietnam. (Communists believe in a system of government where the nation's leaders are selected by a single political party that controls all aspects of society. Private ownership of property is eliminated and government directs all economic production. The goods produced and accumulated wealth are, in theory, shared relatively equally by all. All religious practices are banned.) North Vietnam wanted to overthrow the South Vietnamese government and reunite the two countries under one Communist government. But U.S. government officials worried that a Communist government in Vietnam would increase the power of the Soviet Union and threaten the security of the United States. In the late 1950s and early 1960s the U.S. government sent money, weapons, and military advisors to help South Vietnam defend itself.

Arnett arrived in Vietnam at a time when American involvement in the conflict was increasing rapidly. Though he knew that covering a war could be dangerous, he also believed it would give him an opportunity to prove himself as a journalist. "I wondered whether I had the courage to swim in those turbulent waters or match the legendary exploits of the foreign correspondents I had read about," he noted in his memoir. In 1965 President Lyndon Johnson sent American combat troops to join the fight on the side of South Vietnam. But deepening U.S. involvement in the war failed to defeat the Communists. Instead, the war turned into a bloody stalemate that became increasingly unpopular among citizens of the United States.

Arnett filed numerous reports from battlefields across Vietnam over the next few years. Like many other American reporters, he was sometimes criticized by U.S. government officials for presenting grim facts about the war and its effect on American soldiers and the Vietnamese people. Though some of his stories were controversial, Arnett claimed that he had an obligation to report what he saw. "From the beginning of the war to the end I looked at Vietnam as a news story, not a crusade for one side or the other," he said in *Live from the Battlefield*. "I believed that gathering information was a worthwhile pursuit, and truth the greatest goal I could aspire to."

The U.S. government withdrew the last American troops from Vietnam in 1973. Two years later North Vietnam captured the South Vietnamese capital city of Saigon to win the war. Fearing for their safety, most American journalists and many South Vietnamese people fled from the city as the North Vietnamese troops approached. But Arnett decided to remain in Saigon to cover the historic event. "Because I was in Vietnam at the beginning, I felt it was worth the risk to be there at the end to document the final hours," he explained in his memoir.

The Vietnam War helped establish Arnett's reputation as a daring and resourceful journalist. He earned several awards for his coverage of the conflict, including the prestigious Pulitzer Prize in 1966 and the George Polk Memorial Award from the Overseas Press Club in 1970.

Broadcasts live from Baghdad during the Persian Gulf War

Arnett left Vietnam following the fall of Saigon in 1975. For the next few years he traveled around the United States and the world to report on a wide range of subjects for the Associated Press. He left AP in 1981 after twenty years of service in order to join CNN, a new television network dedicated to providing continuous twenty-four-hour news coverage. Arnett began his new career as CNN's White House correspondent, but he soon found himself longing for the excitement of reporting from the world's war zones. He covered a series of conflicts in Central America, Eastern Europe, and the Middle East over the next few years.

On August 2, 1990, Iraqi leader **Saddam Hussein** (see entry) had ordered his military forces to invade the neighboring country of Kuwait. Hussein argued that Iraq had a historical claim to Kuwait's territory. He also wanted to control Kuwait's oil reserves and to gain access to Kuwait's port on the Persian Gulf. Countries around the world condemned the invasion and demanded that Iraqi leader Saddam Hussein immediately withdraw his troops from Kuwait. Many of these countries then began sending military forces to the Persian Gulf region as part of a U.S.-led coalition against Iraq. In November 1990, the United Nations Security Council established a deadline of January 15, 1991, for Iraq to withdraw from Kuwait or face war.

During the fall of 1990, journalists from around the world rushed to the Persian Gulf region to cover the military buildup and possible war. Arnett was working as a CNN correspondent in Jerusalem, Israel, at this time. Network executives initially asked Arnett to remain there and cover the war from Israel. But Arnett was eager to go to the Iraqi capital of Baghdad, where he could be in the middle of the action. As the UN deadline approached, many foreign journalists decided to leave Iraq for their own safety. A number of CNN reporters and technical support crew also chose to return home. But the network remained committed to covering the war from Baghdad if possible. CNN officials asked Arnett to go to Baghdad to replace some of the departing staff members. He arrived in Iraq on January 11, 1991, just four days before the UN deadline.

CNN news anchorman Bernard Shaw was already in Iraq, waiting for permission to interview Hussein. CNN correspondent John Holliman was there as well, along with producer Robert Wiener. Arnett and his colleagues established a base of operations at the fancy Al Rasheed Hotel in downtown Baghdad. Arnett knew that Baghdad would be a major target for coalition bombing once the war began, but he felt confident that the U.S. military would not target the hotel. He decided to remain in Baghdad and try to provide live coverage of the start of the war.

When Iraq failed to withdraw its troops from Kuwait by the UN deadline, the U.S.-led coalition launched a series of air strikes against Baghdad on January 17. Arnett, Holliman, and Shaw provided live coverage of the bombing from the ninth floor of the Al Rasheed Hotel. They used a special high-quality voice transmission link to report the action to CNN headquarters in Atlanta, Georgia. The reporters allowed TV viewers around the world to watch and listen as explosions shook the hotel and lit up the sky behind them. It marked the first time that a major American military action had been broadcast live on television. This dramatic coverage fascinated people around the world and turned Arnett and his colleagues into celebrities.

War reports create controversy

Arnett stayed in Iraq for the remainder of the Persian Gulf War. Iraqi officials gave him access to many sites that had been damaged by coalition bombs. Unlike his early reports from the Al Rasheed Hotel, Arnett's later reports were all cleared by Iraqi censors. Some people criticized Arnett for re-

U.S. Military Censorship of the Press

The Persian Gulf War marked the first major international military conflict in the age of satellite communications. Journalists planned to use this new technology to bring live reports of the action to television viewers around the world. They succeeded in dramatic fashion during the first coalition air strikes against the Iraqi capital of Baghdad, which were broadcast live on CNN by Peter Arnett and others.

As the war progressed, however, reporters found their activities restricted by U.S. military authorities. The Department of Defense claimed that the restrictions were necessary to maintain the secrecy of coalition strategy and protect the troops from undue risks. American officials also claimed that unchecked TV coverage of the war could create opposition in the United States and around the world.

For these reasons, U.S. military leaders decided to conduct the war largely outside of the view of journalists. They restricted reporters' access to the troops and prevented the media from traveling to combat areas. Most journalists were forced to participate in "pool" reporting. This meant that they depended on briefings by U.S. military officials as their main source of information about the progress of the war. The military briefings tended to focus on the positive aspects of the war, such as the bravery of American soldiers or the successful use of high-tech weaponry. Although the pool reporters were allowed to share the stories of the few journalists who were allowed to witness the fighting, these stories were routinely read and changed by military censors.

Although many journalists resented the restrictions, most ended up accepting under these conditions and felt that he could not present an objective (unbiased) view of the war. As a result, some of Arnett's stories from Iraq created controversy. One such report concerned a visit to an industrial plant that had been destroyed by U.S. air strikes. Iraqi officials claimed that the factory had produced powdered milk for babies, but U.S. military leaders said that it had made biological weapons.

After touring the plant on January 23, Arnett broadcast a report that supported the Iraqi government's claims. "I gave details of what I had seen and quoted officials as saying it was the only source of infant formula for Iraqi children," he noted in his memoir. "I had seen no evidence that the factory had ing them in order to do their jobs. After all, reporters who defied the restrictions and tried to operate independently often lost their press credentials. Some critics claimed that the media thus became a part of the U.S. military's public relations effort and reported only what the Department of Defense wanted the world to know. They claimed that media coverage of the war glossed over the boredom and unhappiness felt by some American troops in the Gulf, for example, and rarely talked about the devastating effects of coalition bombing on Iraqi civilians (people not involved in the war, including women and children).

Arnett remained in Baghdad during the war, so his reports were subject to censorship by Iraqi authorities rather than American authorities. But he still came under criticism from U.S. government offi-cials for reporting on the damage caused by coalition air strikes. Like many of his colleagues, Arnett resented the U.S. military's attempts to control media coverage of the Persian Gulf War. He believed that continuing advances in communications technology would make the censorship issue even more important in the future. "The battle I see today is an attempt by some to restrict the technological advances we've made and restrict our coverage in future crises involving American troops," he stated in the *New York Times*. "Live cameras are going to be on the battlefield. It's going to be a matter of how the military works with them."

Sources: Ridgeway, James. The March to War. New York: Four Walls Eight Windows, 1991.

been used for any other purpose." The following morning, U.S. leaders attacked Arnett's report as well as his credibility. "I tuned into the BBC [British Broadcasting Corporation] at daybreak, and heard White House spokesman Marlin Fitzwater call me a liar," he recalled in *Live from the Battlefield*. "The president had watched my report on the baby milk plant and, Fitzwater said, they were not pleased. He said the installation was a 'production facility for biological weapons.' Fitzwater claimed that the infant formula production at the installation was a front; he described CNN as 'a conduit [channel] for Iraqi disinformation [lies].'"

A few days later, Arnett was granted a personal inter-view with Hussein. "I knew that interviewing Saddam Hussein in the middle of this war was going to be controversial," he acknowledged in his memoir. "Those who had already criticized CNN's decision to stay in Baghdad and were angry that we had chosen to show the results of the allied bombing would be further outraged. I vowed to be as uncompromising with Saddam as possible." As Arnett expected, some people criticized him for interviewing Hussein and claimed that he felt sympathy for the enemy.

The Persian Gulf War ended on February 27, 1991, when coalition ground troops liberated Kuwait from Iraqi occupation. Arnett returned to the United States in early March, where he defended his coverage of the conflict. Some people claimed that his reports were one-sided since they had been cleared by Iraqi censors. In fact, hecklers showed up at many of his public appearances and called him anti-American. But Arnett argued that he had fulfilled his duty to CNN and supplied reports of interest to TV viewers worldwide. He said that his job was to gather and present information, not cater to the wishes of the U.S. government or rally support for the American cause.

Arnett continued reporting from the world's war zones during the 1990s, including Haiti, Somalia, and Bosnia. In 1994 he published a memoir about his career as a journalist, *Live from the Battlefield: From Vietnam to Baghdad—35 Years in the World's War Zones*. In 1998 Arnett was fired from CNN over a controversial report in which he accused the U.S. military of using chemical weapons during the Vietnam War.

Arnett returned to Iraq in 2003 to cover the Iraq War for the NBC television network and *National Geographic*. He once again became the center of controversy when he agreed to be interviewed on the official Iraqi government television station. In this interview, Arnett provided his analysis of the U.S. war effort. He claimed that the initial American war plan had failed and that U.S. leaders were scrambling to come up with a new plan. "The war plan has failed because of Iraqi resistance," he said, as quoted by *CNN.com*. "Clearly, the American war planners misjudged the determination of the Iraqi forces."

U.S. government officials criticized Arnett's statements, claiming that he was giving encouragement to the enemy. He was later fired by both NBC and *National Geographic*. He remained in Iraq, however, to cover the conflict for a British newspaper called the *Daily Mirror*. Several months later, Arnett expressed no regrets about his controversial statements. "The best weapon of a reporter is the truth," he told the *Korea Herald*, "and it is desirable for the government and the media to be in a tense relationship."

Arnett married a South Vietnamese woman, Nina Nguyen Thu-Nga, in 1964. They had two children together, Andrew and Elsa, before they eventually divorced. Arnett became a naturalized American citizen in 1986 and remarried in the early 1990s.

Where to Learn More

Arnett, Peter. *Live from the Battlefield: From Vietnam to Baghdad—35 Years in the World's War Zones*. New York: Simon and Schuster, 1994.

"Journalist Visits Korea." *Korea Herald*, September 20, 2003.

"Peter Arnett: U.S. War Plan Has 'Failed.'" *CNN.com*, March 30, 2003. Available online at http://www.cnn.com/2003/WORLD/meast/03/30/sprj.irq.arnett/index.html (accessed on April 1, 2004).

"Peter (Gregg) Arnett." *Contemporary Authors Online*. Reproduced in *Biography Resource Center Online*. Farmington Hills, MI: Gale Group, 2003.

Schmitt, Eric. "Five Years Later, the Gulf War Story Is Still Being Told." *New York Times*, May 12, 1996.

Tariq Aziz

Born 1936
Tell Kaif, Iraq

Iraqi foreign minister during the 1991 Persian Gulf War

T ariq Aziz was one of the most recognizable officials in the Iraqi government. He served as a top advisor to Iraqi leader Saddam Hussein for more than twenty years. During this time, he often appeared in the media and met with world leaders to explain Iraq's policies and negotiate political deals. As Iraq's foreign minister during the 1991 Persian Gulf War, Aziz defended Hussein's decision to invade Kuwait. He blamed the war on the United States, claiming that the U.S. government and its allies were determined to destroy Iraq.

After the 1991 war ended, Aziz remained a top advisor to Hussein as the deputy prime minister of Iraq. As the 2003 Iraq War approached, Aziz repeatedly insisted that Iraq did not possess weapons of mass destruction. As a high-ranking member of the Iraqi government, he was included among the fifty-five "most wanted" officials following the fall of Baghdad, the capital of Iraq. He surrendered to U.S. forces in late April 2003.

Rises through the ranks of the Baath Party

Tariq Aziz was born in 1936 in Tell Kaif, a village near the city of Mosul in northern Iraq. His father worked as a

"The Kuwaitis acted in an arrogant, irresponsible, provocative manner and that led to the deterioration of the situation."

Tariq Aziz in a interview for "Frontline."

Tariq Aziz. ©Francoise de Mulder/Corbis. Reproduced by permission.

31

waiter in a restaurant. Aziz's family was Chaldean, meaning that they were part of the small minority of Arabs who practiced Christianity. About 95 percent of Iraq's population was Muslim, meaning that they practiced the Islamic religion. Aziz's name at birth was Mikhayl Yuhanna, but he changed it to Tariq Aziz, which means "glorious past" in Arabic, to hide his Catholic background.

Aziz received a solid education at schools in Baghdad. He earned a degree in English literature from the Baghdad College of Fine Arts. After working for a few years as a teacher, he became a journalist. He took a job on the staff of an Iraqi newspaper called *Al-jumhuriyah* (*The Republic*) in 1958. Over the next ten years he rose to the position of editor in chief of the paper.

It also was in the late 1950s that Aziz joined the Baath Arab Socialist Party. Baathism was a radical political movement that aimed to unite the Arab world and create one powerful Arab state. The Iraqi Baath Party was a small, disorganized splinter group of this larger movement. It was made up primarily of violent and ruthless men who were willing to do anything to take control of the government.

Aziz joined the Baath Party because he opposed Iraq's leader, King Faisal II, who had been placed in power by British authorities when Iraq was created following World War I (1914–18). "Most of the young people of my generation were not satisfied with the current situation at that time—the British colonial influence on Iraq, the backwardness of our country," he explained in an interview for "Frontline." "When I learned about the Arab Socialist Party, I felt from the very beginning that that's the best choice. It seeks independence and Arab unity."

In 1963 the Baath Party overthrew the Iraqi government. But the Baathists held on to power for less than a year before they were overthrown by the Iraqi military. At this point the Baath Party splintered into factions, and Aziz aligned himself with a group of rebels that included future Iraqi leader Saddam Hussein. When the Baathists returned to power in 1968, Hussein's cousin Ahmad Hassan al-Bakr became president of Iraq and Hussein became the head of the government's internal security. Aziz accepted a position as editor of the Baath Party journal, *Al-thawra* (*The Revolution*).

Aziz gradually rose through the ranks of the Baath Party over the years. In 1974 he was appointed minister of information in Bakr's government, and in 1977 he became a member of the powerful Revolutionary Command Council. When Hussein became president of Iraq in 1979, Aziz was named deputy prime minister. Throughout his rule, Hussein often used violence to eliminate his political opponents and ensure that he would remain in power.

Despite such violence, Aziz claimed that Hussein's government had ambitious goals of turning Iraq into a modern nation for the benefit of the Iraqi people. "Our ambition was to turn Iraq into a very, very developed country, with industry, services, technology, and education," he recalled in the "Frontline" interview. "We genuinely believe that we deserve that, and believe that we can do that. We have the talent as a nation to be a developed country."

Speaks for Iraq on the world stage

In 1982 Aziz added foreign minister to his many duties in Iraq's government. He served as one of Hussein's top advisors on matters of foreign policy. Thanks to his excellent command of English, he also became the main international spokesman for the Iraqi government. He frequently appeared in the media to explain Iraq's policies to the world. He also played the role of a diplomat at key times in Iraq's history, working to negotiate solutions to political problems between Iraq and other nations.

Given his Chaldean background, some people were surprised that Aziz rose to such an important position in Iraq's government. He was the only Christian member of Hussein's administration, which was made up primarily of Sunni Muslims. But other people noted that Aziz's religious background may have helped him become such a valuable advisor to Hussein. As a Christian, Aziz could count very few supporters among the population of Iraq and thus posed no threat to Hussein's rule. This may have made Hussein feel more comfortable about placing Aziz in positions of authority.

In 1980 Iraq became involved in a bitter war against Iran, its neighbor to the east. Iran was a non-Arab state that had recently been torn apart by revolution. A group of Islamic fundamentalists (people who adhere strictly to the principles of the Islamic religion) under a religious leader called the Ayatollah Khomeini had overthrown the government. Khomeini was a Shiite Muslim and an outspoken opponent of Hussein and his Sunni Muslim government. Hussein claimed that he went to war with Iran in order to defend the Arab world against the spread of Islamic fundamentalism.

Aziz emerged as the main Iraqi spokesman on the world stage during the Iran-Iraq War. In fact, his position was so prominent that he became the target of an assassination attempt by Iranian radicals in 1984. The Iranians set off a bomb in Baghdad that killed seven people, but Aziz survived the attack. Later that year Aziz met with U.S. President Ronald Reagan. He convinced the American leader to re-establish diplomatic relations with Iraq and to provide military assistance in its war against Iran. Aziz also negotiated with France to buy fighter planes and established an economic alliance with the former Soviet Union.

Defends Iraq's invasion of Kuwait

In 1988 Aziz traveled to Geneva, Switzerland, to negotiate a treaty to end the Iran-Iraq War. Though the war had left Hussein with a tough, battle-hardened military, the eight-year conflict also left the Iraqi economy in ruins. In fact, by the time the war ended Iraq owed $80 billion to other countries. Hussein's government desperately needed money to help the country recover from the effects of the war.

In Aziz's view, American leaders began to view Iraq as a threat following its victory in the war with Iran. He claimed that the United States resented Iraq's military and political power and worried that it might cause instability in the Middle East. "The United States didn't want Iraq to win that war [against Iran], but it didn't want Iraq to lose it, because Iraq losing the war was a great setback to their allies in the region," he stated in the "Frontline" interview.

As time passed and Iraq's economic problems continued, Hussein began making threatening statements toward his neighbors in the Middle East. In July 1990, for example, he threatened to use force against any Middle Eastern country that pumped excess oil. Many countries in the Middle

East contain some of the world's largest underground oil reserves. These countries make money by pumping and exporting oil (selling it to other countries around the world). In 1960 the world's major oil-producing countries formed the Organization of Oil Exporting Countries (OPEC) in order to coordinate their efforts. OPEC sets limits, or quotas, on the amount of oil its members pump each year in order to ensure stable oil prices in world markets.

Hussein's threat was clearly aimed at Kuwait, which had been pumping more oil than was allowed under OPEC agreements. Kuwait's actions contributed to a decline in oil prices from $20.50 per barrel in early 1990 to $13.60 per barrel in July. Every dollar drop in the price per barrel of oil cost Iraq an estimated $1 billion per year. Hussein thus blamed Kuwait for making Iraq's financial problems worse. "The Kuwaitis started to dump oil," Aziz explained in the "Frontline" interview. "Of course, Iraq was concerned, because that was going to impoverish us. It was going to undermine our economy. Because we came fresh from the war, we had a lot of loans to pay, and we needed some money for our people."

Aziz met with Kuwaiti government officials in an attempt to convince them to stop pumping excess oil. "We did our best to warn them in a friendly, brotherly, responsible manner that they were hurting Iraq very badly and we wanted them to stop," he recalled. "[But] the Kuwaitis acted in an arrogant, irresponsible, provocative manner and that led to the deterioration of the situation." Aziz and other members of Hussein's government came to believe that Kuwait and the United States were working together to destroy Iraq. "We felt there was a plan to undermine Iraq—to conspire against Iraq—because if you break the Iraqi economy at that time, it will end Iraq," he told "Frontline."

In August 1990 the Iraqi army invaded Kuwait. The invasion set in motion a series of events that ultimately led to the Persian Gulf War. Countries around the world condemned the invasion and demanded that Hussein immediately withdraw his troops from Kuwait. Many of these countries then began sending military forces to the Persian Gulf region as part of a U.S.-led coalition against Iraq. In November 1990, the United Nations (UN) Security Council established a deadline of January 15, 1991, for Iraq to withdraw from Kuwait or face war.

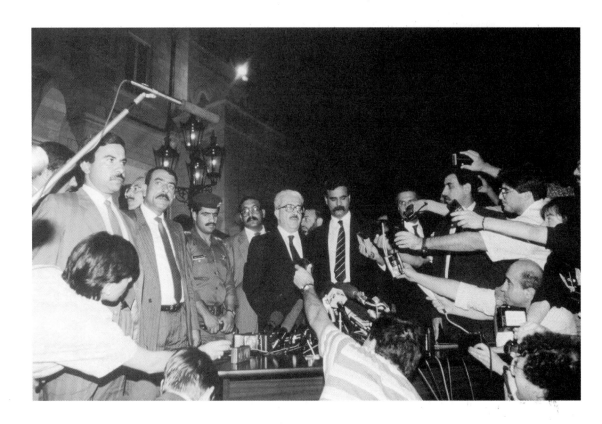

Iraqi Foreign Minister Tariq Aziz speaks to the press after the invasion of Kuwait.
©Francoise de Mulder/Corbis. Reproduced by permission.

Throughout the months between Iraq's invasion of Kuwait and the start of the Persian Gulf War, Aziz frequently appeared in the media to explain the Iraqi side of the situation. He claimed that the invasion was a defensive action taken to protect Iraq from Kuwait's attacks on the Iraqi economy. Aziz also made a round of visits to foreign capitals to try to gather support for a diplomatic solution. A few days before the UN deadline, Aziz met with U.S. Secretary of State **James Baker** (see entry). The two men talked for several hours but failed to reach any agreement. During the meeting, Aziz refused to accept a letter for **Saddam Hussein** (see entry) from U.S. President **George H. W. Bush** (see entry). After reading the letter, he told Baker that it contained threats rather than the type of respectful correspondence that should take place between two heads of state.

Argues over UN weapons inspectors

When Iraq failed to withdraw its troops from Kuwait by the UN deadline, the U.S.-led coalition launched a war.

After six weeks of devastating air strikes against military targets in Iraq, coalition ground troops liberated Kuwait from Iraqi occupation on February 27. The Persian Gulf War ended in a lopsided defeat for Iraq. As part of the agreement that officially ended the war, Iraq agreed to destroy or remove all of its biological, chemical, and nuclear weapons. Hussein also agreed to allow UN weapons inspectors to enter the country in order to monitor its progress.

After the Persian Gulf War ended, Aziz gave up his post as foreign minister but kept his title as deputy prime minister of Iraq. As the years passed, Iraq consistently failed to cooperate with the UN weapons inspectors. In fact, Hussein kicked the inspectors out of Iraq in 1998. Aziz complained about the inspection process during several public appearances. He claimed that Iraq did not possess any weapons of mass destruction. He said that the UN inspectors refused to acknowledge this fact due to pressure from the United States. "Since the first week or month in 1992, until they withdrew from Iraq in 1998, [the inspectors] didn't find in Iraq a gallon of chemicals or biological weapons, or a functional missile, which means there was nothing of the sort. All were destroyed," he stated in the "Frontline" interview. "But they did not report this major fact to the UN Security Council."

In 2002 U.S. President **George W. Bush** (son of the former president who had held office during the 1991 Persian Gulf War; see entry) told the United Nations that Iraq posed a significant threat to world security. He claimed that Hussein still possessed weapons of mass destruction and could provide such weapons to terrorists. Although Iraq allowed the UN inspectors to return in late 2002, Bush was not satisfied and threatened to take military action. Aziz continued to insist that Iraq did not possess any weapons of mass destruction. He claimed that the United States was determined to invade Iraq in order to control the region's oil reserves. In an effort to increase international opposition to a U.S.-led military invasion, he traveled to Rome to meet with Pope John Paul II. "The Holy Father and the Vatican and the leaders in God— Muslims and Christians—are trying their best to stop this aggression," he stated, as quoted by *CNN.com*.

After various diplomatic efforts failed to resolve the crisis, the United States launched another war against Iraq in

March 2003. Aziz remained defiant, proclaiming that he would rather die than be taken into U.S. custody. In the early days of the war, rumors said that Aziz had been killed or had fled the country. But on April 1 Aziz appeared on Iraqi television to prove that the rumors were false. Following the fall of Baghdad, Aziz's home was looted by angry Iraqi citizens. In late April he began suffering from health problems and decided to negotiate his surrender to U.S. forces. As number forty-three on the coalition's list of the fifty-five "most wanted" Iraqi officials, Aziz was expected to provide valuable information about Iraq's financial resources and the whereabouts of other Iraqi leaders. When Hussein was captured in late December, Aziz was called in to verify the Iraqi leader's identity.

Where to Learn More

"Family Says Aziz Surrendered after Hiding at Relative's House." *CNN.com,* April 25, 2003. Available online at http://www.cnn.com/2003/WORLD/meast/04/25/sprj.irq.aziz.custody/index.html (accessed on April 2, 2004).

"Frontline Interview: Tariq Aziz." *PBS.* Available online at http://www.pbs.org/wgbh/pages/frontline/shows/saddam/interviews/aziz.html (accessed on April 2, 2004).

"Profile: Tariq Aziz." *BBC News.* Available online at http://news.bbc.co.uk/go/pr/fr/-/1/hi/world/middle_east/2266978.stm (last accessed on April 2, 2004).

"Tariq Aziz Biography." *Iraqi News.* Available online at http://www.iraqinews.com/people_aziz.shtml (accessed on April 2, 2004).

"Tariq Mikhayl Aziz." *Biography Resource Center Online.* Farmington Hills, MI: Gale Group, 2002.

James Baker

Born April 28, 1930
Houston, Texas

U.S. secretary of state during the Persian Gulf War

As U.S. secretary of state during the Persian Gulf crisis, James Baker played an important role in building the international military coalition made up of more than thirty-five countries that eventually forced Iraq out of Kuwait. In addition, he was a key advisor to President **George H. W. Bush** (see entry) on diplomatic and military strategy throughout the months leading up to the war.

Builds thriving career in law

James Addison Baker III was born April 28, 1930, in Houston, Texas. He was the son of James A. Baker, a banker and attorney, and Bonner (Means) Baker. Raised in an environment of wealth and privilege, Baker attended some of the country's finest private schools. In 1948 he enrolled at Princeton University in New Jersey, and four years later he graduated with a bachelor of arts degree in hand. From there he entered the U.S. Marine Corps, where he fulfilled two years of active duty as a lieutenant. After leaving the marines, Baker studied law at the University of Texas in Austin. He graduated

"I remain unpersuaded that anything we might have done, short of actually moving armed forces to the region, would have deterred Iraq's invasion of Kuwait."

James Baker quoted in *The Politics of Diplomacy.*

James Baker. *AP/Wide World Photos. Reproduced by permission.*

39

with honors in 1957 and quickly secured employment with one of Houston's most prestigious law firms.

Baker worked in corporate law for the next eighteen years, building considerable personal wealth. He and his wife Mary (McHenry) Baker, who were married in 1953, also started a family during this period. They eventually had four sons before she died of cancer in 1970. Baker was remarried three years later to Susan Garrett Winston, who had two sons and a daughter from a previous marriage. In 1977 they had a daughter together.

Baker's thriving career as an attorney kept him very busy, but he still found time to become actively involved in state politics for the Republican Party. He developed a particularly close relationship with George H. W. Bush, who served Texas in the U.S. House of Representatives during the mid-1960s. When Bush decided to run for a seat in the U.S. Senate in 1970, he asked Baker to help run his campaign. Baker agreed, but his efforts came to naught as Bush was defeated.

Moves into world of politics

Despite the disappointment of Bush's defeat in the 1970 elections, Baker found that he enjoyed the excitement of political campaigns. He also was keenly interested in playing a role in shaping the future course of American public policy. As a result, he became an important advisor in the successful 1972 reelection campaign of Republican President Richard Nixon.

In 1975 Baker left his law career behind to accept a job as undersecretary of commerce in the administration of President Gerald R. Ford. The following year, he worked on Ford's election campaign, only to see Democratic nominee Jimmy Carter claim victory. Baker returned to Texas, and in 1978 he ran for the office of state attorney general. Baker's bid for the job, the only time that he ever ran for public office himself, fell short, as he was soundly defeated.

In 1979 Baker's old friend George Bush asked him to manage his upcoming campaign for the Republican Party's 1980 presidential nomination. Bush and Baker mounted a campaign that attracted considerable support from Republican voters, but former California Governor Ronald Reagan eventually clinched the nomination. Once Reagan secured the nomination, he asked Bush to be the Republican Party candidate for vice president. When Bush agreed, Baker became an important advisor to the Reagan-Bush ticket.

In January 1981 Baker became Reagan's first chief of staff. Over the next four years, Baker supervised the daily operations of the White House and became one of Reagan's most trusted advisors. Baker also solidified his national reputation as a smart and well-organized political mind during this period. In January 1985 Reagan began a second term as president. At this time, Baker became the U.S. secretary of the treasury, a position he held until August 1988.

In August 1988 Baker resigned from the Reagan cabinet in order to take the helm of Vice President Bush's presidential campaign. In November 1988 Bush defeated Democratic nominee Michael Dukakis to become the forty-first president of the United States. He subsequently nominated Baker to be secretary of state in his administration. The nomination of Baker was quickly approved by the U.S. Senate, and in January 1989 Baker assumed the duties of secretary of state. For the next four years, Baker was the United States' leading diplomat and chief advisor to the president on foreign affairs.

One of the biggest challenges that confronted Baker during his tenure as Bush's secretary of state was the Persian Gulf War. In August 1990 the Middle Eastern nation of Iraq, a powerful country led by a brutal dictator named **Saddam Hussein** (see entry), staged a surprise invasion of neighboring Kuwait. Hussein argued that Iraq had a historical claim to Kuwait's territory. He also wanted to control Kuwait's oil reserves and to gain access to Kuwait's port on the Persian Gulf. The United States and many other countries expressed outrage about Iraq's attack and demanded that Hussein give up his claim on Kuwait. When he refused, the United States organized a military coalition against Iraq that eventually grew to include five hundred thousand U.S. troops and two hundred thousand soldiers from other nations.

Secretary of State Baker played a major role in lining up the support of other nations. In addition, his diplomatic efforts helped pave the way for a tough United Nations resolution approving the use of military force to free Kuwait from Iraq's army. This resolution, passed in November 1990, established a deadline of January 15, 1991, for Iraq to withdraw from Kuwait or face attack by the U.S.-led forces. When Iraq failed to withdraw its troops from Kuwait by the deadline, the coalition forces began a campaign of air strikes against Iraqi troops and military positions. These air strikes, known as Operation Desert Storm, battered Iraqi military targets for thirty-eight days. The United States then led a massive ground offensive against Iraqi positions in Kuwait and southern Iraq on February 24, 1991. Within one hundred hours, Hussein's forces were chased out of Kuwait and sent fleeing deep into Iraq.

Careful diplomacy during Persian Gulf crisis

Looking back on the Gulf War, Baker has admitted that the Bush administration may not have paid enough attention to Hussein's threats to attack Kuwait. "With the benefit of hindsight, it's easy to argue that we should have recognized earlier that we weren't going to moderate Saddam's behavior, and shifted our policy approach sooner and to a greater degree than we did," he wrote in *The Politics of Diplomacy*. He continued:

> At the least, we should have given Iraqi policy a more prominent place on our radar screen at an earlier date. And while I wish we'd focused more attention on Iraq earlier, given what happened, I remain unpersuaded that anything we might have done, short of actually moving armed forces to the region, would have deterred Iraq's invasion of Kuwait.

Once Iraq invaded Kuwait, however, Baker believes that the Bush administration handled the crisis with great skill. For example, he claims that the U.S.-supported January 15 deadline for Iraq's withdrawal from Kuwait convinced many nations that the United States was willing to let Hussein avoid a military clash.

> [The deadline] helped us bring other nations into the coalition because it was a ... reasonable period of time and it helped us particularly with domestic political opinion in the United States. Which was at the beginning of all this very, very much opposed to the idea of going to war in the Persian Gulf.

Baker also points out that he gave Iraq one last warning of the danger it was in when he met with Iraqi Foreign Minister **Tariq Aziz** (see entry) on January 9, 1991, six days

before the UN deadline. "During the course of the meeting, I made an effort to point out to him that as President Bush's letter to Saddam Hussein pointed out, we were deadly serious about this, that there was no give in opposition," he told the PBS program "Frontline." He went on to say:

> This was now a matter of the credibility of the United Nations, it was a matter of a resolution supported by the overwhelming majority of the international community. [If Iraq did not withdraw from Kuwait] overwhelmingly superior force would be used against them.... [Aziz] didn't buy it. He said something like—you haven't fought in the desert before. Your Arab allies will turn and run, they will not fight their brothers. You will be surprised at the strength and the determination and the force and the courage of the Iraqi military. Things like that. And it was not a particularly productive debate. I think as it turned out our assessments of what our overwhelmingly superior military forces could do were correct.

Baker remains proud of the part the United States played in forcing Iraq out of Kuwait. As he stated in his "Frontline" interview:

Secretary of State James Baker arrives at Kuwait International Airport. Baker visited Kuwaiti officials in the aftermath of Operation Desert Storm. *©Corbis. Reproduced by permission.*

It was the right thing to do and it was the right thing to do morally, politically, and in the national interest. It was what the United States should do as leader of the free world. The diplomatic and political and military decisions that had been made leading up to it had been handled in the right way.... I think that when people look back at this they will see it as a textbook example of the way in which the world community can react to unprovoked aggression in a case where, particularly the United States is willing to offer the leadership required to do so.

Baker spent the last six months of Bush's term in office as the president's chief of staff. In January 1993 Bill Clinton took the presidential oath of office and Baker returned home to Texas. He spent the remainder of the decade dividing his time between his legal practice and political activism on behalf of the Republican Party. In 2000 Baker was asked by Republican nominee **George W. Bush** (see entry), son of Baker's lifelong friend George H. W. Bush, to help monitor the disputed results of the U.S. presidential election. Six weeks after the election was held, Bush was finally declared the winner. Two years later, Baker publicly declared his support for the Bush administration's decision to invade Iraq and remove Hussein from power.

Baker has received numerous prestigious honors for his years of public service over the years. In 1991 he received the Presidential Medal of Freedom, the country's highest award for civilians (people not in the military). Other awards that Baker has received over the years include Princeton University's Woodrow Wilson Award, American Institute for Public Service's Jefferson Award, Harvard University's John F. Kennedy School of Government Award, George F. Kennan Award, and the Department of State's Distinguished Service Award.

Where to Learn More

Baker, James. *The Politics of Diplomacy: Revolution, War and Peace, 1989–1992.* New York: Putnam, 1995.

"James Addison Baker, III." In *Encyclopedia of World Biography,* 1998. Reproduced in *Biography Resource Center,* Farmington Hills, MI: Gale Group, 2003.

"Interview with James Baker." *Frontline: The Gulf War,* available online at http://www.pbs.org/wgbh/pages/frontline/gulf/oral/baker/1.html (accessed on March 24, 2004).

Tony Blair

Born May 6, 1953
Edinburgh, Scotland

**Prime minister of Great Britain during the
2003 Iraq War**

A vocal opponent of **Saddam Hussein** (see entry), British Prime Minister Tony Blair aligned himself with U.S. President **George W. Bush** (see entry) and urged military action to prevent the Iraqi leader from developing weapons of mass destruction. Despite widespread international opposition to the war, Blair committed British military forces to the U.S.-led invasion and postwar stabilization of Iraq. When no evidence of an Iraqi weapons program was found after Hussein was removed from power, Blair defended himself against charges that he misled the British people about the Iraq threat.

A barrister's son

Anthony Charles Lynton Blair was born May 6, 1953, in Edinburgh, Scotland. He was the second of three children born to Leo and Hazel Blair. Leo Blair supported the family by working as a barrister (lawyer). When Tony was very young, his father received an appointment as a law lecturer at Durham University and moved the family to northern England.

"Iraq has chemical and biological weapons."

Tony Blair quoted in *"The Tony Blair Dossier."*

Tony Blair. *Photograph by Adam Butler. AP/Wide World Photos. Reproduced by permission.*

At Durham, Tony's father became prominent in conservative political circles and seemed likely to run for public office as a member of the Tory Party. In addition to his teaching and political networking, Leo Blair maintained a law practice and was a popular public speaker. His energy and political ambition would prove an influence on his son. But Leo Blair also worked long hours and did not spend a great deal of time with his family.

Tony's life changed dramatically when he was ten years old. His father suffered a massive stroke and nearly died. It took three years for Leo Blair to regain his ability to speak. As a result, he was unable to work, and his once-promising political prospects came to a sudden end. The family was dealt a second blow when Tony's younger sister, Sarah, was stricken with rheumatoid arthritis and hospitalized for two years. These family illnesses cast a dark shadow over Blair's early adolescence. In addition, the family's finances clearly suffered as a result of his father and sister's health problems.

Learning and breaking the rules

Blair received a scholarship to attend Fettes College in Edinburgh, Scotland, where he enrolled at age thirteen. (Despite its name, the "college" offered courses similar to those in middle school and high school in the United States.) Blair did well in his studies but had a difficult time adjusting to dormitory life, as well as to the strict rules and traditions of the school.

For instance, in his early years at Fettes, Blair was required to "fag" for the older students, meaning that he had to perform chores for them, such as cleaning their shoes. Blair found the practice degrading, and he also disliked the school's strict guidelines about issues such as hair and dress. Blair earned a reputation for questioning authority, though he never let his protests go too far. "I was never an out-and-out rebel," he recalled in *Tony Blair: The Moderniser*, "but I was a rationalist in the sense that, if certain things were wrong, I would say so." Blair also became known for his acting abilities, assuming lead roles in several school productions.

After completing his studies at Fettes, Blair moved on to St. John's College at Oxford University in 1972, where he studied law. Surprisingly, he showed little interest in joining political organizations while at Oxford. Instead, he filled much of his free time by dating and singing in a rock band. Shortly before he graduated, however, he fell in with a group of students who were interested in public affairs and religious issues. Blair soon joined the Anglican Church. His interest in spiritual concerns became stronger after his mother died of cancer in 1975. Her death also made Blair get serious about pursuing a career in politics.

Joining the Labour Party

Though his father had been a member of the conservative Tory Party, Blair joined the rival Labour Party, which had traditionally been aligned with trade unions and socialist politics. He began building relationships with important Labour officials while completing his law training. It was during this time that he met another aspiring barrister named Cherie Booth, and the two were married in 1980. Blair practiced law through the late 1970s and early 1980s, specializing in employment and industrial cases. Though he was active in Labour Party politics, he did not run for office until 1982. His first attempt to win a seat in Parliament (the British form of government) failed, but a year later he was elected as a representative for Sedgefield, an area near Durham.

At this time the Labour Party was fairing poorly in elections. The Tories, led by Prime Minister **Margaret Thatcher** (see entry), were the party in power. Blair and others within his party felt that Labour needed to change its message if it wanted to reconnect with large numbers of British voters. The change that they pioneered was to move the party more toward the political center. They felt that many voters had turned against Labour because the party was out of touch with current conditions and too closely linked to powerful trade unions and outdated economic policies. At the same time, they wanted to keep their distance from the Tories, whom they felt were too conservative. Blair and his allies proposed a "Third Way" that fell somewhere between socialism and conservatism. (Socialism is an economic system that advocates communal ownership of industry either in the form of state ownership or else in the form of ownership by the workers themselves.) Blair would later coin the term "New Labour" to describe this change in outlook, and he and his associates became known as "the Modernisers." During the 1980s and early 1990s, these lawmakers gradually transformed Labour Party policies and attitudes.

Assuming leadership

Throughout this period, Blair retained his seat in parliament and moved steadily up the ranks of the party. He became a member of the select group that guided Labour's strategy as the opposition party. By the mid-1990s, he was considered one of the party's top figures. When Labour Party leader John Smith died in 1994, Blair replaced him. Under Blair's direction, the party cut its long-standing ties to socialist principles. In the May 1997 elections, the Labour Party won enough parliamentary seats to become the nation's ruling party. Blair, at age forty-three, became one of the youngest prime ministers in British history.

In his first term Blair promoted a political agenda that mixed liberal priorities (such as a strong public education system) with more conservative issues (such as reducing government restrictions on business and cracking down on crime). On the international front, he promoted stronger links between Great Britain and its European neighbors, helped establish a peace agreement in Northern Ireland, and urged the North Atlantic Treaty Organization (NATO) to take action against Serbian leader Slobodan Milosevic, who had presided over a violent program of "ethnic cleansing" in the Eastern European region of Kosovo. In June 2001 Blair won a second term as prime minister. Just a few months later, he faced a new international crisis.

Terror and war

On September 11, 2001, members of a radical Islamic terrorist group known as Al Qaeda hijacked four commercial planes and crashed them into the World Trade Center in New York City, the Pentagon building near Washington, D.C., and a field in Pennsylvania. Nearly three thousand people were killed in these attacks. Immediately after these attacks against the United States, President George W. Bush announced a global war on terrorism that initially focused on Al Qaeda and other known terrorist organizations.

The September 11 attacks made international terrorism an enormous issue for Blair and many other world leaders. Blair quickly pledged his support for Bush's efforts to stamp out terrorism. By early October, British forces were fighting alongside American troops in Afghanistan. The Taliban, Afghanistan's radical Islamic government sheltered Osama bin Laden, the Muslim cleric (religious leader) who masterminded the terrorist attacks, and provided training grounds for Al Qaeda. The invasion of Afghanistan aroused little opposition in the United Kingdom because there was strong evidence showing that the Taliban had supported Al Qaeda.

But there was plenty of controversy when the global war on terrorism moved on to its next major engagement. Beginning in 2002 both U.S. and British officials issued new warnings that Iraqi leader Saddam Hussein posed a dangerous threat to international security. They argued that Hussein had engaged in efforts to create nuclear and chemical weapons, and that he could either use such weapons himself or make them available to terrorist groups. Both governments threatened to use military force to bring an end to the perceived Iraqi threat.

Concerns about Saddam Hussein were nothing new. The Iraqi leader's decision to invade neighboring Kuwait had led to the 1991 Persian Gulf War. In this conflict, a United Nations (UN) coalition that included both the United States and Great Britain had pushed Iraq's army out of Kuwait. The UN resolutions, or formal statements, that ended the war required Iraq to dismantle its weapons program, but Hussein consistently refused to comply with UN inspections to verify Iraq's disarmament. Because Iraq failed to comply with the UN resolutions, it had been placed under economic sanctions (trade restrictions intended to punish a country for breaking international law). In addition, British and American forces carried out periodic aerial bombings and missile attacks against Iraqi targets throughout the 1990s.

The war debate

By 2002 the leaders of the United States and Great Britain were out of patience with Hussein. The Blair and Bush administrations pressured the United Nations to authorize the use of military force to remove Hussein from power in Iraq. Their position created a prolonged international debate. Critics charged that there was not enough evidence to prove that Hussein's government possessed weapons of mass destruction, such as chemical and biological weapons. Others argued that there were no clear links between Iraq and terrorist groups such as Al Qaeda. Some charged that Blair and Bush were using the alleged weapons as an excuse to exert control over a strategic and oil-rich area of the Middle East. While the governments of several nations sided with the American and British opinion, many others were opposed. Officials from France and Russia were among the most powerful and vocal critics of military action against Iraq.

Blair remained undaunted by the opposition, and he continued to recommend tough action against Hussein. On September 24, 2002, Blair released a dossier (file) of intelligence information detailing his administration's findings on Iraq's weapons of mass destruction. Blair addressed the British parliament on the same day to make his argument. "Iraq has chemical and biological weapons," he said, as quoted in "The Tony Blair Dossier." Blair also asserted that Saddam "has existing and active military plans for the use of chemical and biological weapons, which could be activated within 45 minutes," and added that the Iraqi leader "is actively trying to acquire nuclear weapons capability."

In November 2002 a new UN resolution demanded that Iraq disarm or face serious consequences. Hussein accepted the terms of the resolution and agreed to let UN weapons inspectors return to Iraq. As they carried out their investigations, the United States and Great Britain began to station military forces in the region near Iraq. Demonstrations against the impending war took place around the world. Massive protests were staged in London, and opinion polls showed that large numbers of British citizens were opposed to an attack on Iraq.

Reports by Chief UN Inspector Hans Blix in the first three months of 2003 were critical of Iraq's level of cooperation but also found no definite proof of a weapons program. Blix requested more time to complete the investigation, but Blair and Bush continued to push for military action. In February the United States and Great Britain requested another UN resolution, this one specifically authorizing the use of military force against Iraq. The resolution failed to gain the necessary support in the UN Security Council and was dropped.

The lack of UN support left Blair with tough decisions to make. He had to decide whether Great Britain should assist the United States in a military invasion of Iraq without widespread international support. He also had to decide whether to risk the lives of British citizens when so many people in his own country were opposed to the war. His answer to both questions was ultimately yes.

Victory and more questions

The invasion of Iraq began on March 20, 2003 (March 19 in the United States). The majority of British troops were deployed in the southern part of the country, near the city of Basra, which they successfully captured in early April. Most Iraqi towns had fallen to the coalition forces by mid-April, and major combat operations came to an end on May 1. The war had succeeded in removing Saddam Hussein's government from power, but the dictator's whereabouts were unknown.

Despite the rapid victory, the controversy surrounding the causes of the war refused to go away. In the months following the fall of Baghdad, the capital city, no substantial evidence of an active Iraqi weapons program was found. Critics charged that Blair's government had either been wrong in its intelligence assessments of Hussein's weapons programs, or that administration officials had purposefully misled Parliament and the British public.

The issue grew even more heated when a British Broadcasting Corporation (BBC) news story questioned the accuracy of the intelligence dossier Blair had presented to parliament in building his case for the war. The story alleged that the dossier had been exaggerated to make a more compelling case. It also quoted an arms expert with the Ministry of Defense who felt that inaccurate claims had been made in the documents. One point of contention was Blair's claim that Iraq's chemical and biological weapons could be functional in forty-five minutes.

The arms expert was later revealed to be Doctor David Kelly. Shortly after his name was made public, Kelly was found dead after allegedly committing suicide. An independent inquiry into the incident was launched. Meanwhile, spokespersons for the prime minister vigorously disputed the BBC's charges. In December 2003 a former Iraqi military officer declared that he had been the source for the forty-five-minute estimate. He stood by his claim, stating that such warheads had been distributed to Iraqi troops in late 2002.

Growing casualties

The prime minister also faced criticism about the dangerous conditions in postwar Iraq. Though formal military battles came to an end in April, coalition forces continued to endure frequent attacks from guerrilla forces. In addition, nonmilitary installations in Baghdad, such as a hotel and the United Nations headquarters, were targeted in deadly car bombings. The coalition's inability to find Saddam Hussein also followed Blair for many months, until the Iraqi leader was finally captured by U.S. forces in December 2003. In late 2003 the U.S.-led coalition approved a plan to speed the transition to an Iraqi-controlled government, but no timetable was set for the removal of foreign troops. As of early December, fifty-three British soldiers had been killed in Iraq out of a total of 520 coalition deaths.

Opinion polls indicate that Blair's popularity in Britain has dropped as a result of the war. Some British citizens feel that Blair misled them about the Iraqi threat, and there have been widespread complaints that the prime minister is focusing too much attention on Iraq and other international issues and not paying enough attention to his own country. Nonetheless, Blair's government still enjoys significant support.

Despite the difficulties and uncertainty the Iraq War created, Blair stands by his decision to confront Saddam Hussein. "We must affirm that in the face of this terrorism there must be no holding back, no compromise, no hesitation in confronting this menace, in attacking it wherever and whenever we can, and in defeating it utterly," he told Fran Kelly of the Australian Broadcasting Corporation.

Where to Learn More

Foley, Michael. *The British Presidency.* New York: Manchester University Press, 2000.

"In Depth: After Saddam." *BBC News.* Available online at http://news.bbc.co.uk/1/hi/in_depth/middle_east/2002/conflict_with_iraq/default.stm (accessed March 24, 2004).

"Iraq War Debate—2002/2004." University of Michigan Documents Center. Available online at http://www.lib.umich.edu/govdocs/iraqwar.html (accessed March 24, 2004).

Kelly, Fran. "Blair, Bush Reaffirm Vow to Confront Terrorism." *ABC News Online.* Available online at http://www.abc.net.au/am/content/2003/s994099.htm (accessed March 24, 2003).

"Paper Names '45-minute Source.'" *BBC News.* Available online at http://news.bbc.co.uk/1/hi/uk_politics/3297771.stm (accessed March 24, 2004).

Rentoul, John. *Tony Blair: Prime Minister.* Boston: Little, Brown, 2001.

Sopel, Jon. *Tony Blair: The Moderniser.* London: Michael Joseph, 1995.

"Special Report: War in Iraq" *CNN.com.* Available online at http://www.cnn.com/SPECIALS/2003/iraq/ (accessed March 24, 2004).

Stothard, Peter. *Thirty Days: Tony Blair and the Test of History.* New York: HarperCollins, 2003.

"The Tony Blair Dossier." Available online at http://controversy.biogs.com/blair.html (accessed March 24, 2004).

L. Paul Bremer III

Born September 30, 1941
Hartford, Connecticut

U.S. civil administrator in charge of the
postwar reconstruction of Iraq

L. Paul Bremer III is head of the Coalition Provisional Authority, the civilian (nonmilitary) organization in charge of the postwar reconstruction of Iraq. A retired diplomat and former U.S. ambassador, Bremer was selected by President **George W. Bush** (see entry) to oversee the process of rebuilding Iraq and helping the Iraqi people form a democratic government. Bremer faced a difficult task, as U.S. military personnel and international aid workers came under a series of violent attacks during the postwar period. But the Coalition Provisional Authority still managed to achieve some important successes under his leadership.

"America has no designs on Iraq and its wealth. We will finish our job here and stay not one day longer than necessary...."

L. Paul Bremer III in the New York Times.

Builds a career as a diplomat

Lewis Paul Bremer III, known by the nickname Jerry, was born September 30, 1941, in Hartford, Connecticut. He earned a bachelor's degree from Yale University in 1963, then spent a year in France studying at the University of Paris Institute for Political Studies. Upon returning to the United States, he earned a master's degree in business administration from Harvard University in 1966.

L. Paul Bremer III.
Photograph by Murad Sezer.
AP/Wide World Photos.
Reproduced by permission.

Bremer decided to make a career in the U.S. foreign service. In twenty-three years as a diplomat, he served as an assistant to six different secretaries of state. He also worked at the American embassies in Afghanistan, Malawi, and Norway. In 1983 President Ronald Reagan appointed him as U.S. ambassador to the Netherlands. Upon leaving that post in 1986, Bremer became the State Department's ambassador-at-large for counterterrorism. He specialized in monitoring international terrorist activities and helping the United States and other countries prevent terrorist attacks.

In 1989 Bremer retired from government service and began working in the private sector as a consultant. He spent eleven years with Kissinger Associates, a prominent consulting firm run by former U.S. Secretary of State Henry Kissinger. In 2000 Bremer became chairman and chief executive officer of the Marsh Crisis Consulting Company. This firm advises multinational corporations on managing the risks of doing business in foreign countries.

Appointed civilian administrator for Iraq

On September 11, 2001, members of a radical Islamic terrorist group known as Al Qaeda hijacked four commercial planes and crashed them into the World Trade Center in New York City, the Pentagon building near Washington, D.C., and a field in Pennsylvania. Nearly three thousand people were killed that day. Immediately after these attacks against the United States, President George W. Bush announced a global war on terrorism that initially focused on Al Qaeda and other known terrorist organizations. As a recognized counterterrorism expert, Bremer was appointed to Bush's Homeland Security Advisory Council in 2002.

Bush eventually expanded the war on terrorism to include enemy nations that he believed supported terrorist activities. The president claimed that Iraq possessed weapons of mass destruction and could provide these weapons to terrorist groups. He argued that Iraqi leader **Saddam Hussein** (see entry) posed an immediate threat to world security. In early 2003 the United States launched a war against Iraq. The war succeeded in removing Hussein from power after only three weeks of combat, when the Iraqi capital of Baghdad fell to coalition forces on April 9.

On May 6 Bush appointed Bremer as the senior civilian administrator in Iraq. Bremer took charge of the Coalition Provisional Authority (CPA), the U.S.-run civil agency in charge of Iraq's postwar reconstruction. He replaced retired U.S. Army General Jay Garner, who coordinated the military's Office of Reconstruction and Humanitarian Aid during and immediately after the war. Although Bremer reported to U.S. Secretary of Defense **Donald Rumsfeld** (see entry), his appointment symbolized the transition from military to civilian control over Iraq's political and economic reconstruction.

Many people praised the selection of Bremer, an experienced diplomat with proven managerial skills, to oversee the process of rebuilding Iraq and helping the nation form a democratic government. Upon arriving in Baghdad, he outlined his goal of restoring stability and turning over power to the Iraqi people as quickly as possible. "We are committed to establishing the conditions for security, prosperity, and democracy," he told the *New York Times*. "America has no designs on Iraq and its wealth. We will finish our job here and stay not one day longer than necessary.... Once our work is over, the reward will be great: a free, democratic, and independent Iraq that stands not as a threat to its neighbors or the world, but as a beacon of freedom and justice."

Struggles to solve Iraq's postwar problems

But Bremer's postwar plans for Iraq soon ran into trouble. Security became a concern as Iraqi insurgents (people who fight against an established government or occupation force) and foreign fighters launched a series of violent attacks against American troops and international aid workers in Iraq. U.S. officials knew that Hussein's fall from power would create a power vacuum, or gap, in Iraq, so they expected some security issues to arise during the postwar period. But the situation turned out to be much different and more complicated than they anticipated.

Critics claimed that some of Bremer's decisions worsened the situation. For example, one of his first acts as head of the Coalition Provisional Authority was to disband Iraq's army and security forces. He did this because he worried that Iraqi civilians would not trust the people who had been responsible

Sergio Vieira de Mello, United Nations Special Representative to Iraq

Sergio Vieira de Mello was appointed as the UN Special Representative to Iraq in May 2003, shortly after the end of combat in the Iraq War. He thus became the main person representing the interests of the international community during the U.S.-led occupation. His mission was to help the Iraqi people make a peaceful transition to democracy. His four-month assignment was cut short, however, when he was killed in a car bomb attack against the UN offices in Baghdad.

De Mello was born March 15, 1948, in Rio de Janeiro, Brazil. He was educated in Brazil and in Paris. De Mello chose to build a career as a diplomat with the United Nations. He accepted his first UN assignment in 1969. During the next thirty years, he served in humanitarian and peacekeeping missions around the world.

De Mello rose through the ranks of the United Nations. He was appointed Assistant High Commissioner for Refugees in 1996 and Under-Secretary-General for Humanitarian Affairs and Emergency Relief Coordinator in 1998. One of his proudest moments was overseeing the peaceful election of Xanana Gusmao as president of the newly independent nation of Timor-Leste in 2002. Afterward, he was appointed the UN High Commissioner for Human Rights. "I view the position … as a daunting challenge that I face personally, that the United Nations face collectively, to make our work in the field of human rights have true meaning," he stated.

In early 2003 despite a lack of UN support, the United States launched a military invasion of Iraq. The war succeeded in removing Iraqi leader Saddam Hussein from power after only a few weeks of combat. Once the war ended, the United Nations pressured President George W. Bush to allow the international community to participate in the reconstruction of Iraq, especially the process of forming a new Iraqi government. The Bush administration welcomed UN assistance with humanitarian aid, but declared that the United States would handle Iraq's political transition.

In late May UN Secretary-General Kofi Annan asked de Mello to serve as the UN Special Representative to Iraq. His mission involved overseeing humanitarian aid, refugee return, economic development, legal reform, and civil administration on behalf of the international community. Upon arriving in Baghdad, de Mello expressed sympathy for the plight of the Iraqi people under U.S. military occupation. "It must be one of the most humiliating periods in their history," he acknowledged in Biography Resource Center. "Who would like to see their country occupied?"

As the reconstruction process continued, security became a major concern in Iraq. Iraqi insurgents and foreign fighters launched a series of violent attacks against American troops and international aid workers. In a July report to the UN Security Council, de Mello emphasized the need to speed up the transfer of power to the Iraqi people. "Iraqis need to know that the current state of affairs will come to an end soon," he stated. "They need to know that

Sergio Vieira de Mello. *Photograph by United Nations. Getty Images. Reproduced by permission.*

stability will return and that the occupation will end."

On August 19, a week before de Mello was scheduled to leave Iraq, a truck bomb exploded beneath his office at the UN compound in Baghdad. Much of the building was destroyed. A U.S. Army unit that responded to the attack found de Mello trapped alive in the rubble, but they did not have proper equipment to extract the survivors quickly. As he awaited rescue, de Mello repeatedly asked about the welfare of his UN colleagues. He also conveyed a message to Annan requesting that the United Nations remain in Iraq and continue helping the Iraqi people build peace and democracy.

De Mello was freed from the rubble after several hours, but he lost consciousness and died soon afterward. The terrorist attack against the UN headquarters in Baghdad killed twenty-two other people and wounded one hundred more. Members of the United Nations and the international community expressed grief and outrage at de Mello's loss. "The death of any colleague is hard to bear, but I can think of no one we could less afford to spare, or who would be more acutely missed throughout the United Nations system, than Sergio," said Annan on the UN web site.

In September 2003 the United Nations withdrew most of its six hundred staff members from Baghdad and stationed them in Amman, Jordan. Some people expressed sympathy for the United Nations' security concerns, but others criticized the move for playing into the hands of terrorists.

By the time of his death, de Mello was one of the United Nations' most respected diplomats. He was often mentioned as a possible successor to Annan as Secretary-General of the United Nations. Several world leaders said that he should be nominated for a Nobel Peace Prize. According to *CNN.com* U.S. Secretary of State Colin Powell called him "a hero who dedicated his life to helping people in danger and in difficulty. His loss is a terrible blow to the international community." Following a memorial service in Rio de Janeiro, de Mello's remains were taken to the Cemetery of Kings in Switzerland. He is survived by his wife and two sons.

Sources: "Sergio Vieira de Mello." Biography Resource Center Online. *Farmington Hills, MI: Gale Group, 2003; "Sergio Vieira de Mello: Biographical Note." United Nations, August 29, 2003. Available online at http://www.un.org/News/dh/iraq/demello-bio.htm (accessed on November 14, 2003).*

for enforcing Hussein's rules. When unrest broke out in Baghdad and other cities, however, some observers questioned Bremer's decision. Critics claimed that a trained Iraqi security force could have prevented much of the violence.

The Iraqi resistance seemed to become more determined and organized as time went on. Bremer claimed that the insurgents grew desperate as the Iraqi people embraced freedom. "This is not yet a full democracy, but freedom is on the march, from north to south," he told the *New York Times*. He went on to say:

> Sadly, this progress is despised by a narrow band of opponents. A small minority of bitter-enders—members of the former regime's instruments of repression—oppose such freedom. They are joined by foreign terrorists, extreme Islamists influenced by Iran, and bands of criminals.... These shadowy figures are killing brave Iraqis working with us, attacking soldiers and civilians, and trying to sabotage the fragile infrastructure.

The lack of security made it difficult for humanitarian aid, such as food, to reach the Iraqi people, so conditions in the country were slow to improve. For example, many Iraqis suffered from shortages of gasoline, electricity, and safe drinking water. Some people criticized the Bush administration for failing to adequately plan for reconstruction, and the United Nations began pushing for a larger role in the process.

Coalition Provisional Authority makes progress
As time passed, however, Bremer made significant progress on several fronts. He established the first transitional government in Iraq following the fall of Saddam Hussein, the Iraq Governing Council (IGC). Its membership included twenty-five prominent Iraqis whose political, ethnic, and religious backgrounds reflected the diversity of Iraq's population. The IGC held its first meeting on July 13. The group created a temporary constitution that established broad civil rights for the Iraqi people.

In October the Bush administration announced its intention to speed up the transfer of power to the Iraqis. Bremer and the IGC set a goal of handing over power to an independent Iraqi government by July 1, 2004. "We will hand over to a sovereign Iraq government on June 30," he said in a *Time* interview. "The shape and structure of that government isn't yet defined."

In a major concession to Shiite religious leaders, Bremer agreed to allow the Iraqi people to elect a new government before drafting a new constitution. Several prominent Shiites had refused to cooperate with the political process because they believed that only an elected Iraqi government should have the power to create a constitution. The Bush administration, on the other hand, preferred to see its hand-picked interim government, the IGC, draft the constitution.

The Coalition Provisional Authority also made progress in rebuilding Iraq's economy. By late 2003, sewage treatment systems had been improved and electric power had been restored to prewar levels. Thousands of roads, bridges, schools, and hospitals had been repaired or rebuilt. Material goods were widely available in Iraq's cities, and unemployment levels declined. The CPA also established an Iraqi security force and trained seventy thousand new police officers.

On December 13, 2003, Bremer held a press conference in which he announced that coalition military forces had captured former Iraqi leader Saddam Hussein. "This is a great day in Iraq's history," he stated to Associated Press. "For decades, hundreds of thousands of you suffered at the hands of this cruel man. For decades, Saddam Hussein divided you citizens against each other. For decades, he threatened and attacked your neighbors. Those days are over forever. Now it is time to look to the future, to your future of hope, to a future of reconciliation."

In March 2004, on the one-year anniversary of the start of the Iraq War, Bremer emphasized the CPA's many accomplishments in rebuilding Iraq and establishing a democratic government. But he also acknowledged the difficult tasks remaining to complete the transfer of power to the Iraqi people. "I expect in the run-up period to the transition of June 30 that we will have some really bad days," he told the Associated Press. "The terrorists are going to continue and even accelerate their attacks, particularly on Iraqi men, women, and children."

Once he completes his job with the CPA, Bremer plans to retire permanently from government service. "I feel like I'm in a fast-moving car on a slippery mountain road. I don't spend a lot of time looking in the rearview mirror," he noted in an interview with *Time*. "I really am planning to retire this time. I think this will have worn me out sufficiently for the rest of my life." Bremer makes his home in Chevy Chase, Maryland. He has been married to the former Frances Winfield for nearly forty years and has two children.

Where to Learn More

"Ambassador Paul Bremer." Coalition Provisional Authority biography, undated. Available online at http://www.cpa-iraq.org/bios (accessed on March 19, 2004).

Bremer III, L. Paul. "The Road Ahead in Iraq—and How to Navigate It." *New York Times,* July 13, 2003. Available online at http://usinfo. state.gov/topical/pol/conflict/03071301.htm (accessed on March 24, 2004).

"L. Paul Bremer III." *Biography Resource Center Online.* Farmington Hills, MI: Gale Group, 2003.

"One Year after War, Bremer Reflects on Ups and Downs in Iraq." *Associated Press,* March 19, 2004. Available online at http://news.yahoo. com/news?tmpl=story&u=/afp/20040320/pl_afp/iraq_war_1year_us _bremer_040320043214 (accessed on March 24, 2004).

Walt, Vivienne. "Interview: L. Paul Bremer." *Time,* March 7, 2004. Available online at http://www.time.com/time/covers/1101040315/bremer. html (accessed on March 19, 2004).

George H. W. Bush

Born June 12, 1924
Milton, Massachusetts

President of the United States during the
1991 Persian Gulf War

George Bush was the forty-first president of the United States, serving one four-year term from 1989 to 1993. One of the highlights of his time in office was the victory of American-led military forces in the Persian Gulf War, which forced the Middle Eastern nation of Iraq to end its nine-month occupation of neighboring Kuwait. Bush was the world leader most responsible for convincing the international community to oppose Iraq's invasion of Kuwait, and the swift and decisive defeat of Iraq's army marked the United States' biggest military triumph since World War II (1939–45).

In 2000 Bush was proud to see his eldest son, **George W. Bush** (see entry), elected as the forty-third president of the United States. The former president supported his son's decision to launch a second war against Iraq in 2003, which ultimately succeeded in removing Iraqi leader **Saddam Hussein** (see entry) from power.

"Everyone has his place in the sun—large country or small, they should be consulted, their opinions considered. Then when the United States makes a move and I make a decision [about going to war against Iraq], we are more apt to have solid support."

George H. W. Bush quoted in All the Best.

George H. W. Bush. *Courtesy of The Library of Congress. Reproduced by permission.*

Leaves life of privilege for military service

George Herbert Walker Bush was born on June 12, 1924, in Milton, Massachusetts. His parents were Prescott Sheldon Bush, a banker and U.S. senator, and Dorothy Walker Bush. One of five children, Bush was raised in Greenwich, Connecticut, in wealthy and comfortable surroundings. His parents ensured that he received a fine education, enrolling him in Phillips Academy, a private school in Andover, Massachusetts. "[Our parents] were our biggest boosters, always there when we needed them," recalled Bush in his 1987 autobiography *Looking Forward*. "It taught me to be the same way with my own children."

Bush excelled at Phillips Academy. He was a fine student and top athlete who captained the school's soccer and basketball teams. He also was named class president his senior year. After graduating from Phillips in 1942, he was accepted at Yale University, a prestigious school located in New Haven, Connecticut. As soon as he turned eighteen years old, however, Bush decided that he needed to offer his services to his country in World War II. "The country was unified," Bush recalled in a letter published in his memoir, *All the Best*. "It seemed that everyone wanted to do his part—do his duty. Having said that I did not really have any idea when I enlisted what kind of experiences lay ahead. I had never flown before, though I knew I wanted to be a Navy pilot. I had always loved the sea and the idea of flying off a carrier really appealed to me."

Triumph and tragedy in the U.S. Navy

Eager to be a fighter pilot, Bush enlisted in the U.S. Navy Reserve. After completing flight training school, he became a member of the navy's Torpedo Bomber Squadron. He was stationed in the war's "Pacific Theater," a geographic region encompassing the Pacific Ocean and surrounding lands, where American forces were engaged in a fierce struggle against enemy forces from Japan.

By the end of 1943, Bush was the youngest fighter pilot in the entire U.S. Navy. He performed bravely throughout his tour of duty, enduring dangerous fire from enemy forces on numerous occasions. His closest brush with death came on September 2, 1944, when the plane he was piloting was raked by Japanese anti-aircraft fire. "It felt as if a giant fist had crunched into the belly of the plane," Bush wrote in a letter later published in *All the Best.* After being hit, Bush dropped all four bombs that he was carrying on their intended targets, then steered the burning plane out to sea. As flames spread throughout the plane, Bush ordered the other two crewmen in the plane to bail out, then he ejected from the plane himself. He never saw the other two crewmen again.

Bush spent the next several hours floating alone in the sea. He was greatly concerned that he might still be captured by Japanese forces in the region, who had a reputation for torturing prisoners. But after several anxious hours, he was instead rescued by an American submarine. Bush eventually received the Distinguished Flying Cross medal from the U.S. government in recognition of his ordeal.

In December 1944 Bush was released from further military duty. Shortly after returning home to the United States, on January 6, 1945, he married Barbara Pierce, his longtime sweetheart. But even as he began a new stage in his life, the memories of his World War II experiences stayed with him. "I experienced great joy and great sadness," he recalled in a 1998 letter included in *All the Best.* "I laughed a lot, and when my squadron mates were killed, and quite a few were, I wept.... When I look back at my life I put my experience as a 'combat Navy flier' right up at the top of the list of experiences that truly shaped my life."

Successful careers in business and politics

In 1945 Bush enrolled at Yale University, where he earned a bachelor's degree in economics in three years. He then moved to Texas and established a successful business developing offshore oil drilling equipment. George and Barbara Bush also started a family around this time. They eventually had six children, but one of them—daughter Robin—died from leukemia, a form of cancer, in 1953 at age three. "To this day, like every parent who has lost a child—we wonder why," Bush wrote in *Looking Forward.* "Yet we know that whatever the reason, she is in God's loving arms."

During the 1960s Bush became a leading activist in the Texas Republican Party. In 1964 he earned the Republican nomination for a seat in the United States Senate, but he was defeated in the general election. Two years later he won election to the U.S. House of Representatives. He easily won re-election in 1968, but in 1970 he abandoned his Congressional seat to make another bid for a spot in the U.S. Senate. Despite active support from Republican President Richard M. Nixon, however, Bush lost to Democrat Lloyd Bentsen.

In 1971 Bush was named U.S. ambassador to the United Nations, and he spent the next two years working at the UN's New York City headquarters. In 1973 he was named chairman of the Republican National Committee, an organization dedicated to helping Republicans in elections and policy discussions. His biggest challenge as chairman was dealing with the Watergate scandal, in which it was revealed that President Richard Nixon and members of his staff engaged in numerous illegal activities during and after his re-election campaign of 1972. Nixon's personal involvement in the scandal eventually convinced most Americans, including political figures such as Bush, that he was unfit to hold public office. On August 9, 1973, Nixon resigned and Vice President Gerald R. Ford took the oath of the presidency.

In October 1974 President Ford named Bush his chief diplomat to China. Bush and his family enjoyed their time in China. They were fascinated by Chinese culture and loved traveling throughout the country. But in December 1975 Bush was called back to the United States to take over the Central Intelligence Agency (CIA). The CIA is responsible for gathering information, often through spying, on the activities of other countries and organizations that might affect the United States. Bush served as director of the CIA until Ford lost to Democratic candidate Jimmy Carter in the 1976 election.

After leaving the CIA, Bush and his family returned to Texas. In 1980 Bush ran for the Republican Party's presidential nomination. He was a popular choice among many Republican voters but was eventually defeated by former California governor Ronald Reagan. Mindful of Bush's popularity, Reagan asked him to be the party's vice presidential nominee, and Bush accepted. A few months later, the Reagan-Bush ticket easily defeated President Jimmy Carter and Vice President Walter Mondale to claim the White House.

Reagan and Bush took their respective oaths of office on January 21, 1981. They kept these positions for the next eight years, for Reagan-Bush easily won reelection in 1984, winning forty-nine of the fifty states. Throughout Bush's eight years as vice president, he publicly defended all of Reagan's positions, even when he privately disagreed with the president.

In 1988 the Republican Party chose Bush to be their candidate to succeed Reagan, who was nearing the end of his last term in office. Bush had campaigned hard to be the Republican candidate, and he was delighted to earn the nomination. "I may not be the most eloquent [candidate]," he admitted in his acceptance speech at the Republican National Convention. "I may sometimes be a little awkward. But there is nothing self-conscious in my love of country. I am a quiet man—but I hear the quiet people others don't. The quiet people who raise the family, pay the taxes, meet the mortgage. I hear them, and their concerns are mine."

Bush easily won the 1988 presidential election, defeating Democratic candidate Michael Dukakis. He took the oath of office to be the forty-first president of the United States on January 20, 1989. Bush's highest priorities as president included improving education, helping businesses, and reducing the huge federal budget deficit that he inherited from the Reagan administration. In 1990, however, he was forced to turn his attention to a brewing crisis in the Middle East.

The Persian Gulf War

On August 2, 1990, Iraqi leader Saddam Hussein had ordered his military forces to invade the neighboring country of Kuwait. Hussein argued that Iraq had a historical claim to Kuwait's territory. He also wanted to control Kuwait's oil reserves and to gain access to Kuwait's port on the Persian Gulf. The United States and many other countries expressed outrage about Iraq's attack and demanded that Hussein give up his claim on Kuwait. When he refused, the United States organized a military coalition against Iraq that eventually grew to include five hundred thousand U.S. troops and two hundred thousand soldiers from other nations. In addition, the Bush administration successfully lobbied the United Nations

President George H. W. Bush speaking to the press about Iraq's invasion of Kuwait. Bush is flanked by his Middle East advisors, Defense Secretary Dick Cheney (left) and Chairman of the Joint Chiefs of Staff Colin Powell (right).
Photograph by Doug Mills. AP/Wide World Photos. Reproduced by permission.

to pass a tough resolution approving the use of military force to free Kuwait from Iraq's army.

According to Bush, the United States played a vital role in shaping the decisive international response to Iraq's aggression. "The importance of the United States leadership is brought home to me clearly," he wrote in a September 7, 1990, letter reprinted in *All the Best*. The letter went on to say:

> It's only the United States that can lead.... But it is my theory that the more they [smaller, less powerful countries] are included on the take-off, the more we get their opinion, the more we reach out no matter what is involved, in terms of time involved, the better it is. Everyone is proud. Everyone has his place in the sun—large country or small, they should be consulted, their opinions considered. Then when the United States makes a move and I make a decision [about going to war against Iraq], we are more apt to have solid support.

The stalemate between Iraq and the U.S.-led coalition forces continued through the end of 1990. Bush admitted in a December 31 letter to his family reprinted in *All the Best*:

I have thought long and hard about what might have to be done.... As I write this letter at Year's end, there is still some hope that Iraq's dictator will pull out of Kuwait. I vary on this. Sometimes I think he might, at others I think he simply is too unrealistic—too ignorant of what he might face. I have the peace of mind that comes from knowing that we have tried hard for peace. We have gone to the UN; we have formed an historic coalition; there have been diplomatic initiatives from country after country.... I guess what I want you to know as a father is this: Every human life is precious. When the question is asked, 'How many lives are you willing to sacrifice'—it tears at my heart. The answer, of course, is none—none at all. We have waited to give sanctions a chance, we have moved a tremendous force so as to reduce the risk to every American soldier if force has to be used; but the question of loss of life still lingers and plagues the heart.

On January 16, 1991, Bush approved the launch of Operation Desert Storm, a major bombing campaign against Iraqi military positions in Kuwait and Iraq. "I have never felt a day like this in my life," he wrote in *All the Best*. "My mind is a thousand miles away. I simply can't sleep. I think of what other Presidents went through. The agony of war. I think of our able pilots, their training, their gung-ho spirit. And also what it is they are being asked to do." But despite his anxiety about the lives of American soldiers, he expressed a deep conviction that he had made the right decision. "For me this [conflict against Iraq] is good versus evil," he wrote in a January 22, 1991, letter included in *All the Best*. "It is right versus wrong. It is the world versus Iraq's brutal dictator, with his cruelty, his international arrogance, his thumbing his nose at the rest of the world."

The American-led bombing campaign lasted for thirty-eight days before giving way to a ground assault on Iraqi positions in Kuwait and southern Iraq. This ground attack crushed Iraq's remaining military forces in less than one hundred hours. As Iraq's tattered forces retreated to Baghdad, Iraq's capital city, Bush decided to call off the attack. A short time later, Iraq agreed to all of the coalition demands, including giving up all claims to Kuwait. "I was convinced, as were all our Arab friends and allies, that Hussein would be overthrown once the war ended," Bush stated in *All the Best*. "We underestimated his brutality and cruelty to his own people and the stranglehold he has on his country. We were disappointed, but I still do not regret my decision to end the war when we did.... Our mission, as mandated [declared] by the

Texan "Red" Adair Corrals Kuwaiti Oil Well Fires

As Iraqi military forces fled Kuwait in the final days of the Persian Gulf War, they set fire to hundreds of Kuwaiti oil wells. This despicable act of environmental terrorism created a terrible air pollution hazard for the Kuwaiti people. Smoke and oil carried on the wind from the ruined oil wells poisoned trees and grazing livestock, contaminated fresh water supplies, and threatened the health of people throughout the Persian Gulf. Desperate to deal with this emergency situation, the U.S. government called in "Red" Adair, the world's most famous oil well firefighter. Some analysts thought that the damaged oil wells would burn for years. But working together, Adair's crew and other firefighting companies capped every well within nine months.

Paul N. "Red" Adair was born June 18, 1915, in Houston, Texas. He dropped out of high school to help support his family, and over the next several years took a wide assortment of jobs. In 1945 he was inducted into the U.S. Army, where he achieved the rank of staff sergeant. He returned to the Houston area after completing his military service and secured a job with Myron Kinley, one of the country's early pioneers in controlling oil wells that "blow out," spray large volumes of oil into the air or water, or catch on fire.

Adair worked for Kinley's company until 1959, when he decided to form his own company to control oil well fires and blowouts. Over the next three decades, he gained international fame for his success in controlling major oil well fires and blowouts, both on land and on oil rigs located far out at sea. He also developed some of the oil industry's most effective machines for controlling underwater oil wells that catch on fire or blow out.

One of the notable achievements of Adair's career was his role in neutralizing oil field fires in Kuwait following the Gulf War. Adair and his team extinguished 117 oil well fires across Kuwait, including many wells located in the country's most valuable oil fields. When the crisis first erupted, some analysts thought that it might take up to five years to cap all of the burning wells. They pointed out that shortages of water and equipment posed tremendous challenges to Adair and the other firefighting companies arriving in Kuwait. But Adair's company worked tirelessly to put out the fires, and the legendary firefighter and his crews completed their task in only nine months. A few months later, President George H. W. Bush sent Adair a Special Letter of Recognition thanking him for his help.

In 1994 Adair sold his business for an estimated $10 million and retired, saying that he wanted to spend more time with his family. Even after retiring, however, he continued to advise the oil industry on a wide range of oil well safety issues.

Sources: "Paul N. 'Red' Adair." Available online at http://www.redadair.com/bio.html (accessed April 2, 2004); "Red Adair." Contemporary Newsmakers *1987. Reproduced in* Biography Resource Center. *Farmington Hills, MI: Gale Group, 2003; Singerman, Philip.* Red Adair: An American Hero. *New York: Bloomsbury, 1989.*

United Nations, was clear: end the aggression. We did that. We liberated Kuwait and destroyed Hussein's military machine so that he could no longer threaten his neighbors."

Loses 1992 election

The U.S. victory in the Persian Gulf War made Bush enormously popular with the American people. But as time passed, the weak U.S. economy eroded his standing with American voters. In addition, Bush struggled to erase a widely held public perception that he was out of touch with the challenges facing average American families. As a result, Democratic presidential candidate Bill Clinton was able to defeat Bush in the November 1992 presidential election.

Bush held office until January 20, 1993, when Clinton took over. On his last day as president, Bush felt a range of emotions. "And so time goes on and I'm sitting here now alone, the desk is clear and the pictures are gone," he wrote in a diary entry that appeared in *All the Best*. Bush's diary entry continued:

> I leave a note on the desk for Bill Clinton. It looks a little lonely sitting there. I don't want it to be overly dramatic, but I did want him to know that I would be rooting for him.... I feel the same sense of wonder and majesty about this office today as I did when I first walked in here. I've tried to serve here with no taint or dishonor; no conflict of interest; nothing to sully [stain] this beautiful place and this job I've been privileged to hold.

After leaving the White House, Bush retired from public life. He and his wife Barbara divided their time between homes in Houston, Texas, and Kennebunkport, Maine. In 2000 he was delighted to see his son George W. Bush defeat Democratic candidate Al Gore in the most closely contested presidential election in U.S. history. In 2003 the United States invaded Iraq and seized control of the country within a matter of weeks. President George W. Bush thus succeeded in removing Saddam Hussein from power nearly a dozen years after his father had defeated Hussein in the Persian Gulf War.

Where to Learn More

Bush, George. *All the Best, George Bush: My Life in Letters and Other Writings.* New York: Scribner, 1999.

Bush, George, with Victor Gold. *Looking Forward.* Garden City, NJ: Doubleday, 1987.

"George Bush." *American Decades CD-ROM.* Reproduced in *Biography Resource Center,* Farmington Hills, MI: Gale Group, 2003.

Price, Sean. "The Mother of All Battles." *New York Times Upfront,* March 28, 2003.

Sufrin, Mark. *George Bush: The Story of the Forty-First President of the United States.* New York: Dell, 1989.

George W. Bush

Born July 6, 1946
New Haven, Connecticut

President of the United States during the 2003 Iraq War

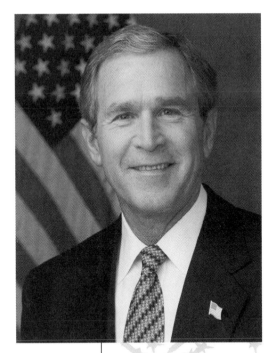

George W. Bush served as president of the United States during the 2003 Iraq War. He is the son of former President **George H. W. Bush** (see entry), who led the United States during the 1991 Persian Gulf War. The younger Bush launched a second war against Iraq in March 2003 with the goal of removing Iraqi leader **Saddam Hussein** (see entry) from power. The younger Bush described Hussein as a brutal dictator who possessed weapons of mass destruction and could provide such weapons to international terrorist groups.

The war succeeded in liberating Iraq from Hussein's rule, but a massive search failed to uncover any weapons of mass destruction. In addition, U.S. troops struggled to maintain security in the face of violent Iraqi resistance during the reconstruction process. Considering the postwar problems, some analysts questioned the Bush administration's ability to create a stable, democratic Iraq.

Enjoys a privileged upbringing

George Walker Bush was born on July 6, 1946, in New Haven, Connecticut, but his family moved to Texas when he

"The history, the logic, and the facts lead to one conclusion: Saddam Hussein's regime is a grave and gathering danger."

George W. Bush in a speech before the UN General Assembly.

George W. Bush. *Courtesy of The White House. Reproduced by permission.*

was two years old. He grew up in Midland and Houston while his father, George Herbert Walker Bush, made a fortune in the oil industry. A strong-willed boy, George sometimes proved difficult for his mother, Barbara Pierce Bush, to handle. In elementary school and junior high, George was a popular student who earned only mediocre grades. He also was a huge baseball fan who enjoyed playing Little League and memorizing the statistics of his favorite major-league players.

In 1961 Bush was sent back east to attend Phillips Academy, a prestigious prep school located in Andover, Massachusetts. He became known for his outgoing nature and good humor in the face of the school's competitive atmosphere. He played a variety of sports while in school. Although his grades remained average, he used his family connections to get into Yale University in 1964. Two years later his father was elected to the U.S. House of Representatives. During his years at Yale, Bush served as the president of Delta Kappa Epsilon fraternity. He enjoyed going to parties, drinking, playing football, and dating, but did not show much concern about his academic performance.

After earning his bachelor's degree in 1968, Bush received a coveted spot in the Texas Air National Guard. At that time, thousands of young American men were being drafted into the U.S. military to serve in the Vietnam War. Since the National Guard provided an opportunity to complete military service without much danger of being sent to Vietnam, many young men tried to secure positions in this branch of the service. Some critics claimed that Bush used his family connections to move ahead of others on the waiting list.

In any case, Bush trained as a pilot in F-102 fighter jets and was eventually stationed at Ellington Air Force Base in Houston. Bush has long claimed that he fulfilled all of his National Guard service obligations. But during his years as president, opponents charged that he missed months of duty so that he could help out a family friend's political campaign.

Finds religion and changes course

In 1970 Bush's father campaigned for a seat in the U.S. Senate but lost the election. The elder Bush was later appointed U.S. ambassador to the United Nations and chairman of the Republican National Committee. In 1972 George W. Bush went to Harvard Business School, earning a master's degree in 1975. He then returned to Texas, where he met and married librarian Laura Welch. The couple eventually had twin daughters, Barbara and Jenna. In 1977 Bush surprised many people by announcing his intention to run for a seat in the U.S. Congress. He won the Republican primary but lost the election.

Bush then began working in the oil industry. But his company, Arbusto Energy, failed to strike oil and experienced severe financial problems over the next few years. In 1980 his father was elected vice president of the United States under President Ronald Reagan. The following year Texas-based Harken Energy Corporation, which was run by powerful friends of his father, purchased Arbusto Energy and offered Bush a job on its board of directors. Critics claimed that Harken bailed out the younger Bush's struggling company so that the vice president would steer lucrative government contracts its way. The deal led to an investigation by government regulators, but no charges of wrongdoing were ever filed.

In 1985 George W. Bush met with evangelist Billy Graham at the Bush family home in Kennebunkport, Maine. He later claimed that the meeting led to a "personal conversion" and he became a born-again Christian. A year later, following a raucous fortieth birthday party, Bush quit drinking alcohol. After he became president, he explained that discovering his religious faith marked a major turning point in his life. "I had a drinking problem," he admitted, as quoted in *The Right Man.* "Right now I should be in a bar in Texas, not the Oval Office. There is only one reason that I am in the Oval Office and not in a bar. I found faith. I found God."

Elected governor of Texas

In 1988 Bush worked on his father's successful presidential election campaign. He then organized a group of investors to buy the struggling Texas Rangers baseball franchise. Over the next several years, Bush became the most visible of the team's owners. He helped turn the franchise around by arranging a lucrative deal in which taxpayers financed a new stadium for the team.

In 1991 Bush's father led the United States during the Persian Gulf War. The war succeeded in forcing the Middle Eastern nation of Iraq to withdraw its army from neighboring Kuwait after only six weeks of fighting. Despite the impressive military victory, President Bush faced criticism for his decision to end the war before U.S. troops reached Baghdad, which allowed Iraqi leader Saddam Hussein to remain in power. In addition, many Americans felt that the president did not understand their concerns about the U.S. economy and other domestic issues. In 1992 the elder Bush lost his bid for reelection to Democrat Bill Clinton.

With his father's career effectively over, George W. Bush felt free to pursue his own political ambitions. In 1994 he resigned from the Rangers job to run for governor of Texas. After securing the Republican Party nomination, he defeated the incumbent Ann Richards with 53.5 percent of the vote. As governor, Bush became known for his ability to build coalitions and reach compromises with members of the opposing political party. His major accomplishment was reforming public education in Texas.

In 1998 Bush was reelected governor of Texas with 68.6 percent of the vote. Later that year his group of investors sold the Rangers baseball franchise. Bush earned nearly $15 million on the deal, which he used to run for president of the United States in 2000. As a presidential candidate, Bush appealed to fiscally conservative Republicans as well as to socially conservative Christians. He also enjoyed support from big business, especially the oil industry. He collected more campaign contributions than any previous candidate, which was a big factor in his victory over U.S. Senator John McCain in the Republican primary.

Becomes president in a disputed election

During the presidential race, Bush presented himself as a "compassionate conservative." He was criticized for his lack of experience in foreign policy, his close ties to special interest groups and big business, and his tendency to misspeak and jumble his words. But many praised his folksy appeal, which they claimed made his opponent, Vice President Al Gore, seem stiff by comparison. Some voters also appreciated the Bush campaign's focus on domestic issues like education reform and tax cuts.

The 2000 election turned out to be the closest in American history. Gore won the popular vote (the actual number of individuals who cast their ballots) by more than five hundred thousand. But Bush won a narrow victory in the electoral college (an institution that converts the popular vote into delegates awarded from each state). Questions arose about the process used to count votes in Florida, where Bush's brother Jeb served as governor. These questions were ultimately decided by the U.S. Supreme Court, which voted 5 to 4 to award Bush the presidency.

Upon taking office, Bush surrounded himself with an administration full of experienced politicians, including Vice President **Dick Cheney** (see entry), Secretary of State **Colin Powell** (see entry), and Secretary of Defense **Donald Rumsfeld** (see entry). Still, Bush had trouble finding his stride during his first eight months in office. The United States entered an economic recession, and a wave of corporate scandals caused a decline in the stock market. But then a national crisis caused the American people to rally around the president. On September 11, 2001, members of a radical Islamic terrorist group called Al Qaeda hijacked four commercial airplanes and crashed them into the World Trade Center towers in New York City, the Pentagon building near Washington, D.C., and a field in Pennsylvania. Nearly three thousand people were killed in the attacks.

That evening, Bush appeared on national television to reassure the American people. "Today, our fellow citizens, our way of life, our very freedom, came under attack in a series of deliberate and deadly terrorist attacks," he stated. "Terrorist attacks can shake the foundations of our biggest buildings, but they cannot touch the foundation of America. These acts shattered steel, but they cannot dent the steel of American resolve. America was targeted for attack because we're the brightest beacon for freedom and opportunity in the world. And no one will keep that light from shining."

In the wake of September 11, Bush announced a global war on terrorism that initially focused on the people directly responsible for the attacks, Muslim cleric (religious leader) Osama bin Laden and his Al Qaeda terrorist organization. U.S. intelligence experts quickly tracked bin Laden to

Afghanistan, a country on the outskirts of the Middle East that was led by a radical Islamic government called the Taliban. The Bush administration demanded that the Taliban turn over bin Laden and members of Al Qaeda so that they could be punished for organizing the September 11 terrorist attacks. But the Taliban viewed bin Laden as a hero to the fundamentalist Islamic cause and refused to cooperate.

In October 2001 Bush launched Operation Enduring Freedom, a series of air strikes that targeted Taliban military capabilities and Al Qaeda training facilities in Afghanistan. The United States also provided military support to the Northern Alliance, an Afghan opposition group that had long fought against the Taliban. Although the U.S. troops and their Afghan allies soon succeeded in removing the Taliban from power, bin Laden managed to escape. Still, Bush administration officials claimed that they had completed the first phase in their global war against terrorism by destroying the home base of Al Qaeda.

Launches an invasion of Iraq

In early 2002 Bush expanded the fight against terrorism to include nations that he described as harboring terrorists or providing weapons, training, or financial support for their activities. Among the countries that he accused of supporting terrorism was Iraq. Ever since Bush's father had led the United States to victory in the 1991 Persian Gulf War, Iraqi leader Saddam Hussein had failed to comply with the UN peace agreement that had ended the war. Part of this agreement required Iraq to destroy its biological and chemical weapons and allow UN weapons inspectors to monitor its progress. But Hussein consistently failed to cooperate with the inspectors and threw them out of Iraq in 1998. Although there was no clear link between Hussein's government and Al Qaeda, Bush claimed that Iraq possessed weapons of mass destruction and could provide such weapons to terrorists. He argued that Hussein posed an immediate threat to world security and should be removed from power in Iraq.

In September 2002 Bush challenged the United Nations to enforce its resolutions calling for Iraq to destroy its weapons of mass destruction and submit to international weapons inspections. He also made it clear that the United States would act alone to disarm Iraq by force if necessary. "The history, the logic, and the facts lead to one conclusion: Saddam Hussein's regime is a grave and gathering danger," he said in a speech before the UN General Assembly. "To suggest otherwise is to hope against the evidence. To assume this regime's good faith is to bet the lives of millions and the peace of the world in a reckless gamble. And this is a risk we must not take."

Bush's threat to invade Iraq created a great deal of controversy in the international community. Some of America's longtime allies, including France and Germany, strongly opposed a U.S. military invasion of Iraq. Large-scale antiwar protests took place in many countries around the world. While some Americans appreciated Bush's firm stand in the face of international opposition, others criticized him for using "cowboy diplomacy." Some people questioned his motives for going to war in Iraq. Critics claimed that he wanted to remove Hussein from power because of personal resentment, or in order to gain access to Iraq's vast oil reserves.

As the threat of American military action increased, Iraq agreed to allow the UN weapons inspectors to return "without conditions." In November the UN Security Council responded to Bush's calls for action by unanimously passing a new resolution regarding Iraq. Resolution 1441 declared Iraq in violation of earlier UN resolutions, authorized a new round of weapons inspections, and promised that Iraq would face serious consequences if it failed to comply.

UN weapons inspectors returned to Iraq on November 18, 2002. Their reports over the next few months contained mixed results. Sometimes Iraqi authorities were very cooperative. At other times, however, they seemed to be hiding information from the inspectors. The Bush administration was dissatisfied with the reports and continued to pressure the UN Security Council to authorize the use of military force to disarm Iraq and remove Hussein from power. But many nations objected to Bush's calls for an invasion of Iraq. After a series of tense diplomatic negotiations, it became clear that France would use its veto power to block a new resolution authorizing the use of military force in Iraq. The United States and its allies decided not to seek a new resolution, instead arguing that military force was permitted under resolution 1441.

On March 17, 2003, Bush gave Saddam Hussein and his two sons forty-eight hours to leave Iraq or face a U.S.-led military invasion. "The danger is clear," he said in a nationally televised speech. President Bush went on to say:

> Using chemical, biological, or one day nuclear weapons, obtained with the help of Iraq, the terrorists could fulfill their stated ambitions and kill thousands or hundreds of thousands of innocent people in our country or any other. The United States and other nations did nothing to deserve or invite this threat, but we will do everything to defeat it. Instead of drifting along toward tragedy, we will set a course toward safety. Before the day of horror can come, before it is too late to act, this danger will be removed.

Removes Saddam Hussein from power

When Hussein ignored the ultimatum to leave Iraq, Bush ordered the invasion of the country. Operation Iraqi Freedom began with a series of punishing air strikes against the Iraqi capital of Baghdad. Thousands of tanks and other military vehicles then moved into Iraq as part of a major ground attack. From the beginning of the conflict, coalition troops faced less organized resistance from the Iraqi army than they expected. But they also received a more hostile reception from the Iraqi people than they anticipated. In fact, they faced a surprising number of sneak attacks from Iraqi resistance fighters using tactics of guerilla warfare (an unconventional fighting style that uses methods like ambushes, booby traps, and sniper attacks). As the situation in Iraq grew more complicated, the Bush administration faced increasing criticism of its war plan.

In early April the coalition forces prepared to fight for control of Baghdad. U.S. military officials worried that the troops might face stiff resistance from Iraqi Republican Guard forces, as well as the possibility of chemical weapons attacks, as they neared the capital. But Operation Iraqi Freedom continued to proceed rapidly and the Iraqi capital fell to coalition forces on April 9, after only three weeks of combat. Over the next week, coalition forces went on to capture Mosul and Tikrit in northern Iraq and secure the southern city of Basra. On May 1, 2003, Bush made a historic speech aboard the aircraft carrier USS *Abraham Lincoln* in which he declared an end to major combat operations in Iraq.

As soon as the war ended, the Bush administration began working to reconstruct Iraq and help the Iraqi people establish a democratic government. But the U.S. government's postwar plans soon ran into trouble. Security became a concern as Iraqi insurgents (people who fight against an established government or occupation force) and foreign fighters launched a series of violent attacks against American troops and international aid workers in Iraq. Although Saddam Hussein and most high-ranking members of his regime were eventually captured or killed, the postwar violence continued. The lack of security made it difficult for humanitarian aid to reach the Iraqi people, so conditions in the country were slow to improve. Despite massive searches, no evidence of weapons of mass destruction was found in Iraq, which raised questions about the Bush administration's stated reasons for going to war.

The Iraq War accomplished several important goals for the Bush administration. It removed a brutal dictator from power, ended decades of repression for the Iraqi people, and demonstrated the strength of U.S. military forces. But it also cost the United States billions of dollars, committed its military to a long and uncertain process of nation-building, and strained the alliances that the United States had depended on since World War II (1939–45). Bush said that he invaded Iraq in order to make the world safer for America's interests. Afterward, however, some analysts claimed that U.S. actions in Iraq had caused widespread resentment in the Arab world and made it easier for terrorist groups to recruit new members.

The majority of Americans supported Bush's decision to invade Iraq, and his approval ratings exceeded 70 percent at the beginning of the conflict. But the postwar problems in Iraq—combined with concerns about domestic issues like unemployment, health care, and a growing national budget deficit—dropped his approval ratings to around 50 percent in early 2004. Many people felt that the 2004 presidential elections would provide the final assessment of Bush's performance.

Where to Learn More

Alterman, Eric, and Mark J. Green. *The Book on Bush: How George W. (Mis)leads America.* New York: Viking, 2004.

Frum, David. *The Right Man: The Surprise Presidency of George W. Bush.* New York: Random House, 2003.

"George W. Bush." *Encyclopedia of World Biography,* vol. 21, 2001. Reproduced in *Biography Resource Center.* Farmington Hills, MI: Gale Group, 2004.

"George W. Bush." *Worldmark Encyclopedia of the Nations: World Leaders,* 2003. Reproduced in *Biography Resource Center.* Farmington Hills, MI: Gale Group, 2004.

Gormley, Beatrice. *President George W. Bush.* New York: Aladdin, 2001.

Purdum, Todd S., and the staff of the *New York Times. A Time of Our Choosing: America's War in Iraq.* New York: Times Books, 2003.

Sifry, Micah L., and Christopher Serf, eds. *The Iraq War Reader.* New York: Simon and Schuster, 2003.

Ahmad Chalabi

Born c. 1945
Baghdad, Iraq

Exiled Iraqi opposition leader who founded the Iraqi National Congress

A hmad Chalabi is one of the best-known members of the Iraqi opposition to Saddam Hussein's government. After living in exile abroad for most of his life, Chalabi returned to Iraq in 1992 to form the Iraqi National Congress, an influential coalition of major opposition groups. In the years leading up to the 2003 Iraq War, he was often mentioned as a possible future leader of Iraq.

Known for his intelligence, charm, and ambition, Chalabi gained the support of many U.S. leaders over the years, particularly within military circles. But many others questioned his honesty and integrity. "Some American officials, particularly leading Pentagon hawks [military leaders who favor an aggressive policy toward war], regard him as a true democrat and a paragon [perfect model] of Iraqi patriotism, an aristocrat who gave up a potential life of comfort and ease to fight against Hussein at a time when few others dared," wrote Christopher Dickey and Mark Hosenball in *Newsweek*. "Critics, including officials from the CIA and State Department, characterize Chalabi as a corrupt and unreliable ally."

"There is no substitute for an Iraqi political process ... to give legitimacy to a provisional government."

Ahmad Chalabi in an interview for Online NewsHour.

Ahmad Chalabi. *Photograph by Chris Hondros. Getty Images. Reproduced by permission.*

When the 2003 war concluded, Chalabi was named a member of Iraq's provisional government. But he remained a controversial figure within his homeland and seemed to lack the popular support required to lead the new Iraq.

Wealthy family forced into exile

Ahmad Chalabi was born around 1945 in Baghdad, Iraq. He came from a wealthy and influential family of Shiite Muslims. In fact, his family was connected to the Hashemite royal dynasty that British leaders had installed as the rulers of Iraq in 1921. Both Chalabi's father and grandfather served as government ministers under King Faisal II. But when a military coup (a sudden violent overthrow of a government) removed the king from power in 1958, Chalabi and his family were forced to flee from Iraq. The teenager spent the remainder of his youth living in exile in Jordan, Lebanon, Great Britain, and the United States.

Chalabi earned an undergraduate degree in mathematics from the Massachusetts Institute of Technology (MIT) in the mid-1960s, and he added a doctorate in mathematics from the University of Chicago in 1969. He spent the next several years teaching at American University in Beirut, Lebanon, where he met his wife.

In 1977 Chalabi used his own and his family's money to found Petra Bank in Amman, Jordan. With Chalabi as chairman, the bank grew rapidly by introducing such innovations as automated teller machines and credit cards to its customers. In 1989, however, the bank was seized by the government of Jordan and Chalabi was forced to flee the country. He was later tried and convicted in his absence on charges of embezzlement (stealing) and fraud (deception).

Chalabi proclaimed his innocence on these charges. He said that he used his banking connections to help fund Iraqi opposition groups and to block money that **Saddam Hussein** (see entry) needed to finance his war against Iran (1980–88). Chalabi claimed that the Iraqi leader pressured King Hussein of Jordan to seize the bank as revenge for Chalabi's political activities.

Founds the Iraqi National Congress

After leaving Jordan in 1989, Chalabi lived in London for a few years. In August 1990 Iraq invaded its smaller neighbor to the south, Kuwait. Hussein argued that Iraq had a historical claim to Kuwait's territory. He also wanted to control Kuwait's oil reserves and to gain access to Kuwait's port on the Persian Gulf. In early 1991 the United States joined forces with a number of other countries to push the Iraqi army out of Kuwait. The Persian Gulf War ended in a dramatic victory for the U.S.-led coalition in February 1991, when Iraqi troops were forced to withdraw from Kuwait after six weeks of fighting.

Shortly after the 1991 Persian Gulf War ended, Chalabi moved to Iraqi Kurdistan, a semi-independent region in northern Iraq that was protected by a U.S.-patrolled "no-fly zone." In 1992, with the support of the U.S. Central Intelligence Agency (CIA), Chalabi created the Iraqi National Congress (INC). The INC was intended to act as an umbrella organization for all of the major Iraqi opposition groups. A statement of its purpose, quoted in *The Iraq War Reader,* said that it "provides an institutional framework so that the popular will of the Iraqi people … can be democratically determined and implemented."

In its early stages the INC was a genuinely representative political organization aimed at overthrowing Hussein and creating a democratic Iraqi government. It originally included 234 members representing 90 percent of all the Iraqi opposition groups. Chalabi led an active opposition movement in northern Iraq that developed its own newspapers, radio stations, and military force.

In 1996 the INC launched a military offensive intended to remove Hussein from power. But the effort lost crucial assistance from the CIA at the last minute and also failed to attract support from disgruntled members of the Iraqi military. As a result, the coup attempt ended disastrously, with the deaths of thousands of INC supporters. Afterward the INC lost much of its power and ended up relocating its headquarters to London.

Over the next two years, Chalabi spent a great deal of time in Washington, D.C., lobbying for U.S. military action to remove Hussein from power. Although the U.S. government did not provide direct military support to Chalabi's cause, it did supply financial assistance to the Iraqi opposition movement. In 1998 the U.S. Congress passed the Iraq Liberation Act, which gave the INC and other opposition groups

Ahmad Chalabi (right), leader of the Iraqi National Congress, is supported by several bodyguards as he attends the funeral ceremony for Ayatollah Mohammed Baqr al-Hakim. Hakim, leader of the Supreme Assembly of the Islamic Revolution in Iraq, was killed by a car bomb on **August 29, 2003.** *Ahmad al-Rubaye/AFP/Getty Images. Reproduced by permission.*

$97 million to fight Hussein. The following year, however, the INC was accused of using the funds unwisely. Chalabi was demoted from leader to regular member of the INC, and a seven-member leadership group took his place.

Supports U.S. efforts during the 2003 Iraq War

The United Nations (UN) agreement that officially ended the 1991 Persian Gulf War required Iraq to destroy all of its biological, chemical, and nuclear weapons. In the decade after the war ended, however, Hussein consistently refused to honor certain terms of this peace agreement. Most notably, Hussein repeatedly interfered with the UN inspectors sent to verify that Iraq had abandoned its weapons programs. The international community tried a number of different approaches to force Hussein to cooperate with UN weapons inspectors, but instead he kicked the inspectors out of Iraq in 2000. After taking office in 2001, President **George W. Bush** (see entry) claimed that Iraq possessed weapons of mass destruction and posed an immediate threat to world security. In early 2003 the United States launched a second war against Iraq with the goal of removing Hussein from power.

Immediately before the 2003 Iraq war began, Chalabi returned to northern Iraq, where he recruited and trained a small militia. During the war the U.S. military flew him and his forces to Nasiriyah, where they took part in the fighting. The war succeeded in removing Hussein from power after only three weeks of combat, when Baghdad fell to coalition forces on April 9. As soon as the major combat ended, Chalabi moved his base of operations to Baghdad's elite Hunting Club. Chalabi's presence in Baghdad was controversial because many Iraqis viewed him with suspicion. Some criticized him for living comfortably in exile abroad while they suffered under Hussein's rule. Others distrusted him because of his reputation for shady business dealings, his close ties with the United States, and his apparent hunger for power in postwar Iraq.

Member of the Iraq Governing Council

Thanks to his prominent position in the Iraqi opposition movement, however, Chalabi assumed a leading role in Iraq's postwar politics. U.S. civil authorities in Iraq selected him as a member of the Iraq Governing Council (IGC)—an interim (temporary) government composed of twenty-five prominent Iraqis from a range of political, ethnic, and religious backgrounds. Like Chalabi, many members of the IGC were leaders of groups that had opposed Saddam Hussein's government.

From its initial meeting on July 13, the IGC showed its determination to be a positive force for change in Iraq.

Powerful Iraqi Shiite Leader Grand Ayatollah Ali al-Sistani

The Grand Ayatollah Ali al-Husseini al-Sistani is the most powerful Shiite Muslim cleric (religious leader) in Iraq. Muslims (people who practice the religion of Islam) worship one God, called Allah. They believe that Allah revealed himself to man through the Koran, a holy book written in Arabic. The prophet Muhammad founded Islam and began spreading Allah's word in the year 622. Over the next few centuries Muslims divided into two main branches, Sunni and Shiite. The two branches differ mainly over which prophets they recognize as successors (people who rightfully inherit a title) to Muhammad. Today the religion of Islam is practiced by one billion people around the world. Although Shiites account for only about 15 percent of the world's Muslims, they make up about 60 percent of Iraq's population. As a result, al-Sistani holds a great deal of influence over the nation and its future.

Al-Sistani was born around 1930 near the holy city of Masshad in Iran. He began studying the Koran at the age of five. In 1952 he moved to the holy city of Najaf in Iraq, where he studied with some of the most important Shiite clerics of the time. When his mentor, the Grand Ayatollah Imam Abul Qassim al-Khoei, died in 1992, al-Sistani was selected to head an important network of schools in Najaf. He gradually rose through the ranks to reach marjah (object of emulation), the highest level of Shiite religious leadership.

Al-Sistani has written many books on Islamic law and is widely viewed as one of the top Shiite religious authorities in the world. Most Iraqi Shiites look to him for guidance on how to live their lives in accordance with Islamic law. His teachings generally fall within the quietist or moderate tradition, which says that clerics should not be involved directly in government, but should instead provide an independent religious authority.

Throughout the decades of Saddam Hussein's rule, his Sunni-led government oppressed the Shiite majority in Iraq. Therefore, like most Iraqi Shiites, al-Sistani opposed Hussein's regime. He was tolerant of the 2003 U.S.-led invasion of Iraq because it removed Hussein from power. Both during and after the war, al-Sistani encouraged his Shiite followers to cooperate with the coalition forces. In fact, some experts credit al-Sistani's influence for preventing violent opposition to the U.S. occupation from spreading to Shiite-controlled areas of Iraq.

But al-Sistani's goals for Iraq's future do not necessarily match those of U.S. leaders. He wants the new Iraq to be an Islamic state, where Islam is formally recognized as the religion of the majority of Iraqis and no laws are created that conflict with Islamic principles. In contrast, the Bush administration prefers the new Iraq to be led by a secular (nonreligious) government that would tend to be more supportive of American interests. Some experts believe that al-Sistani could support a moderate Islamic democracy that would allow elections, freedom of religion, and other civil rights.

Al-Sistani gained international prominence during the postwar period as U.S. leaders worked to form a new Iraqi government. He publicly disagreed with the American plans at several critical moments in the process. In June 2003 al-Sistani issued a fatwa (religious ruling) saying that only those who were elected by the Iraqi people, rather than appointed by U.S. officials or its hand-picked interim government, the Iraq Governing Council, had the authority to draft a new constitution. U.S. civil administrator L. Paul Bremer initially said that elections would take too long, but he later agreed to speed up the process.

In November 2003 al-Sistani called for direct popular elections, instead of the system of nationwide caucuses proposed by Bremer, to choose Iraq's transitional government. He argued that elections were necessary because then "the parliament would spring from the will of the Iraqis and would represent them in a just manner and would prevent any diminution [reduction] of Islamic law." Since Shiites make up the majority of Iraq's population, al-Sistani believed that elections would ensure that the

government would represent his followers' interests. In January 2004 al-Sistani called upon Shiites to demonstrate in favor of elections. After thirty thousand people took to the streets of Basra in peaceful protest, Bremer agreed to drop the caucus plan.

Due to security concerns, al-Sistani is rarely seen in public. He meets with visitors at his office in Najaf and expresses his opinion by issuing fatwas. He has consistently refused to speak with L. Paul Bremer or other U.S. officials because he does not want to appear too close to the American occupation forces. But al-Sistani's power and influence over Iraq's Shiite population make it impossible for the Bush administration to ignore his wishes. If they attempt to create a new Iraqi government without his approval, it might very well collapse as soon as American troops withdraw from Iraq.

Sources: Ahrari, Ehsan. "When Sistani Speaks, Bush Listens." Asia Times, 2004. Available online at http://www.atimes.com/atimes/Middle_East/FA17Ak 02.html (accessed on March 24, 2004); Fahs, Hani. "Behind Ayatollah Ali al-Sistani's Tactics." Al-Hayat, January 23, 2004. Available online at http://www.worldpress.org/Mideast/1773.cfm (accessed on March 14, 2004); Guggenheim, Ken. "Newsview: Cleric Is Wild Card for Washington." Newsday.com, March 17, 2004. Available online at http://www.newsday.com/news/nationworld/world/ wire/sns-ap-us-iraqi-cleric,0,2748416.story?coll=sns- ap-world-headlines (accessed on March 24, 2004); Otterman, Sharon. "Grand Ayatollah Ali al-Sistani." Council on Foreign Relations, January 16, 2004. Available online at http://www.cfr.org/background/ background_iraq_sistani.php (accessed on March 24, 2004).

The group's first official act was to ban six national holidays that had been put in place under Hussein's rule. They declared that Iraq's new national day would be April 9, the anniversary of the fall of Baghdad to coalition forces. They also sent diplomats to visit foreign governments, set up a budget, and formed a war crimes court to put former members of Hussein's government on trial.

Over the next several months the IGC continued its efforts to form a democratic government in Iraq. They faced pressures from various groups within Iraq that wanted to advance their own interests. They also struggled to perform their duties in the face of continuing instability and violence in Baghdad and other parts of central Iraq. Chalabi became a leading voice calling for a timely transfer of political power to the Iraqi people. "We believe an Iraqi political process must be started," he said in an interview for *Online NewsHour*. "There is no substitute for an Iraqi political process ... to give legitimacy to a provisional government."

The next steps in the political process include selecting a transitional assembly of 250 members representing Iraq's provinces, drafting and ratifying a new constitution, and holding free elections. Coalition leaders established a goal of handing over power to an Iraqi government by June 30, 2004. But they acknowledged that it would be difficult to transfer political power to the Iraqi people if they could not reduce the instability and violence within Iraq.

Where to Learn More

"Ahmad Chalabi." *Biography Resource Center Online*. Gale Group, 2003.

"Ahmad Chalabi." *Online NewsHour,* June 11, 2003. Available online at http://www.pbs.org/newshour/bb/middle_east/jan-june03/chalabi_6-11.html (accessed on January 7, 2004).

"Ahmad Chalabi Biography." *Iraqi News,* 2003. Available online at http://www.iraqinews.com/people_chalabi.shtml (accessed on March 24, 2004).

Dickey, Christopher, and Mark Hosenball. "Banker, Schmoozer, Spy." *Newsweek,* May 12, 2003. Available online at http://msnbc.msn.com/id/3068557/ (accessed on March 24, 2004).

Purdum, Todd S., and the staff of the *New York Times*. *A Time of Our Choosing: America's War in Iraq*. New York: Times Books, 2003.

Singer, Max. "After Saddam: The Controversy over Ahmad Chalabi." *National Review,* June 20, 2002. Available online at http://www.national review.com/comment/comment-singer062002.asp (accessed on March 24, 2004).

"A Who's Who of the Iraqi Opposition." In Sifry, Micah L., and Christopher Serf, eds. *The Iraq War Reader.* New York: Simon and Schuster, 2003.

Dick Cheney

Born January 30, 1941
Lincoln, Nebraska

Served as U.S. secretary of defense during the 1991 Persian Gulf War and vice president during the 2003 Iraq War

Dick Cheney's work as U.S. secretary of defense under President **George H. W. Bush** (see entry) was a milestone in his long and distinguished political career. He helped plan and carry out Operation Desert Shield and Operation Desert Storm, the two main phases of the U.S. military campaign against Iraq that became known as the 1991 Persian Gulf War. In addition, Cheney spent a great deal of time explaining the Bush administration's military and political goals to the American people throughout the conflict.

Cheney's term as secretary of defense came to an end in 1994. But seven years later he became vice president of the United States in the administration of **George W. Bush** (see entry), son of the former president. In this new position, Cheney helped convince the younger Bush to launch a military invasion of Iraq in 2003. This war succeeded in removing Iraqi leader **Saddam Hussein** (see entry) from power.

Early interest in politics

Richard "Dick" B. Cheney was born in Lincoln, Nebraska, on January 30, 1941. His parents were Richard H. Ch-

"Saddam Hussein's pursuit of weapons of mass destruction poses a grave danger, not only to his neighbors, but also to the United States...."

Dick Cheney on CNN.

Dick Cheney. *AP/Wide World Photos. Reproduced by permission.*

eney, a worker for the U.S. Department of Agriculture, and Marjorie L. Dickey. Cheney spent most of his childhood in Casper, Wyoming, where he excelled in his school work. He continued his schooling at Connecticut's Yale University, one of the country's finest colleges. But he struggled with his studies and dropped out during his sophomore year. Cheney returned home to Casper, where he worked for two years before deciding to return to school. He enrolled at the nearby University of Wyoming, where he earned a bachelor's degree in 1965 and a master's degree in political science in 1966.

Keenly interested in building a career in politics, Cheney worked hard to establish relationships with Wyoming lawmakers. He accepted internships with several legislators and even worked on the staff of the state governor. Cheney's performed so well in these roles that the leadership of the national Republican Party decided that he deserved a real opportunity to develop his talents. In 1968 he was appointed a special assistant to **Donald Rumsfeld** (see entry), who at that time was director of the Office of Economic Opportunity in the administration of President Richard Nixon. Cheney spent the next few years working closely with Rumsfeld, who worked in several important positions in the Nixon administration.

In 1973 Cheney left politics to work for an investment company. But when Republican President Gerald R. Ford took office in 1974, he returned to Washington, D.C., as a special assistant to the White House. In 1975 Ford asked him to serve as chief of staff. This was an enormous honor for the thirty-four-year-old Cheney, for the chief of staff supervises the daily operations of the White House and its staff.

Cheney served as White House chief of staff from 1975 to early 1977. During this time, Cheney gained a reputation as a hard-working, loyal, intelligent, and effective counselor to the president. In January 1977 Democrat Jimmy Carter was sworn in as president, so Cheney returned to his home state of Wyoming.

Powerful member of Congress

In 1978 Cheney ran for political office for the first time. First he clinched the Republican nomination for Wyoming's lone seat in the U.S. House of Representatives, even though he suffered a mild heart attack in the middle of the campaign. He then defeated the Democratic Party's nominee in the general election, giving him the opportunity to represent the people of Wyoming back in Washington, D.C.

Once Cheney took office, he quickly established himself as one of the most powerful and conservative members of the House. He served from 1978 to 1989, successfully defending his seat against Democratic challengers in five straight elections. During this period he emerged as a recognized leader of the national Republican Party and a strong supporter of President Ronald Reagan, who served from 1981 to 1989. Health problems continued to hound him, however, and in 1988 he was forced to undergo quadruple-bypass heart surgery. The operation was a success, but Cheney has suffered four heart attacks over the years, and questions about his health have followed him throughout his career.

In 1989 Cheney received a new political challenge when President George H. W. Bush asked him to serve as secretary of defense in his new administration. As Bush's defense secretary, Cheney would be responsible for supervising all aspects of the U.S. military. Some people criticized Bush for selecting Cheney, who had never served in the military and did not have much experience dealing with the leadership of the army, air force, navy, and marines. But Bush and many other people defended the choice. They pointed out that Cheney enjoyed the respect of both Republicans and Democrats in Congress, and they claimed that his calm but decisive style made him ideally suited to manage the U.S. military.

Soon after Cheney's nomination was approved by the U.S. Senate, the Bush administration faced its first major international test. American officials became convinced that General Manuel Noriega, the dictator of a Central American nation called Panama, was allowing drug dealers to take shipments of drugs through Panama on their way to the United States. The Bush administration also expressed concern about Noriega's refusal to honor the results of Panamanian elections and about Panama's treatment of American soldiers stationed in the country.

By December 1989, relations between the United States and Panama had reached a crisis point. Bush ordered Cheney and other U.S. military leaders to devise a strategy to

Secretary of Defense Dick
Cheney meets with Saudi
officials during the 1991
Persian Gulf War. ©Liaison
Agency. Reproduced by
permission.

invade Panama and arrest Noriega. On December 20, 1989,
this plan, called Operation Just Cause, was launched. The
nighttime invasion by U.S. forces destroyed Noriega's headquarters and other important military posts. On January 3,
1990, Noriega surrendered to the United States, and he remains in the U.S. prison system.

Confrontation with Iraq

In August 1990 the Bush administration turned its attention to a region of the world known as the Middle East,
where Iraq, a country with a large and powerful military, had
staged a surprise invasion of neighboring Kuwait. Iraqi leader
Saddam Hussein had ordered his military forces to invade
Kuwait because he believed that Iraq had a historical claim to
Kuwait's territory. He also wanted to control Kuwait's oil reserves and to gain access to Kuwait's port on the Persian Gulf.
The United States and many other countries expressed outrage

about Iraq's attack. They demanded that Hussein remove his forces from Kuwait or face the consequences. When he refused, many of these countries sent military forces to the Persian Gulf region to join a U.S.-led coalition against Iraq. The coalition eventually grew to include five hundred thousand U.S. troops and two hundred thousand soldiers from other nations.

Many of these coalition forces were placed in Saudi Arabia, a long-time ally of the United States. The leaders of Saudi Arabia had expressed deep reservations about letting U.S. soldiers into their country. But Cheney and a small team of other American officials convinced the Saudi leaders to host the U.S. troops. Cheney pointed out that Hussein had repeatedly threatened to attack Saudi Arabia, and he stressed that the entire Middle East region would suffer if Iraq's invasion went unpunished.

Cheney played a major role in the campaign to protect Saudi Arabia, which came to be known as Operation Desert Shield. In addition, he approved the military campaign known as Operation Desert Storm, in which U.S.-led planes pounded Iraqi military positions with thousands of bombs. The bombing campaign began on January 16, 1991, and lasted for thirty-eight days. American forces then began the second phase of Desert Storm, a ground attack that destroyed most of Iraq's remaining military forces in less than five days. Iraq surrendered on February 26, 1991, and gave up all claims to Kuwait.

After helping guide the United States to victory in the Persian Gulf War, Cheney returned to his administrative duties as defense secretary. He made several major changes to the U.S. military in 1992 and 1993, the first year of Democrat Bill Clinton's presidency. For example, Cheney closed several unneeded military bases and reduced the overall size of the armed forces. But he also approved major investments in new high-technology weapons programs.

In 1994 Cheney resigned from his post as defense secretary. A few months later he was named president and chief executive officer (CEO) of Halliburton, one of the largest oil exploration and development companies in the world. He led Halliburton for the next five years, using his organizational skills and international business and political contacts to help the company reach new levels of success.

Returns to public service

In 2000 Cheney returned to the political arena once again. Texas Governor George W. Bush, a son of former President George H. W. Bush, for whom Cheney had served as secretary of defense, clinched the Republican Party's nomination for president of the United States. Governor Bush initially asked Cheney to lead a group to find a good candidate to be the vice presidential nominee for the Republican Party. But as the weeks went by, Bush decided that he wanted Cheney to take the nomination himself.

Cheney accepted Bush's offer and promptly began campaigning across the country for the Bush-Cheney presidential ticket. In November 2000 American voters went to the polls to choose between Bush-Cheney and the Democratic ticket of presidential nominee Al Gore and vice-presidential nominee Joseph Lieberman. The vote was the closest in U.S. history, and problems with the vote tally in the deciding state of Florida touched off six weeks of legal clashes to see who America's next president and vice president would be. Finally, however, the U.S. Supreme Court issued a ruling that paved the way for Bush and Cheney to claim victory. They took their oaths of office on January 20, 2001.

In 2002 Iraq once again became a major topic of conversation in Washington, D.C. President Bush and his advisors claimed that Saddam Hussein and his generals were holding chemical weapons and were seeking to acquire nuclear weapons, despite their promises to the United Nations that they would not do so. "Saddam Hussein is continuing his decade-old game of defiance, delay, and deception," Cheney charged in a speech to Republican leaders that was broadcast on CNN. "Saddam Hussein's pursuit of weapons of mass destruction poses a grave danger, not only to his neighbors, but also to the United States.... He could decide secretly to provide weapons of mass destruction to terrorists for their use against us."

In late 2002 and early 2003, the United States engaged in a heated debate with other countries over Iraq's future. The Bush administration argued that Hussein's government was dangerous and should be removed from power, but other nations claimed that Iraq did not pose an immediate threat. In March 2003 the Bush administration decided to launch a major offensive against Iraq. U.S. forces, joined by a smaller number of troops from Great Britain and other allies, seized control of Iraq after a few weeks of fighting. Since that time, the United States has been engaged in a program to help the people of Iraq rebuild their battered country and install a new government.

Cheney is married to Lynne Cheney, a conservative activist and writer whom he met in high school. They have two daughters.

Where to Learn More

Andrews, Elaine. *Dick Cheney: A Life in Public Service.* Brookfield, CT: Millbrook Press, 2001.

Cohen, Richard E., and James Kitfield. "Cheney: Pros and Cons." *National Journal,* July 29, 2000.

Evans, Rowland, and Robert Novak. "Cheney for the Defense." *Reader's Digest,* December 1991.

Gibbs, Nancy. "Double-Edged Sword." *Time,* December 30, 2002.

"Richard B. Cheney." *Encyclopedia of World Biography, 1998;* reproduced in online *Biography Resource Center,* Farmington Hills, MI: Gale Group, 2003.

Jacques Chirac

Born November 29, 1932
Paris, France

President of France who led international opposition to the 2003 Iraq War

Frenche President Jacques Chirac emerged as the most outspoken opponent of the U.S.-led military invasion of Iraq in 2003. His position angered the United States and Great Britain, two of France's longtime allies, but proved very popular within France. Once the Iraq War ended, Chirac pushed for greater United Nations involvement in reconstruction efforts and a rapid transfer of political power back to the Iraqi people.

Receives political and diplomatic schooling

Jacques Rene Chirac was born in Paris on November 29, 1932. He was the only child of Francois Chirac, an aircraft company executive, and Marie-Louise (Valette) Chirac, a homemaker. He attended Lycee Carnot, a prestigious prep school, and was later accepted to the Lycee Louis-le-Grand, a school roughly equivalent in the United States to high school plus two years of college. He graduated with honors in 1950.

Chirac served briefly in the French military but soon returned to Paris on his father's advice and enrolled at the Institut d'Etudes Politiques, a political and diplomatic universi-

"The war, launched without the authorization of the Security Council, [has shaken] the multilateral system [a system that operates using the input of multiple countries]. The [UN] has just been through one of the most grave crises in its history."

Jacques Chirac addressing the United Nations.

Jacques Chirac. *Photograph by Michel Lipchitz. Reproduced by permission.*

101

ty. During the summer of 1953 he studied at Harvard University in Boston, Massachusetts. Eager to sample a variety of American experiences, he also worked at a Howard Johnson's restaurant in Boston and toured the country by car in his spare time.

Upon his return to France, Chirac was drafted into the French army. He was wounded in action during a colonial war in Algeria. Afterward, he enrolled at the Ecole Nationale d'Administration, an elite government service school, graduating in 1959.

Launches a long and distinguished political career

Chirac got his start in politics in 1960 as an auditor in the accounting office of the French government. In 1962 he joined the staff of Prime Minister Georges Pompidou and later became undersecretary of state for social affairs. In 1967 he was elected to the National Assembly (one of two houses of the French parliament, in which members are elected by popular vote to five-year terms).

When President Charles De Gaulle resigned in 1969, Pompidou became president and appointed Chirac secretary of state for the economy and finance. Chirac moved to several cabinet positions over the next few years. In 1973 he became minister of agriculture and rural development, and in 1974 took the position of minister of the interior. When Valery Giscard d'Estaing was elected president of France, he appointed Chirac prime minister. (In the French government, the president serves a seven-year term as head of state and controls foreign affairs. The president appoints the prime minister, who oversees the activities of parliament and concentrates on domestic affairs.)

Chirac served as prime minister from 1974 to 1976. He then formed his own political party, Rassemblement pour la Republique (Rally for the Republic). In 1977 Chirac was elected mayor of Paris. He held this position for nearly twenty years, during which time his political influence grew considerably. He successfully launched several urban renewal projects, including restoration of the Eiffel Tower and a citywide clean-up. A believer in government support for social and educational causes, he presided over the construction of libraries, the installation of public swimming pools, and the opening of no-cost children's nurseries.

Chirac ran for president of France in 1981 but was defeated by Francois Mitterrand. He was appointed prime minister of France for the second time in 1986 and served in this position until 1988. Encouraged by his popularity in Paris, Chirac made a second bid for the French presidency that year. His political views centered on lower taxes, severe punishment for terrorism and crime, the elimination of price controls, and the transfer of government-run businesses into private control. At the time, however, the French people strongly supported the nation's Socialist Party and reelected Mitterrand instead. Chirac remained mayor of Paris and an active member of parliament.

Chirac finally achieved his goal of becoming the president of France in 1995, defeating Lionel Jospin. Despite his two earlier defeats, Chirac had never lost hope. "I never doubted this rise would come," he told *Time* magazine. "I have been preparing [for this] a long time."

Faces problems as president of France

France's new president inherited severe social unrest. At the heart of the country's problems was unemployment. The national unemployment rate was 12.2 percent, a staggeringly high figure for an industrialized country. As president, Chirac faced the difficult task of restoring public confidence and generating enough economic growth to reduce unemployment. Critics claimed that Chirac failed to deliver on his promises regarding France's economy. The nation's unemployment rate remained among the highest in Europe throughout his first term in office, and Chirac's ratings in opinion polls stayed low as a result.

Chirac also faced several difficult foreign policy challenges during his first term. One example was the civil war in the former Yugoslavian republic of Bosnia. Terrible violence erupted between Bosnia's two main ethnic groups after the republic declared its independence in 1991. Ethnic Serbs, with the support of former Yugoslav President Slobodan Milosevic, began a systematic campaign of arrests, torture, and murder to eliminate the Muslims who formed the ethnic minority in Bosnia. This savage and bloody conflict pulled in forces from France and other European countries. Many French soldiers were killed during a UN peacekeeping mission to Bosnia.

Another foreign policy challenge involved the controversy surrounding France's decision to resume nuclear weapons testing in 1995. More than twenty nations protested against the tests, and demonstrations were staged all over the world. Opponents organized boycotts of wine and other French products. Riots broke out around the test site in Tahiti, causing millions of dollars in property damage and injuring forty people. Although the tests continued as scheduled, Chirac promised to sign the Comprehensive Test Ban Treaty and use computer simulations in the future.

Second term brings disagreements over war in Iraq

In 2002 Chirac used his political skills and the popularity of his Rally for the Republic party to win reelection to a second term as president. Within a short time, he led France into a major confrontation with the United States over its plans to use military force against Iraq. Iraq had first gained international attention a dozen years earlier when it invaded its smaller neighbor, Kuwait. In 1991 France joined a U.S.-led coalition of more than thirty-five countries that sent military troops to fight in the Persian Gulf War. The coalition succeeded in forcing Iraqi leader Saddam Hussein to withdraw his army from Kuwait.

The United Nations (UN) agreement that ended the war required Iraq to destroy all of its biological, chemical, and nuclear weapons. In the decade after the war ended, however, Hussein consistently refused to honor the terms of this peace agreement. The international community tried a number of different approaches to force Hussein to cooperate with UN weapons inspectors, but instead he kicked the inspectors out of Iraq in 2000.

On September 11, 2001, terrorist attacks killed nearly three thousand people in the United States. France immediately expressed its support for the victims and their families. One French newspaper ran a large headline proclaiming "We

Are All Americans." U.S. President George W. Bush responded to the attacks by launching a global war on terrorism. This effort initially focused on known terrorist groups, but it eventually expanded to include countries that Bush believed supported terrorist activities, including Iraq. Bush claimed that Iraq possessed weapons of mass destruction and could provide such weapons to terrorists. He argued that Hussein posed an immediate threat to world security and should be removed from power in Iraq.

In September 2002 Bush challenged the United Nations to force Iraq to honor the agreement that had ended the Persian Gulf War. Bush also made it clear that the United States would act alone to disarm Iraq by force if necessary. A series of tense discussions followed in the UN Security Council. As one of five permanent members of the council, France threatened to use its veto power to prevent the UN from supporting an invasion of Iraq. Chirac soon rallied support from Russia and China, two of the council's other permanent members. The remaining two permanent members, the United States and Great Britain, strongly supported the use of military force in Iraq. But France's opposition made them decide against seeking a formal UN resolution authorizing military force. Instead, they argued that the use of force was justified under previous UN resolutions.

Leads worldwide opposition to Iraq War

Several members of the international community expressed outrage at the Bush administration's willingness to act against the will of the UN Security Council. Chirac became the unofficial leader and spokesman for the countries opposed to war in Iraq. He argued that UN weapons inspections could effectively disarm Iraq and prevent Hussein from threatening world security. He also claimed that by acting alone, the United States would defy international law, reduce the power of the United Nations, and increase political instability around the world.

Some analysts pointed to other possible reasons for France's opposition to war in Iraq. For example, France is home to five million Muslims, the largest concentration in Europe. Many Muslims around the world criticized the U.S. plan to invade Iraq, viewing it as an attack upon a Muslim nation. Therefore, Chirac may have worried about angering this segment of the French population. In addition, French companies have acquired oil from Iraq for decades, and this oil is important to France's economy. Total Petroleum, France's biggest company and the fourth-largest oil corporation in the world, held development rights to many southern Iraq oil fields. Finally, France loaned billions of dollars to Iraq over the years and faced the possibility that it would never recover the money if Hussein's government were overthrown.

All of these factors made Chirac's opposition to the war hugely popular within France. After a rocky first term and low numbers in French opinion polls, Chirac finally struck a chord with his countrymen. His approval ratings soared to 65 percent, up from 19 percent only a year before.

Despite widespread international opposition and a lack of UN support, U.S. military forces invaded Iraq on March 19, 2003. Chirac was outraged. "No one can act alone in the name of all and no one can accept the anarchy [chaos] of a society without rules," he said in a speech before the Unite Nations. "The war, launched without the authorization of the Security Council, [has shaken] the multilateral system [a system that operates using the input of multiple countries]. The [UN] has just been through one of the most grave crises in its history."

The U.S.-led invasion of Iraq succeeded in removing Hussein from power after only a few weeks of fighting. On May 1, 2003, Bush announced the end of major combat operations. The U.S. military remained in Iraq as an occupying force and began working to rebuild the country and install a new government.

Pushes for a quick transfer of power to Iraqis

As the reconstruction of Iraq got underway, France once again found itself at odds with the United States. Chirac insisted that total control of Iraq be transferred as quickly as possible to the Iraqi people and stressed that the UN must assume a "key role" in the transition. He argued on *CNN.com* that it was "up to the United Nations to assist with the gradual transfer of administrative and economic responsibilities to the present Iraqi institutions according to a realistic timetable and to help the Iraqis draft a constitution and hold elections."

Chirac proposed a two-stage plan for the transfer of power from the U.S. military occupation forces to an independent Iraqi government. The first stage would be a "symbolic transfer" of power from the United States to an Iraqi Governing Council. The second stage, implemented six to nine months later, would involve the actual handing over of control. France promised to train Iraqi police officers and soldiers to aid in the peaceful transition.

But U.S. leaders were determined to maintain control over the reconstruction process. President Bush wanted the UN to play a role in providing food, medicine, and humanitarian aid to the people of Iraq, but he declared that the United States would handle Iraq's political transition.

Views on the Iraq War divide Europe

Throughout its opposition of the war, France enjoyed the support of Germany and its leader, Chancellor Gerhard Schroder. But Great Britain and its leader, Prime Minister **Tony Blair** (see entry), stood firmly on the side of the United States. The war in Iraq thus divided Europe. On September 23, 2003, France, Britain, and Germany held a one-day summit in Berlin in an attempt to settle their differences. "Whatever the differences there have been about the conflict, we all want to see a stable Iraq," Blair told CNN after the meeting.

But Schroder and Chirac felt that significant disagreements remained over the transfer of power to the Iraqi people. Like Chirac, Schroder believed that the United Nations should be given a more prominent role in the quick transition of power to an Iraqi authority. Richard Whitman, a professor at the University of Westminster in London, called the meeting a "major disappointment." He told CNN that they had "hoped for a real push towards some firm agreement, at least among European states. It is very difficult to see where we are going to see some common ground."

Chirac's staunch opposition to the Iraq War led some critics to call him anti-American. Some people in the United States organized boycotts of French goods in protest against

Chirac's policies. "When I hear people say I'm anti-American, I'm sad—not angry, but really sad," Chirac told *Time*. In fact, the French president has long shown a taste for American culture. "When you're in the U.S. with Chirac, there's always a problem," Prime Minister Alain Juppe told *Time*. "As soon as he sees a fast-food place, he has to stop the car, rush up to the counter and order a hamburger." Chirac also enjoys American music and film and counted the legendary American actor Gregory Peck among his closest friends.

Chirac's opposition to the Iraq War led to a huge increase in his popularity in France. But this increase soon proved to be temporary. His popularity began to decline again after the war ended, as the French people shifted their focus back to domestic issues.

Through victories and setbacks, Chirac has enjoyed unwavering support from his wife, Bernadette. The couple lives in the Elysee Palace, a beautifully decorated eighteenth-century home reserved for French presidents. They have three children. Chirac credits his youngest daughter, Claude, for his election to the presidency of France. She helped him appeal to young voters during his 1995 campaign by organizing town meetings where he could discuss his goals with the people of France.

Where to Learn More

"Chirac: No Veto on Iraq Resolution." *CNN.com*, http://www.cnn.com/2003/WORLD/europe/09/22/chirac.iraq/index.html http://www.cnn.com/2003/WORLD/europe/09/22/chirac.iraq/ index.html (accessed on March 26, 2004).

"Chirac: U.S. Action Brought Crisis." *CNN.com*, http://www.cnn.com/2003/WORLD/europe/09/23/sprj.irq.un.chirac/index.html (accessed March 26, 2004).

Dickey, Christopher. "Iraq's Mr. Popularity: The French Have Staked Out a Position as the Un-America." *Newsweek*, October 6, 2003.

Jeffrey, Simon. "War with Iraq." *Guardian Unlimited*, October 4, 2002.

Lawday, David. "The Gallic Spanner in the U.S. War Works: France and America Are Almost Alone These Days in Believing They Have a Civilizing Mission in the World." *New Statesman*, February 24, 2003.

Turback, Gary. "With France Like These, Who Needs Enemies?" *VFW Magazine*, October 2003.

Rhonda Cornum

Born October 31, 1954
Dayton, Ohio

U.S. Army flight surgeon who was held
prisoner in Iraq during the Persian Gulf War

Rhonda Cornum served as a doctor in the U.S. Army during the Persian Gulf War. On the final day of the conflict, she took part in a helicopter search-and-rescue mission to locate an American pilot who had been shot down behind enemy lines. The helicopter she was flying in was shot down as well. Cornum survived the crash but suffered severe injuries. She was captured by Iraqi soldiers and held for eight days as a prisoner of war (POW). Upon her safe return to the United States, she wrote a book about her experiences and became an unofficial spokesperson for expanding combat roles for women in the military.

"I remember very distinctly thinking as I was crashing, 'I have had a great life,' because I thought it was ending then."

Rhonda Cornum in the Seattle Post-Intelligencer.

Becomes a doctor in the U.S. Army

Rhonda Leah (Scott) Cornum was born October 31, 1954, in Dayton, Ohio. Her father, Donald Scott, was an engineer who designed toys, and her mother, Jeanne Scott, was a clerk and homemaker. Rhonda was the oldest of their four children. Her family moved to a small town near Buffalo, New York, when she was a young girl. "Growing up, I was

Rhonda Cornum. *©Corbis. Reproduced by permission.*

what most people would call a tomboy," she recalled in her autobiography, *She Went to War.* "I built dams in the creek and floated on rafts and collected frogs, toads, and snakes."

Cornum was a strong-willed and independent girl who occasionally showed a rebellious streak. But she was also a good student who always planned to go to college. Science was her favorite subject, and for many years she hoped to become a veterinarian. Cornum earned a bachelor's degree from Cornell University in 1975. She married her first husband, Marvin Fawley, during her senior year of college. She then went on to earn a doctorate degree in nutrition and biochemistry from Cornell in 1978. Her daughter, Regan, was born while she was in graduate school.

During her college years, Cornum and her family lived a simple life in upstate New York. "I lived in a log cabin and had my kid at home and raised chickens and goats," she noted in the *Seattle Post-Intelligencer.* "I wasn't a druggie, but I wasn't exactly establishment." Joining the military never crossed her mind. But then one day she presented the results of a research project at a scientific conference. After her lecture, she was approached by a man in uniform who offered her a job doing medical research for the U.S. Army.

Cornum accepted the job, joined the military, and received the rank of first lieutenant. By the time she completed the officer basic training course, she realized that she enjoyed army life. "In three months, I became an Army person—push-ups and sit-ups and running and all that," she stated in *U.S. News and World Report.* "And I was pretty good at it." Her husband did not share her enthusiasm for the military, however, and they divorced in 1980 as her career advanced.

From 1978 to 1982, Cornum worked as a medical research scientist at the Letterman Army Institute for Research in San Francisco, California. In 1983 she attended a flight surgeon training course. "Flight surgeons are medical doctors who have extra training and experience in aviation, altitude physiology, field sanitation, and combat medicine," she explained in her autobiography. As part of this course, Cornum learned to fly helicopters and to parachute out of airplanes. She also met her second husband, Kory Gene Cornum, who was a doctor in the U.S. Air Force.

Cornum earned her medical degree from the Uniformed Services University of Health Science in 1986. She then spent a year as a medical intern at Walter Reed Army Medical Center in Washington, D.C. In 1987 she took a job as a physician at the U.S. Army Aeromedical Research Laboratory at Fort Rucker, Alabama. Her husband became a flight surgeon at Eglin Air Force Base in the Florida panhandle around the same time. They bought a farm in northwestern Florida, about halfway between the two military bases, where they raised Thoroughbred horses.

Serves as a flight surgeon in the Persian Gulf War

In August 1990 the Middle Eastern nation of Iraq invaded its smaller neighbor, Kuwait. Iraqi President Saddam Hussein argued that Iraq had a historical claim to Kuwait's territory. He also wanted to control Kuwait's oil reserves and to gain access to Kuwait's port on the Persian Gulf. Countries around the world condemned the invasion and demanded that Hussein immediately withdraw his troops from Kuwait. Many of these countries then began sending military forces to the Persian Gulf region as part of a U.S.-led coalition against Iraq. The United States sent more than four hundred thousand troops to the Persian Gulf over the next six months. This massive military buildup received the code name Operation Desert Shield.

By mid-August Cornum learned that her army unit would be sent to Saudi Arabia as part of Operation Desert Shield. She welcomed the challenge of using her skills in a real military operation. "Nobody's looking for war," she said in *U.S. News and World Report.* "But if [it happens], then you would like to put into practice all the stuff you've learned." Cornum, who had earned the rank of major by this time, served as the flight surgeon for the U.S. Army's 2/229 Attack Helicopter Battalion, which was attached to the 101st Air Assault Division. She was stationed near Dhahran, Saudi Arabia, where she was responsible for the medical care of more than three hundred soldiers. Her husband's air force unit was sent to a different area of Saudi Arabia.

In November 1990, the United Nations Security Council established a deadline of January 15, 1991, for Iraq to withdraw from Kuwait or face war. When Hussein failed to meet the deadline, the U.S.-led coalition launched a series of air strikes against military targets in Iraq. This military action received the code name Operation Desert Storm. The air war went on for nearly six weeks and caused major damage to Iraq's military capability. On February 24 the coalition launched a dramatic ground assault to force the Iraqi troops out of Kuwait. It met with little resistance from Hussein's army and succeeded in liberating Kuwait after only four days of fighting.

On the last day of the coalition ground assault, U.S. Air Force Captain William Andrews was shot down in his F-16 fighter plane behind enemy lines. Andrews was able to parachute safely to the ground and provide U.S. military officials with his location. Cornum learned about the situation while she was sitting in a Blackhawk helicopter waiting to fly off on a different mission. The army decided to send Cornum's helicopter on an emergency combat search-and-rescue mission to pick up the downed pilot before he was captured by Iraqi forces. Cornum's job as flight surgeon on this mission was to provide medical care to the injured pilot.

Cornum was part of an eight-person crew on the helicopter. Accompanied by two Apache attack helicopters, the Blackhawk flew low over coalition troops for half an hour. As they approached the F-16 crash site, they began taking fire from Iraqi antiaircraft guns on the ground. The Blackhawk suffered severe damage to its tail and crashed into the desert at 140 miles per hour. "I remember very distinctly thinking as I was crashing, 'I have had a great life,' because I thought it was ending then," Cornum told the *Seattle Post-Intelligencer*. "I really got to do more stuff than most people do, so I should not complain."

Captured and taken prisoner by the Iraqis

Five of the eight crew members on board the Blackhawk died in the impact. Their bodies were later recovered by army investigators. Cornum and two enlisted men, Sergeant Troy Dunlap and Staff Sergeant Daniel Stamaris, miraculously survived the crash. Cornum suffered two broken arms, torn ligaments in one knee, a gunshot wound to the shoulder, and multiple cuts and bruises. Stamaris also suffered severe injuries, but Dunlap only had minor wounds. The three Americans were captured by Iraqi soldiers within minutes of the crash, before a rescue could be attempted. As a result, the U.S. Army did not know what happened to them and informed their families that they were missing in action. Andrews, the pilot they were looking for, was captured as well.

For the next eight days, Cornum was held by the Iraqis as a prisoner of war. She became one of twenty-three American POWs to be held during the Persian Gulf War, and one of only two women prisoners. During their first few days of captivity, Cornum and Dunlap were transported across the desert from bunker to bunker in the back of a truck. They were repeatedly questioned by the Iraqis and refused to reveal any classified military information. Cornum was sexually molested by an Iraqi guard during this time. She later said that the abuse she suffered was not nearly as bad as her constant fear of death. "It didn't make a big impression on me," she told *Time*. "You're supposed to look at this as a fate worse than death. Having faced both, I can tell you it's not. Getting molested was not the biggest deal of my life."

Cornum was eventually taken to an Iraqi hospital, where the bullet was removed from her shoulder and her broken arms were set. She tried to think positively and kept her spirits up by singing songs whenever she was alone in her Baghdad hospital room. Some of her fellow POWs later reported that they had heard her singing and that it cheered them up as well.

Cornum was released by the Iraqis along with all the other coalition prisoners on March 6, 1991. She flew to Riyadh, Saudi Arabia, on a plane sent by the International Red Cross relief organization. When they landed, she struggled to walk down the steep metal stairs with her injured knee and both arms in casts. "Step by cautious step, I made it to the ground, and the first person to greet me was General **H. Norman Schwarzkopf** (see entry) [the commander of coalition forces during Operation Desert Storm]," she recalled in her book. "I had never met him before, but instinctively, I tried to snap off a salute. My arm was stopped short by the plaster cast. 'I'm sorry, sir,' I said with a big smile. 'I normally salute four-star generals.'" A short time later, Cornum had a joyous reunion with her husband on board a U.S. Navy hospital ship in the Persian Gulf.

Becomes a spokesperson for women in the military

Cornum returned home in the spring of 1991 to parades and celebrations. She was interviewed for newspapers and magazines, and she spoke about her ordeal as a POW in a number of public appearances. Cornum's yellow POW uniform and the slings that held her broken arms became part of an exhibit at the National Museum of American History in Washington, D.C. In 1992 she published a book about her experiences, *She Went to War: The Rhonda Cornum Story.* The book received positive reviews and was declared one of the most notable books of the year by the *New York Times.*

All the attention surrounding her POW experience made Cornum one of the best-known women in the U.S. military. Without intending to do so, she became an unofficial representative of female members of the armed services. During the Persian Gulf War, women were prohibited from serving in a number of positions that might expose them to combat. One reason for this policy, according to U.S. government officials, was to reduce the risk of capture, rape, and torture of women soldiers by enemy forces. Cornum supported giving women the opportunity to serve in combat roles, and she rejected this common argument against it. "Every 15 seconds in America, some woman is assaulted," she pointed out in *Time.* "Why are they worried about a woman getting assaulted once every ten years in a war overseas? It's ridiculous. It's clearly an emotional argument they use [to keep women out of combat] because they can't think of a rational one."

In 1992 Cornum testified before a presidential commission in support of allowing women to serve in combat positions. The air combat roles for women in the U.S. military were expanded a short time later. Some people felt that Cornum's courageous conduct as a POW in Iraq helped change the views of U.S. leaders. "This was a validation that if women are in combat and something like this happens, they do have the strength, the stamina, the mental courage to meet the demands," said retired air force Brigadier General Wilma Vaught in *U.S. News and World Report.*

Cornum earned a number of awards for her military service, including the Distinguished Flying Cross, Bronze Star, Purple Heart, and Prisoner of War Medal. After recovering from the injuries she received during the Persian Gulf War, she attended command and staff college in Alabama and was promoted to the rank of colonel. She was stationed at Fort Bragg in North Carolina, where she became commander of a Combat Support Hospital for the 18th Airborne Corps. In 2001 Cornum was sent to Bosnia for six months as part of a U.S. peacekeeping mission. Upon her return to the United States, she attended the War College in Washington, D.C. Many people speculated that she was being groomed to become a general, which would make her one of only eleven women to hold that rank in the U.S. Army.

Despite occasional frustration, Cornum loves the opportunities and challenges presented by her military career. "Where else could a 46-year-old woman who is also a physician and a surgeon get paid to jump out of an airplane?" she said in the *Seattle Post-Intelligencer*. "I feel exactly like I felt 10 years ago, when I thought I was going to die in the middle of the desert. Every day is a gift. I feel really lucky."

Where to Learn More

Chase, Randall. *Seattle Post Intelligencer,* Jan. 16, 2001. Available online at http://www.pownetwork.org/gulf/cd070.htm (last accessed on March 26, 2004).

Cornum, Rhonda, with Peter Copeland. *She Went to War: The Rhonda Cornum Story.* Novato, CA: Presidio Press, 1992.

Gleick, Elizabeth. "Combat Ready." *People Weekly,* August 10, 1992.

Perry, Joellen. "Rhonda Cornum: The Iraqi Army Couldn't Quash Her Fighting Spirit." *U.S. News and World Report,* August 20, 2001. Available online at http://www.usnews.com/usnews/doubleissue/heroes/cornum.htm (accessed March 26, 2004).

Ramirez, Adam. "Task Force Med Eagle Commander Has Made Her Mark since Days as POW in Iraq." *Stars and Stripes,* April 8, 2001. Available online at http://ww2.pstripes.osd.mil/01/apr01/ed040801k.html (accessed on March 26, 2004).

"Rhonda (Leah Scott) Cornum." *Contemporary Authors Online,* 2002. Reproduced in *Biography Resource Center.* Farmington Hills, MI: Gale Group, 2003.

"A Woman's Burden." *Time,* March 28, 2003. Available online at http://www.time.com/time/nation/printout/0,8816,438760,00.html (accessed on March 26, 2004).

Michael Donnelly

Born February 3, 1959
Orange, California

American fighter pilot who became a champion for veterans suffering from Gulf War syndrome

As a fighter pilot in the U.S. Air Force, Major Michael Donnelly flew forty-four combat missions over Iraq during the Persian Gulf War. Once he returned home, however, he began experiencing mysterious health problems that were eventually diagnosed as amyotrophic lateral sclerosis (ALS). This rare disease destroys nerve cells in the brain and spinal cord, causing paralysis and eventually death. Donnelly learned that an unusually high number of Gulf War veterans suffered from ALS, and he became convinced that the disease was directly related to their wartime service. With the support of his family, he fought to force the U.S. government to acknowledge the link.

Love of planes leads to career in the U.S. Air Force

Michael William Donnelly was born on February 3, 1959, in Orange, California, the second of Thomas and Raffaela Donnelly's four children. His family moved to Connecticut when he was a child. Donnelly was an active boy who de-

"Even today, as I sit, paralyzed by ALS, Lou Gehrig's disease, unable to speak, eat, or even scratch my head, I consider myself a patriot."

Michael Donnelly in Contemporary Authors.

Michael Donnelly.
Photograph by Dennis Cook.
AP/Wide World Photos.
Reproduced by permission.

veloped a fascination with airplanes. "I was a child of the out-doors and the physical. I lived to run, to bike, to play Army and guns, and later, every sport imaginable," he recalled in his memoir, *Falcon's Cry*. "And from a young age, I was fasci-nated by the jets that streaked across our innocent suburban skies.... I spent hours holed away in our damp basement, glu-ing model airplanes, affixing the U.S. insignia just so. My bedroom ceiling was the site of a permanent mock dogfight—the air above my bed prickled with jet models and fighters of every description."

Donnelly's father was an attorney who had flown heli-copters for the U.S. Marines during the Korean War. Tom Don-nelly remembered his military service with pride and remained deeply patriotic. Each day he raised the American flag and the Marine Corps flag in front of the family's house. When he re-turned home from work in the evening, his children greeted him at the flagpole and sang the marines' fight song.

Thanks to his father's influence, Donnelly began con-sidering a career in the military at an early age. He joined the U.S. Air Force in 1981, a few months after he earned a bache-lor's degree from Fairfield University. He underwent intensive flight training and eventually qualified to be a fighter pilot. "I was top gun in my class and a distinguished graduate of the program. An ace fighter pilot in the making," he recalled in his memoir. "I had never been happier in my life because I was where I was supposed to be, doing what I was meant to do." Donnelly started out flying A-10 Warthogs and later pro-gressed to F-16 Falcons. In 1984 he married his longtime girl-friend, Susan Allen. They eventually had two children, Erin and Sean. Over the next few years, Donnelly's air force career took him across the United States and all over the world.

Serves as a fighter pilot in the Persian Gulf War

On August 2, 1990, Iraqi leader **Saddam Hussein** (see entry) had ordered his military forces to invade the neighbor-ing country of Kuwait. Saddam argued that Iraq had a histori-cal claim to Kuwait's territory. He also wanted to control Kuwait's oil reserves and to gain access to Kuwait's port on the Persian Gulf. Countries around the world condemned the invasion and demanded that Hussein immediately withdraw his troops from Kuwait. Many of these countries then began sending military forces to the Persian Gulf region as part of a U.S.-led coalition against Iraq. The United States sent more than four hundred thousand troops to the Persian Gulf over the next six months. This massive military buildup received the code name Operation Desert Shield.

Donnelly was stationed in Germany when Operation Desert Shield began. His unit, the 10th Tactical Fighter Squadron, was sent to Saudi Arabia in December 1990. They arrived two weeks before the deadline set by the United Nations Security Council for Iraq to withdraw from Kuwait. When Hussein failed to meet the deadline, the U.S.-led coalition launched a series of air strikes against military targets in Iraq. The war became known as Operation Desert Storm.

The air war went on for nearly six weeks and caused major damage to Iraq's military capability. Donnelly flew forty-four combat missions over Iraq during this time. "Our targets changed throughout the war," he recalled in *Falcon's Cry*. "Some days we would be after something strategic like an airfield, or just tanks, or armored vehicles. Or else they would send us out for bridges on one of the two rivers—the Tigris and the Euphrates—or we would be given sections of river to patrol. If we saw any sort of river crossing or bridge building going on, we would try to hit it." Donnelly's squadron also bombed Iraqi oil production facilities, radar installations, Scud missile launchers, and suspected chemical and biological weapons factories.

On February 24, 1991, the coalition launched a dramatic ground assault to force the Iraqi troops out of Kuwait. It met with little resistance from Hussein's army, which had been devastated by the air strikes. The Persian Gulf War ended on February 27, when coalition forces succeeded in liberating Kuwait from Iraqi occupation. Donnelly earned a number of honors for his service in the Persian Gulf War, including the Meritorious Service Medal, the Air Medal with three oak leaf clusters, the Air Force Commendation Medal with four oak leaf clusters, the Aerial Achievement Medal, and the Air Force Achievement Medal.

Suffers mysterious illness upon returning home

Donnelly returned to the United States after the war ended and became a flight instructor at Sheppard Air Force

Base in Texas. Over the next few years, he often noticed that he did not feel completely healthy. Though annoying, his health problems never became so severe that he needed to seek medical treatment.

In the summer of 1995, however, Donnelly came into contact with a pesticide that was used to control mosquitoes. He saw a truck spraying the chemical while he was jogging around the base. "I remember clearly the first night I encountered the truck as I was out running," he noted in his book. "It passed me, exhaling its poison, and I tasted the Malathion on my tongue, a sharp, bitter taste almost like citrus. I remember wondering vaguely, surely they wouldn't spray something poisonous or hazardous in the base housing area, where people lived with their families."

Immediately after his encounter with the fogging truck, Donnelly's health problems took a sudden turn for the worse. He began to suffer a number of strange symptoms, including an irregular heartbeat, insomnia (difficulty sleeping), short-term memory loss, difficulty concentrating, and weakness in his legs. After undergoing months of medical tests, he was finally diagnosed with amyotrophic lateral sclerosis (ALS) in the spring of 1996. Also known as Lou Gehrig's disease (after a legendary professional baseball player who died from it), ALS is a progressive neurological disease that destroys nerve cells in the brain and spinal cord. The cause of ALS is not known, and there is no cure. The disease leads to total paralysis and eventually death, usually within five years of diagnosis. ALS does not affect the mind, however, so sufferers are fully aware of the progression of their illness.

ALS is a relatively rare disease that strikes people at an average age of fifty-seven. Donnelly was thirty-five at the time his symptoms appeared. Within a short time, he learned that at least forty other Persian Gulf War veterans also suffered from the disease, despite the fact that military service members generally tended to be young and healthy. Under normal circumstances, a group of people the size of the American forces that served in the war should see only one or two cases of ALS. The unusually high rate of ALS among Gulf War veterans is known as a "cluster" in medical terminology.

ALS is linked to Gulf War syndrome

As his illness progressed, Donnelly was forced to retire from the air force in 1996 with the rank of major. By this time he and his family had begun to suspect that the cluster of ALS was somehow related to service in the Persian Gulf War. Thousands of American soldiers had developed unexplained health problems after returning from the war. Some of the most common symptoms included headaches, blurred vision, insomnia, short-term memory loss, abdominal pain, diarrhea, skin rashes, and aching joints. The collection of mysterious ailments suffered by these veterans eventually became known as Gulf War syndrome.

No one knew what had caused the Gulf War veterans to become ill. Some things that were mentioned as possible causes included exposure to chemical weapons, bad reactions to the vaccinations and experimental drugs given to the American forces, and inhaling toxic smoke from Kuwaiti oil well fires. Some experts felt that some combination of these toxic substances could have damaged the soldiers' nervous and immune systems.

At first the U.S. Department of Defense (DOD) insisted that there was no connection between the veterans' unexplained health problems and their service in the Persian Gulf War. Military officials initially denied that the troops had been exposed to chemical or biological weapons during their time in Saudi Arabia, Iraq, and Kuwait. In 1996, however, the U.S. government admitted that thousands of American soldiers may have been exposed to the toxic nerve gas sarin during the war.

Donnelly and his family conducted their own research and talked to numerous other veterans who were suffering from Gulf War syndrome. They became convinced that Donnelly had been exposed to nerve gas as he flew his F-16 over Iraqi chemical weapons factories that were destroyed in coalition bombing raids. This low-level exposure did some damage to his nervous system, but not enough to cause ALS. The onset of the disease was triggered a few years later by his exposure to the pesticide Malathion, which comes from the same chemical family as the poisons released in Iraq.

In 1997 the U.S. House of Representatives held hearings into the possible causes of Gulf War syndrome. Although Donnelly was using a wheelchair by this time, he testified be-

Michael Donnelly with his wife, Susan, and his parents. Donnelly is paralyzed as a result of ALS, or Lou Gehrig's disease, which was diagnosed a few years after he served in the 1991 Persian Gulf War. *Photograph by Steve Miller. AP/Wide World Photos. Reproduced by permission.*

fore Congress about the link between ALS and wartime service. The House later released a report that was highly critical of the DOD and the Veterans Administration (VA). The report claimed that these agencies ignored veterans' complaints and refused to declassify documents that would have helped to explain what happened to them.

Fights for victims of Gulf War syndrome

Despite the devastating physical effects of ALS, Donnelly fought to force the U.S. government to acknowledge that his illness, as well as those suffered by fellow veterans, was a direct result of their service in the Persian Gulf War. By the end of the 1990s, more than 110,000 American veterans suffered from recognized symptoms of Gulf War syndrome. Hundreds had contracted rare cancers and neurological diseases, and their children were born with birth defects at a rate between two and ten times higher than the national average. Donnelly wanted the military to provide full health care and disability benefits to all of these people.

In 1998 Donnelly published *Falcon's Cry: A Desert Storm Memoir.* In this book, which was co-written by his sister Denise, he tells about his early love of flight, his years in the air force, and his combat experiences during the Persian Gulf War. He also describes the onset of mysterious symptoms that were eventually diagnosed as ALS, and his constant struggle against the effects of the disease. Finally, he chronicles his fight to force the military to recognize the connection between his illness and his wartime service. "I wrote this book so that you would know the real story of what has happened to yet another generation of patriots, and so that you might be moved to act, to prevent it from happening again, so that you might be moved to do whatever it takes to protect the ideals for which I risked my life, ideals which I believe most Americans still truly value," he explained in *Contemporary Authors.*

Donnelly and his family achieved a major victory in 2001. On December 10, VA Secretary Anthony Principi announced that a government study had found that Gulf War veterans were more than twice as likely to suffer from ALS as American soldiers who had not served in the war. Principi also stated that the VA would provide full benefits to all Gulf War veterans diagnosed with the condition. "We are pleased that they did this, but this is really bittersweet for us," Tom Donnelly told *WebMD.* "This is something that they could have done years ago if they had been more concerned about helping veterans and less concerned about denying Gulf War illness existed."

By this time Donnelly was completely paralyzed. He received nutrition through a feeding tube and breathed with the support of a ventilator. His only form of communication involved blinking his eyes at specific letters as his caregivers recited the alphabet. Yet despite his limitations, he continued fighting to raise money to help Gulf War veterans and find a cure for ALS. "Even today, as I sit, paralyzed by ALS, Lou Gehrig's disease, unable to speak, eat, or even scratch my head, I consider myself a patriot," he told *Contemporary Authors.* "Even as I hear the sad bureaucrats who populate the seats of power in the Pentagon continue to lie about what happened to me and to more than 110,000 other Persian Gulf War veterans, I can say that I do not regret my service. I am proud to have risked my life for the principles for which this country stands."

Where to Learn More

Arnold, David. "Victory for Gulf War Family Who Persisted on Link to ALS." *Boston Globe,* December 16, 2001. Available online at http://www.rideforlife.com/archives/000049.html (accessed on April 9, 2004).

Boyles, Salynn. "Feds Acknowledge Lou Gehrig's Disease a Gulf War Illness." *WebMD Medical News.* Available online at http://www.focusonals.com/feds_acknowledge_lou_gehrigs_disease_a_gulf_war_illness.htm (last accessed on March 26, 2004).

Donnelly, Michael, with Denise Donnelly. *Falcon's Cry: A Desert Storm Memoir.* Westport, CT: Praeger, 1998.

Michael Donnelly." *Contemporary Authors Online,* 2000. Reproduced in Biography Resource Center. Farmington Hills, MI: Gale Group, 2003.

"Michael Donnelly Biography." *Hope for ALS.* Available online at http://www.hopeforals.com/html/mdonnelly.html (accessed on March 26, 2004).

Stolberg, Sheryl Gay. "Campaign by Pilot's Family Secures Benefits for Gulf War Veterans." *New York Times,* December 25, 2001.

Fahd ibn Abdul Aziz Al-Saud

Born 1923
Riyadh, Saudi Arabia

King of Saudi Arabia during the Persian Gulf War

K ing Fahd ibn Abdul Aziz Al-Saud, the ruler of Saudi Arabia, steered his country through the events surrounding the 1991 Persian Gulf War. The Arab leader's decision to side with the U.S.-led coalition and oppose Iraq played an important role in the war's outcome. For example, King Fahd allowed coalition forces to use Saudi Arabia as a base of operations. He also contributed billions of dollars to help pay for the conflict.

The king's choices during the Gulf crisis were a continuation of the sometimes-unconventional behavior he displayed throughout his life. Although he was a devout Muslim and the head of a very conservative Islamic nation, the king maintained close relationships with Western nations, including the United States. This made King Fahd a controversial figure in the Arab world. His actions earned him both devoted followers and dedicated opponents.

Royal heritage

The future King Fahd was born in 1923 around the time when his father, Abdul Aziz ibn Saud, was founding the

Fahd ibn Abdul Aziz Al-Saud. Photograph by Tannen Maury. AP/Wide World Photos. Reproduced by permission.

nation of Saudi Arabia. Before this time, the people of the Arabian Peninsula were divided into small tribal groups, and the region had been controlled for several centuries by the Ottoman Empire and other foreign powers. The Kingdom of Saudi Arabia was officially established in 1932, and Fahd's father became its first ruler, King Abdul Aziz.

Young Prince Fahd was raised at the king's court in the city of Riyadh, but he was by no means the only prince in the family. His father had forty-five sons by several different wives. However, preference was given to the male children born to Hassa al-Sudeiri, Prince Fahd's mother. As one of the chosen few, Prince Fahd was educated in a special school in Riyadh. Saudi Arabia's vast oil reserves were discovered when he was a teenager, and petroleum revenues soon made the kingdom very prosperous. After completing his education in Riyadh, Prince Fahd undertook Islamic studies in the holy Muslim city of Mecca.

Prince Fahd's religious education is a sign of how important the religion of Islam is in Saudi Arabia. The country's unity is based on the widespread acceptance of Wahabbism, a very pure and conservative form of Muslim belief that dates to the 1700s. The Muslim holy book, the Koran, serves as the country's constitution. The *Sharia*, a strict code of justice based on the Koran, is the law of the land. It includes rigid guidelines about the role of women in society and also forbids the population from engaging in such activities as drinking alcohol and gambling.

The prince of the party

As a young man, Prince Fahd often rebelled against his strict Islamic upbringing. While in his early twenties, he became known as an international playboy. He gambled enormous sums in Europe's fashionable Monte Carlo casinos, attended nightclubs in Beirut, Lebanon, and developed a taste for fine Scotch. Such behavior got him in trouble with his older brothers, especially Prince Faisal. Faisal eventually told Fahd that if he continued to live the wild life he would give up his chance to one day serve as king. This warning brought an end to Prince Fahd's rowdy ways.

Fahd developed other nontraditional interests, how-
ever. In 1945 he accompanied Prince Faisal to San Francisco,
California, for the initial meeting of the United Nations.
Prince Fahd admired the vibrant and modern surroundings of
the United States, and he developed a lifelong interest in
American culture.

After King Abdul Aziz died in 1953, Prince Fahd's
older brother Saud took power. Prince Fahd, then in his early
thirties, was appointed minister of education—the first one
his country ever had. Prior to his appointment, there were
very few schools in Saudi Arabia, and most were only concerned with elementary instruction. Under Prince Fahd's direction, schools were established for students at all levels,
from preschool to higher education. In one of his most progressive initiatives, he made education available to women—
a startling development in Saudi Arabia, where women have
traditionally been considered second-class citizens. In 1962
he was given another important post, minister of the interior.

As the years passed, two more of Prince Fahd's brothers took turns as king. During the reign of both Faisal and
Khalid, Prince Fahd had great responsibilities. He served in a
series of important positions and attended high-profile meetings around the world. When Khalid took power in 1975,
Fahd assumed the title of crown prince, which meant he
would be the next king. Because Khalid was in poor health
for much of his reign, Prince Fahd assumed many of the
country's leadership responsibilities even before he officially
took the throne in 1982.

Becomes king of Saudi Arabia

When Khalid died, Fahd became the fifth king of
Saudi Arabia. As monarch, he tried to strike a balance between modernizing the country and staying true to its devout
Islamic traditions. This task did not always prove easy. Many
people in the country believed that if the king promoted any
trappings of Western culture or reached out to non-Islamic
nations, he was moving away from the teachings of Muhammad, the great prophet of Islam. If the people of Saudi Arabia
felt that the king was moving too far in that direction, he
risked losing power.

Despite these dangers, King Fahd cultivated close relations with the United States during the 1980s. At the same time, he took a leading role in issues important to the Arab world. He assumed the official title of Custodian of the Two Holy Mosques, a reference to his role as the overseer of Islam's two holiest sites, which are located in the Saudi Arabian cities of Mecca and Medina. In international relations, he was a strong supporter of the Palestinians in their struggle with Israel and also was involved in efforts to bring an end to the civil war in Lebanon. During the war between Iran and Iraq (1980–88), Saudi Arabia provided financial support to Iraq but did not involve its army in the dispute. Soon after that conflict came to an end, however, Saudi Arabia became involved in another crisis involving Iraq.

Persian Gulf War

The 1991 Persian Gulf War came as a result of Iraq's invasion of Kuwait on August 2, 1990. Most experts believe that Iraqi president **Saddam Hussein** (see entry) decided to take over Kuwait so that he could control that country's large oil resources. Iraq had just ended its long war with Iran, and its economy was in shambles. In official statements, the Iraqi government maintained that they had a historical claim on the territory that made up Kuwait. They also complained that Kuwait was pumping more oil than was allowed under international agreements, thereby keeping petroleum prices low and reducing Iraq's oil income.

The Iraqi army quickly overwhelmed Kuwait. Hussein's forces then took up threatening positions near the Saudi Arabian border, raising the prospect that Iraq might invade King Fahd's country. Saudi Arabia maintained a small army that was thought to be no match for the larger Iraqi force. Sensing the urgency of the situation, U.S. President **George H. W. Bush** (see entry) moved quickly. Within a day of the initial invasion of Kuwait, the United States offered to send troops and weapons to help defend Saudi Arabia.

Iraq's invasion of Kuwait placed King Fahd in a difficult position. On the one hand, his country faced a very real threat from Hussein's troops. On the other, he was reluctant to open his country to a foreign army. In accepting assistance

from outsiders, he would be admitting that he had failed to protect his people on his own, which might weaken his hold on power. It also was politically risky for any Arab leader to become too closely aligned with the United States, which was Israel's closest ally.

King Fahd also had to consider the effect that contact with large numbers of foreigners would have on his people. Many Muslims in Saudi Arabia are opposed to the presence of non-Muslims in their land, which they consider to be sacred. In recognition of such feelings, King Fahd's government had limited the number of foreigners it allowed to visit and work in the country. Saudi Arabia was isolated in other ways, as well. For example, the government placed heavy restrictions on the types of newspaper and television information allowed into Saudi Arabia. Most Western forms of entertainment, such as music and movies, were forbidden. In many ways, Saudi Arabia kept itself walled off from the outside world in order to keep its people from being corrupted by for-

King Fahd (center) reviews troops of the Royal Saudi Landing Force. Saudi forces played a part in reclaiming Kuwait from Iraqi occupation during Operation Desert Storm. *©Corbis. Reproduced by permission.*

eign influences. Allowing hundreds of thousands of foreign soldiers into the country would change that.

Meets with Cheney

King Fahd did not have much time to make his choice. On August 5, U.S. Secretary of Defense **Dick Cheney** (see entry) arrived in Riyadh to discuss the situation. Cheney told King Fahd that if he wanted U.S. military assistance, then he needed to act immediately. After a brief consultation with other Saudi officials, the king gave his answer: U.S. forces were welcome in Saudi Arabia. American troops began to arrive within days and were soon joined by soldiers from other countries. An estimated six hundred thousand non-Saudis were based in the country during the Persian Gulf War.

The Saudi government put several plans in place to try and lessen the impact of the foreigners. Most soldiers were based in remote locations away from cities to reduce their contact with Saudi citizens. The foreign troops also were subject to many of the strict rules that had been applied to foreign visitors for many years in Saudi Arabia. For instance, they were not allowed travel freely around the country or to drink alcohol.

The Saudi government also made some concessions to accommodate the outsiders. Female soldiers were allowed to serve in Saudi Arabia, and they were not forced to observe the country's strict rules that require women to keep their faces and bodies fully covered, at least while stationed at their military camps. When traveling elsewhere, however, the women soldiers sometimes found it necessary to wear an *abaya* (a black robe) and to cover their heads with a scarf in order to avoid hostile reactions from local Saudis.

In addition to hosting the foreign troops, the king committed a large amount of money to the war effort. The Saudi government spent an estimated $37.5 billion on the Gulf crisis. Even a country as wealthy as Saudi Arabia found it difficult to pay this bill. In the years following the war, the Saudi government struggled with budget shortfalls due to the high cost of the conflict.

Though it was the primary staging area for the coalition war effort, Saudi Arabia suffered relatively little damage.

Iraqi forces fired more than forty Scud missiles into Saudi Arabia during the war. One struck a military camp in Al Khobar, killing twenty-eight U.S. soldiers, but otherwise the missiles did little harm. Face-to-face fighting took place at the Saudi town of Khafji, along the border of Kuwait, after Iraqis invaded the area in the second week of the war. A coalition force composed largely of Saudi Arabian troops repelled the Iraqis after several days of fighting. Saudi troops also participated in other engagements. An estimated 47 Saudi Arabian soldiers were killed in the war, and another 220 wounded.

Growing dissent

While Saudi Arabia was largely spared from combat damage, the Gulf War still had a powerful effect on the country. In the years following the conflict, King Fahd faced greater opposition from groups inside Saudi Arabia. The greatest threat came from radical Muslims who felt that King Fahd's government no longer upheld the strict version of Islam that they thought appropriate. One of their strongest complaints was the king's decision to allow foreign troops to operate in Saudi Arabia during the Gulf crisis and their continued presence after the war.

While some of the Saudi opposition groups expressed their views peacefully, others did not. In 1995, a bomb went off at a building in Riyadh used by the U.S. military, killing six people. In 1996, a U.S. military housing complex in Dhahran was the target of a truck bomb that killed nineteen U.S. soldiers. Though the attacks have been attributed to different groups, both were opposed to the U.S. presence in Saudi Arabia. Osama bin Laden, a Saudi native, is another extremist who was offended by King Fahd's close relations with the United States. His anger at the Saudi monarchy is seen as one of the motivations for his role in a series of terrorist incidents, including the September 11, 2001, attacks on the World Trade Center in New York and the Pentagon in Washington, D.C.

King Fahd's government jailed some leaders of the religious opposition in the years following the war. But ever mindful of the power of religious groups, the government has been careful not to alienate Islamic clerics. Many of those imprisoned were later freed, and the *matawain,* or religious police who enforce Islamic law, have been given more power on several occasions since the war.

Over the years, King Fahd also has granted more authority to leaders outside the royal family. He created a consultative council called the *Majilis al-Shura* in 1992. Its members, which include both religious elites and secular (nonreligious) figures, give advice to the ruler on important issues. The council has grown larger and more powerful in the years since it was first established, but ultimate authority still rests with the ruling family.

An ailing king

In 1995 King Fahd suffered the first of several strokes, and he has been in poor health ever since. His ailments include diabetes and arthritis, and he underwent cataract (eye) surgery in 2002. He officially remains Saudi Arabia's king, but it is thought that Crown Prince Abdullah, Fahd's half-brother, has assumed most leadership duties.

King Fahd's poor health has contributed to the government's gradual drift toward a more conservative stance in recent years. Whereas King Fahd is considered moderate by Saudi standards, Crown Prince Abdullah is seen as more religious and has been very critical of the United States in its support of Israel.

The relationship between the governments of Saudi Arabia and the United States also soured because of events that followed the September 11 terrorist attacks. As a result of these attacks, the United States led an invasion into Iraq to remove Saddam Hussein from power. The Saudis opposed this U.S.-led invasion of Iraq in 2003, and the future of U.S. military installations in Saudi Arabia is unclear. Uncertainty also clouds the long-term future of King Fahd's country. Both Fahd and Abdullah are elderly, and it is not clear who will lead the country in coming decades.

Where to Learn More

Beyer, Lisa. "Lifting The Veil: A Secretive and Deeply Conservative Realm, Saudi Arabia Suddenly Finds Itself on the Sword Edge of Change." *Time*, September 24, 1990.

"Causes of 9/11: U.S. Troops in Saudi Arabia." *Terrorism Questions & Answers.* Available online at http://www.terrorismanswers.com/causes/saudiarabia3.html (accessed March 27, 2004).

Church, George J. "An Exquisite Balancing Act: Onetime Playboy King Fahd Tries to Mingle Modernity and Feudalism." *Time,* September 24, 1990.

"Fahd ibn Abdul Aziz Al-Saud." *Encyclopedia of World Biography,* 2nd ed. 17 Vols. Gale Research, 1998. Reproduced in *Biography Resource Center.* Farmington Hills, MI: The Gale Group, 2003.

"Fahd Bin Abdul Aziz Al-Saud, King and Prime Minister of Saudi Arabia." *Worldmark Encyclopedia of the Nations: World Leaders,* 2002. Reproduced in *Biography Resource Center.* Farmington Hills, MI: The Gale Group, 2003.

Janin, Hunt. *Saudi Arabia.* New York: Marshall Cavendish, 1993.

"King Fahd Bin Abdul Aziz." Available online at http://www.kingfahd binabdulaziz.com (accessed March 27, 2004).

Rashid, Nasser Ibrahim and Esber Ibrahim Shaheen. *Saudi Arabia and the Gulf War.* Joplin, MO: International Institute of Technology, 1992.

Teitelbaum, Joshua. "Deserted: Why Riyadh Stiffs America." *New Republic,* October 22, 2001.

Teitelbaum, Joshua. Executive summary for *Holier than Thou: Saudi Arabia's Islamic Opposition.* Available online at http://www.washington institute.org/pubs/exec/teitelexec.htm (accessed March 27, 2004).

Weiss, Joanna. "Gulf War Veterans Recall Muslim Distrust." *Boston Globe,* November 11, 2001.

April Glaspie

Born April 26, 1942
Vancouver, British Columbia, Canada

U.S. ambassador to Iraq before the 1991
Persian Gulf War

A pril Glaspie served as the U.S. ambassador to Iraq in the years leading up to Iraq's 1990 invasion of Kuwait. A week before the invasion occurred, Glaspie was called to a meeting with Iraqi leader **Saddam Hussein** (see entry). They discussed a number of matters, including the increasing tension between Iraq and its smaller neighbor. When the Iraqi government released a transcript (written record) of the meeting following the invasion of Kuwait, it created a huge controversy. Some people claimed that Glaspie's comments had encouraged Hussein to send his military forces into Kuwait. But Glaspie argued that the Iraqis had edited the transcript in a misleading way in order to make her comments sound more supportive than they actually were.

Becomes U.S. ambassador to Iraq

April Catherine Glaspie was born on April 26, 1942, in Vancouver, British Columbia, Canada. She earned a bachelor's degree from Mills College in 1963, and a master's degree from Johns Hopkins University in 1965. The following year

"I hope my credibility is at least as great as Saddam Hussein's."

April Glaspie quoted in New Republic.

April Glaspie. *©Reuters NewMedia Inc./Corbis. Reproduced by permission.*

she entered the foreign service with the U.S. Department of State. Her job involved maintaining friendly relations and representing American interests with other countries around the world.

Glaspie served as political officer (a deputy ambassador) at the U.S. Embassy in Cairo, Egypt, from 1973 to 1977. She received a citation as the State Department's top political reporting officer for her work there in 1975. Glaspie also served at the U.S. Embassies in England, Tunisia, and Syria over the years. From 1985 to 1987 she was director of the Office of Jordan, Lebanon, and Syrian Affairs in Washington, D.C.

As Glaspie's career as a diplomat progressed, she gained a reputation as one of the State Department's leading Arabists (scholars specializing in Arabic language and culture) and an expert in Middle Eastern affairs. In 1987 she was named U.S. ambassador to Iraq. She thus became the first woman to serve as American ambassador to an Arab country.

Tension builds between Iraq and Kuwait

At the time Glaspie arrived in Iraq, the country was just concluding a bitter eight-year war against its neighbor to the east, Iran. During this war, Iraqi leader Saddam Hussein purchased weapons from the United States and other countries and developed a tough, battle-hardened military. But the costs of the conflict left the Iraqi economy in ruins. In fact, by the time the war ended Iraq owed $80 billion to other countries. Hussein desperately needed money to help his country recover from the effects of the war.

The Iraqi leader argued that he had fought the war against Iran in order to protect the Arab world from the Islamic fundamentalists (people who strictly adhere to the basic principles of Islam) who had taken over Iran. He felt that his Arab neighbors should forgive Iraq's debts (not require repayment of loans) since Iraq fought to defend all Arab interests in the Persian Gulf region. Some countries did forgive Iraq's war debts, though Kuwait, a small but very wealthy country located to the south of Iraq, refused to do so.

Iraq's financial problems grew worse in 1990 because of a steep decline in world oil prices. Many countries in the

Middle East, including Iraq and Kuwait, contain some of the world's largest underground oil reserves. These countries make money by pumping and exporting oil (selling it to other countries around the world). The Organization of Oil Exporting Countries (OPEC) sets limits, or quotas, on the amount of oil its member countries pump each year in order to ensure stable oil prices in world markets.

Hussein believed that some OPEC countries were involved in a conspiracy to reduce Iraq's power in the Middle East. He argued that these countries, which included Kuwait, pumped more oil than was allowed under OPEC agreements in a deliberate attempt to lower world oil prices and harm Iraq's economy. He considered these actions by his fellow Arab states to be an "economic war" against Iraq.

Iraq and Kuwait also were involved in a longstanding dispute over the border between the two countries and the ownership of offshore islands in the Persian Gulf. Hussein claimed that Kuwait was trying to expand into Iraqi territory and was stealing oil from underground oil fields on the Iraqi side of the border. On July 17, 1990, Hussein made a fiery speech in which he threatened to use force against any country that pumped excess oil. He also began sending military troops south to the Kuwaiti border.

Attends famous meeting with Saddam Hussein

On July 25, Glaspie was called to a meeting with Hussein. Although she had served as the U.S. ambassador to Iraq for three years, she had never before met the Iraqi president. As a result, Glaspie was very surprised to learn that Hussein wanted to speak with her. She had only a few minutes to prepare for the meeting before she was led into the Iraqi president's office.

Glaspie was aware of the growing tension between Iraq and Kuwait, and she knew that Iraq had recently sent military troops to the Kuwaiti border. This situation was the main topic of discussion during her two-hour meeting with Hussein. The Iraqi leader outlined a long list of complaints against Kuwait. He discussed the ongoing border disputes between the two countries, for example, and he also accused Kuwait of pursuing policies that were intended to harm Iraq's economy. Glaspie listened to Hussein's concerns and expressed sympathy for Iraq's financial problems. She also emphasized the U.S. government's wish to maintain friendly relations with Iraq.

Eight days later, on August 2, 1990, Iraq launched a military invasion of Kuwait. Countries around the world condemned the invasion and demanded that Hussein immediately withdraw his troops from Kuwait. Many of these countries then began sending military forces to the Persian Gulf region as part of a U.S.-led coalition against Iraq. The meeting between Glaspie and Hussein had marked the last official high-level contact between the Iraqi and American governments before the invasion. Glaspie had left Iraq a few days later and was vacationing in London, England, when she learned about the invasion. She was not allowed to return to Iraq afterward.

Iraqi transcript of meeting creates controversy

On September 2, a month after the invasion of Kuwait, the Iraqi government released a transcript of the meeting between Glaspie and Hussein to British journalists. The transcript created a huge controversy when it became public. After reviewing it, some people felt that Hussein had informed Glaspie of his intention to attack Kuwait. They also claimed that Glaspie had led the Iraqi leader to believe that the United States would not get involved in his dispute with his neighbor.

According to the transcript, Glaspie expressed U.S. concern about the Iraqi troops gathered near the Kuwaiti border. But she also said that the U.S. government had no official position on border disputes in the Middle East and no special defense commitments with Kuwait. Some people criticized her comments and claimed that she had encouraged Iraq's aggression.

As it turned out, the United States and most other countries around the world objected strongly to Hussein's invasion of Kuwait. In November 1990, the United Nations Security Council established a deadline of January 15, 1991, for Iraq to withdraw from Kuwait or face war. When Hussein failed to meet the deadline, the coalition launched a series of punishing air strikes against military targets in Iraq. The Persian Gulf War ended on February 27, when coalition ground forces liberated Kuwait from Iraqi occupation.

Testifies before the U.S. Senate

In March 1991, following the U.S.-led coalition's victory over Iraq, Glaspie was asked to testify before the U.S. Senate Foreign Relations Committee. She answered a series of questions about her meeting with Hussein. During her testimony, Glaspie pointed out that the transcript of the meeting had been prepared by the Iraqi government. She claimed that the Iraqis edited her comments in a misleading way in order to make her seem supportive of Hussein's invasion of Kuwait. She told the committee members that the transcript did not reflect the true nature of her comments, and argued that she was the victim of "deliberate deception" by the Iraqi government.

Glaspie said that the Iraqis had removed strongly worded warnings she issued to Hussein about the American reaction to an invasion of Kuwait. "I told him orally we would defend our vital interests, we would support our friends in the Gulf, we would defend their sovereignty [independence] and integrity," she told the senators, as quoted in the *New Republic*. She expressed "astonishment" that anyone would give weight to the Iraqi version of the meeting, and concluded by saying that "I hope my credibility is at least as great as Saddam Hussein's."

Glaspie's appearance before the Senate Foreign Relations Committee helped turn public opinion in her favor. Supporters claimed that she had taken the blame for the Bush administration's failed policies toward Iraq. But the controversy continued when the State Department released a secret cable that Glaspie had sent to Washington containing her account of the meeting with Hussein. Although the cable differed somewhat from the Iraqi transcript, it also did not fully support her testimony before the Senate. The cable only created more questions about what actually took place during Glaspie's meeting with Hussein.

Years later, Glaspie's version of events received some support from Tariq Aziz, the Iraqi foreign minister who had been present at her 1990 meeting with Hussein. In an interview for "Frontline," Aziz said that the meeting with Glaspie had no influence on Hussein's decision to invade Kuwait. According to Aziz:

> It was a routine meeting. There was nothing extraordinary in it. She didn't say anything extraordinary beyond what any professional diplomat would say without previous instructions from his government. She did not ask for an audience with the president [Saddam]. She was summoned by the president.... He wanted her to carry a message to George Bush—not to receive a message through her from Washington.

Lingering questions about Glaspie's performance as U.S. ambassador to Iraq had a negative effect on her career. She was never offered another ambassadorship or any other position that required confirmation by the U.S. Congress. Glaspie served in several lower-level diplomatic posts over the next ten years, including as U.S. consul general in Cape Town, South Africa. She retired from the State Department around 2002.

Where to Learn More

"April Catherine Glaspie." *The Complete Marquis Who's Who,* 2001. Reproduced in *Biography Resource Center Online.* Farmington Hills, MI: Gale Group, 2003.

Blumenthal, Sidney. "April's Bluff: The Secrets of Ms. Glaspie's Cable." *New Republic,* August 5, 1991.

Cipkowski, Peter. *Understanding the Crisis in the Persian Gulf.* New York: John Wiley, 1992.

Cole, Carlton. "Whatever Happened to U.S. Ambassador April Glaspie?" *Christian Science Monitor,* May 27, 1999. Available online at http://csmweb2.emcweb.com/durable/1999/05/27/p23s3.htm (accessed on March 26, 2004).

"Excerpts from Iraqi Document on Meeting with U.S. Envoy." *New York Times International,* September 23, 1990. Available online at http://www.chss.montclair.edu/english/furr/glaspie.html (accessed on March 26, 2004).

"Frontline Interview: Tariq Aziz." *PBS.* Available online at http://www.pbs.org/wgbh/pages/frontline/shows/saddam/interviews/aziz.html (accessed on March 26, 2004).

Kilgore, Andrew I. "Tales of the Foreign Service: In Defense of April Glaspie." *Washington Report on Middle East Affairs,* August 2002. Available online at http://www.wrmea.com/archives/august2002/0208049.html (accessed on March 20, 2003).

Ogden, Christopher. "In from the Cold." *Time,* April 1, 1991.

Hussein ibn Talal

Born November 14, 1935
Amman, Jordan
Died February 7, 1999
Amman, Jordan

King of Jordan and Middle Eastern statesman who supported Iraq during the 1991 Persian Gulf War

Hussein ibn Talal, king of Jordan was a respected Middle Eastern leader who supported Iraq during the Persian Gulf War. After Iraq invaded Kuwait in August 1990, the king spent the next few months trying to negotiate a peaceful resolution to the crisis. When these efforts failed, he bowed to pressure from Jordan's large Palestinian population and threw his support behind Iraq. King Hussein's decision led to strained relations between his country and members of the U.S.-led coalition that fought against Iraq. But the king was able to repair these relationships over the years, and by the time of his death he was widely regarded as an accomplished statesman.

> "Let war be banished from our lands forever, so that we may engage our minds and energies in the development of the area."
>
> *King Hussein in* Current Leaders of Nations.

Born into a royal family

Hussein ibn Talal was born on November 14, 1935, in Amman, Jordan, the oldest of Prince Talal and Queen Zain's four children. Hussein came from a powerful royal family. He was descended from the Hashemite dynasty, a group of Arabs who could trace their family history back to the prophet

Hussein ibn Talal, king of Jordan. *Photograph by Dirck Halstead. Time Life Pictures/Getty Images. Reproduced by permission.*

Muhammad, founder of the religion of Islam. Hussein's grandfather, King Abdullah, was the ruler of Jordan at the time of his birth.

Jordan is a central state in the Middle East. It is surrounded by Syria to the north, Iraq to the east, Saudi Arabia to the south, and Israel to the west. At 37,700 square miles (60,659 square kilometers), Jordan is about the size of South Carolina. King Abdullah negotiated with British colonial powers to form the country of Jordan (then known as Transjordan) in 1921. When the country gained its independence from Great Britain in 1946, it became the Hashemite Kingdom of Jordan.

Hussein always loved the natural surroundings and rich history of his country. "Jordan itself is a beautiful country," he once said, as quoted in *King Hussein.* "It is wild, with limitless deserts ... but the mountains of the north are clothed in green forests, and where the Jordan River flows it is fertile and warm in winter. Jordan has a strange, haunting beauty and sense of timelessness. Dotted with the ruins of empires once great, it is the last resort of yesterday and tomorrow."

Throughout Hussein's youth, his grandfather Abdullah was the strongest influence in his life. Since Hussein's father suffered from schizophrenia (a form of mental illness), the king always viewed his grandson as the next ruler of Jordan. Hussein spent his youth preparing to become the king of Jordan someday. He studied at a series of exclusive private schools in Jordan and Egypt. He also spent a year at Harrow, a world-renowned prep school in England. He completed his education at the Sandhurst Royal Military Academy in England, where he gained confidence, pride, and leadership skills.

Becomes king of Jordan at the age of eighteen

While Hussein was growing up and preparing to claim the throne, his country was going through some difficult times. In 1948 the United Nations created the nation of Israel as a homeland for all Jewish people. The part of the Middle East that became Israel also was home to an Arab people known as the Palestinians. Their ancestors had lived in the region known as Palestine, located between the Jordan

River and the Mediterranean Sea, since ancient times. The newly created state of Israel covered most of this territory, which Jews also regard as their historic holy land.

The creation of Israel angered many Arabs. In fact, Jordan and four other Arab countries went to war against Israel shortly after it was formed. The Arab-Israeli War lasted for nine months before Israel defeated the Arab armies in early 1949. Although the Arabs lost the war, Jordan succeeded in capturing an area of land on the west bank of the Jordan River. The West Bank was home to five hundred thousand Palestinians, as well as the important religious sites of Jerusalem and Bethlehem. Another five hundred thousand Palestinians fled from Israel after the war ended, and about half of these people became refugees in Jordan. Suddenly Palestinians made up the majority of Jordan's population, which affected the political goals of the country from that time forward.

Some of the displaced Palestinians formed a group called the Palestine Liberation Organization (PLO). The purpose of the PLO was to fight to reclaim lost territory and establish an independent Palestinian state. The PLO often resorted to acts of violence and terrorism in its dispute against Israel. It gained the support of many Arab nations, however, and was eventually recognized by the United Nations as the legitimate government of Palestine.

King Abdullah struggled to keep control of Jordan's government during this time of political turmoil. In 1951 he was assassinated by a Palestinian extremist who resented his close ties to Great Britain. Hussein was there when his grandfather was shot to death during a visit to a mosque (an Islamic place of worship) in Jerusalem. In fact, Hussein was shot in the chest but the bullet bounced off of a medal he was wearing. Hussein mourned the loss of his grandfather, who had taught him a great deal about the duties of a king. "It was he who taught me to understand the minds of my people and the intricacies of the Arab world in which we lived," he explained, as quoted in *King Hussein*. "And he taught me above all else that a leader's greatest duty is to serve."

Immediately after King Abdullah's death, Hussein's father, Talal, became ruler of Jordan. But the pressures of the job caused Talal's mental illness to resurface, making it impossible for him to rule. The Jordanian parliament declared Hussein the king of Jordan in 1952. Since he was still a minor at this time, the parliament established a three-person council to hold the office until he turned eighteen the following year.

Young king struggles to survive

Upon taking the throne, King Hussein proved to be a moderate (less extreme) leader whose policies tended to favor the West (the noncommunist countries of Western Europe and North America). His political views brought him into conflict with some other Arab leaders, however, as well as with Jordan's large Palestinian population. Some people viewed him as an immature ruler who was used as a pawn by the United States and other Western powers. In fact, he survived a dozen assassination attempts during the early years of his rule.

Despite King Hussein's moderate views, Jordan joined its neighbors Syria and Egypt in a war against Israel in 1967. Known as the Six-Day War, this conflict quickly ended in a victory for Israel. As a result of the fighting, the Jewish state regained control over the West Bank, which had once been part of ancient Palestine. This 3,729-square-mile (6,000-square-kilometer) area contained half of Jordan's population as well as a large portion of its industrial base. It also contained a number of important religious sites for Jews, Christians, and Muslims.

The loss of the West Bank angered Jordan's Palestinian population. Palestinian extremists stepped up their efforts to overthrow the king, which resulted in a civil war in Jordan in 1970. But King Hussein maintained control of the national army and held the loyalty of many citizens. He eventually was able to win the war and strengthen his rule. In 1974 the king made an agreement with the PLO that helped ease tensions with the Palestinians in his country. Jordan gave up its claims on the West Bank, which remained under occupation by the Israeli army, and recognized the Palestinians as the rightful owners of the disputed territory.

As King Hussein's relations with the Palestinians improved, Jordan became more stable. The country's economy experienced strong growth during the 1970s and 1980s. The king granted his people greater personal and economic freedom and placed a strong emphasis on education. As King Hussein entered his forties, he emerged as a leading figure in the Middle Eastern affairs. Over the years he developed several proposals aimed at making peace with Israel while also securing greater rights for the Palestinians.

Supports Iraq during the Persian Gulf War

Jordan supported Iraq during its eight-year war with Iran (1980–88). During this conflict, King Hussein developed a friendship with **Saddam Hussein** (no relation to King Hussein; see entry) and came to regard the Iraqi leader as a dedicated fighter for Arab causes. On August 2, 1990, Saddam Hussein had ordered his military forces to invade the neighboring country of Kuwait. Saddam argued that Iraq had a historical claim to Kuwait's territory. He also wanted to control Kuwait's oil reserves and to gain access to Kuwait's port on the Persian Gulf. Countries around the world condemned the invasion and demanded that Saddam immediately withdraw his troops from Kuwait. Many of these countries then began sending military forces to the Persian Gulf region as part of a U.S.-led coalition against Iraq. In November 1990, the United Nations Security Council established a deadline of January 15, 1991, for Iraq to withdraw from Kuwait or face war.

During the months between Iraq's invasion of Kuwait and the start of the Persian Gulf War, King Hussein emerged as one of the main figures behind efforts to negotiate a peaceful resolution to the crisis. He initially declared that Jordan would remain neutral (not take sides) in the conflict and tried to act as a mediator between Iraq and the United States. He stressed the importance of Arab participation in solving the problems in the Middle East, and he traveled widely in the Arab world to try to build support for a diplomatic solution. He also met with Saddam to try to convince him to withdraw from Kuwait. King Hussein desperately wanted to avoid a war, which he felt would have harmful effects throughout the Arab world.

King Hussein respected Kuwait's status as a sovereign (independent) nation and spoke out against Iraq's aggression toward its neighbor. But he also faced a great deal of pressure from within his own country. The PLO openly expressed its

Arab leaders (from left to right) Yemeni Vice President Ali Salem Al Beedh, King Hussein of Jordan, Iraqi President Saddam Hussein, and Palestinian leader Yasser Arafat meet in Baghdad in December 1990 to discuss the Persian Gulf situation. *AP/Wide World Photos. Reproduced by permission.*

support for Saddam and his invasion of Kuwait. Palestinian leaders viewed Saddam as a powerful opponent of Israel and the United States. King Hussein recognized that Jordan's large Palestinian population would likely follow the PLO's lead and support Iraq. In fact, polls showed that 70 percent of Jordanians approved of Saddam's actions. The king felt that he could not ignore the feelings of the majority of his people. He worried that turning against Iraq would cause huge protests in Jordan and put his rule at risk. As a result, Jordan ended up supporting Iraq during the Persian Gulf War.

King Hussein's support of Iraq led to strained relations between Jordan and the more than thirty-five countries that joined the coalition. Many of these countries stopped trading with Jordan and cut off international aid payments. Meanwhile 750,000 refugees made their way into Jordan from Iraq and Kuwait in the months leading up to the war, putting additional stress on King Hussein's government and the Jordanian people.

The world's longest-serving head of state

Once the Persian Gulf War ended, however, King Hussein worked to improve Jordan's economy and also gave his people greater freedoms. His actions helped Jordan regain the favor of its Arab neighbors, as well as Western powers. King Hussein went on to play a leading role in peace negotiations between the Arabs and Israelis. In 1993 Israel and the PLO agreed on principles of Palestinian self-rule in the occupied territories. The following year Jordan signed a peace treaty with Israel, ending a forty-six-year state of war between the two countries.

Although the king experienced success in his peace-keeping efforts, he wasn't so fortunate where his health was concerned. King Hussein was first diagnosed with cancer in 1992. When the cancer reappeared in 1998, he traveled to the prestigious Mayo Clinic in Minnesota to receive treatment for non-Hodgkin's lymphoma. He died on February 7, 1999, at the age of 63. He had ruled Jordan for nearly fifty years, making him the longest-serving leader in the world. By the time of his death, King Hussein was highly regarded throughout the world as a peacemaker. "I want to hear the tracks of bulldozers, not tanks; the footsteps of travelers, not troops," he once stated, as quoted in *Current Leaders of Nations*. "Let war be banished from our lands forever, so that we may engage our minds and energies in the development of the area."

King Hussein was married four times and had eleven children. He married Dina Abdul Hamed in 1955. They had one daughter together before they were divorced two years later. He married Antoinette Gardiner, the daughter of a British army officer, in 1961. She converted to Islam and took the name Muna al-Hussein following their marriage. They had two sons and two daughters before they were divorced in 1973. Later that year the king married Alia Toukan, a Jordanian Palestinian flight attendant. They had a son and a daughter together before she died in 1977. The following year King Hussein married Lisa Halaby, an American citizen who took the name Noor al-Hussein. They had two sons and two daughters together. Upon his death, King Hussein was succeeded on the throne by his son Abdullah II.

Where to Learn More

"Hussein I, King of Jordan." *Current Leaders of Nations,* 1998. Reproduced in *Biography Resource Center.* Farmington Hills, MI: Gale Group, 2003.

"Hussein ibn Talal." *Encyclopedia of World Biography,* 1998. Reproduced in *Biography Resource Center.* Farmington Hills, MI: Gale Group, 2003.

Hussein ibn Talal. *My War with Israel.* New York: Morrow, 1969.

Hussein ibn Talal. *Uneasy Lies the Head.* New York: Bernard Geis, 1962.

Matusky, Gregory, and John P. Hayes. *King Hussein.* New York: Chelsea House, 1987.

Snow, Peter. *Hussein: A Biography.* London: Barrie and Jenkins, 1972.

Saddam Hussein

**Born April 28, 1937
Tikrit, Iraq**

President of Iraq, 1979–2003

S addam Hussein served as the president of Iraq from 1979 to 2003. During his twenty-four years in power, he gained a reputation as a brutal dictator who used intimidation and violence to eliminate all opposition to his rule. Hussein aspired to make Iraq the dominant nation in the Middle East. He built an impressive army and used it against neighboring countries as well as rebellious groups within Iraq.

When Iraq invaded Kuwait in August 1990, Hussein set in motion a series of events that led to the 1991 Persian Gulf War. After months of diplomatic negotiations and military buildup, the U.S.-led coalition went to war to force Iraq to withdraw from Kuwait. Although Hussein suffered a humiliating defeat in the war, he remained in power. He continued to defy world opinion over the next dozen years, as he refused to honor the United Nations agreement that ended the Persian Gulf War. In 2003 the United States launched a military invasion of Iraq that finally succeeded in removing Hussein from power. After nine months in hiding, the former Iraqi leader was captured by U.S. forces in December 2003.

"Iraqis will not forget the saying that cutting necks is better than cutting means of living. Oh, God Almighty, be witness that we have warned them!"

Saddam Hussein as quoted in Understanding the Crisis in the Persian Gulf.

Saddam Hussein. *©Reuters NewMedia Inc./Corbis. Reproduced by permission.*

A difficult childhood

Saddam Hussein al-Tikriti was born on April 28, 1937. He always preferred to be called by his given name, Saddam, which means "he who confronts" in Arabic. Hussein grew up as a peasant near the Sunni Muslim village of Tikrit, which is located about 100 miles (161 kilometers) north of Baghdad along the Tigris River. He lived in a mud hut with no electricity or running water.

During his rise to power, Hussein changed or exaggerated many details of his early life in order to build his image as a powerful and ruthless leader. As a result, some facts about his life are uncertain. It is known that Hussein's father, Hussein al-Majid, either died or left the family before he was born. He was raised by his mother, Subha Talfa al-Majid, and his stepfather, Ibrahim Hassan.

Hussein has said that he endured a difficult childhood in which he was abused and prevented from attending school. His stepfather forced him to steal sheep and chickens to sell in the local market. Some historians claim that his harsh upbringing taught him to view other people with mistrust and to rely only upon himself. Hussein also decided at a young age that intimidation and violence were effective tools to help him get what he wanted.

Hussein's early life improved in 1947, when he was sent to the Iraqi capital of Baghdad to live with his uncle, Khairallah Talfah. Khairallah was a retired army officer who supported the idea of Arab nationalism, a belief that the Arab world should be united to create one powerful Arab state. Hussein learned a great deal about politics while under his uncle's care. He was also encouraged to attend school for the first time.

Joins the Baath Party

In 1957, as a twenty-year-old student, Saddam joined the Iraqi Baath Party. Baathism was a radical Arab nationalist movement founded in the 1940s. Baath means "rebirth" or "renaissance" in Arabic. The Iraqi Baath Party was a small, disorganized splinter group of this larger movement. It was made up primarily of violent and ruthless men who were willing to do anything to take control of the government.

In 1959 Hussein was part of a group of Baath revolutionaries who tried to murder Iraq's military ruler, General Abdul Karim Qassem. When the assassination attempt failed, Hussein left Iraq in order to avoid punishment. He fled to Syria and eventually settled in Cairo, Egypt, where he entered Cairo University and studied law.

In 1963 the Baath Party succeeded in overthrowing the Iraqi government. Hussein immediately returned to Iraq and claimed his place in the new regime. Thanks to the support of his older cousin, Ahmad Hassan al-Bakr, Hussein received a position in the Baath regional command, which was the party's highest decision-making body in Iraq. Also in 1963, Hussein married his first cousin, Sajida Khairallah Talfah. They eventually had two sons, Uday and Qusay, and three daughters, Raghad, Rina, and Hala.

The Baathists maintained control of the government for just nine months before the Iraqi military overthrew them. The new military rulers put Hussein and several other Baath Party leaders in prison. Hussein used his time in prison to think about why his party did not hold on to power. He felt that party leaders had placed too much trust in the Iraqi military. He decided to build his own security force within the party to help the Baathists regain power. Hussein escaped from prison after two years. He then became the security organizer for the Baath Party. He created a large force that used violence in order to intimidate citizens or eliminate rival political leaders.

In 1968 the Baath Party overthrew the Iraqi government and returned to power. Bakr became president of Iraq, and his ambitious younger cousin Hussein became deputy chairman of the party's Revolutionary Command Council. Hussein also served as the head of internal security for the Baathist government. By controlling the forces of violence and terror that helped the party maintain power, Hussein held the most influential position in the government. He forged close relationships with other party leaders during this time. But he later betrayed many of these men in order to further his own career.

Becomes president of Iraq

Hussein spent the 1970s gradually eliminating Bakr's supporters and his own rivals within the Baath Party. On July

17, 1979, he finally managed to push his cousin out of office and seize control of the government. Shortly after becoming president of Iraq, Hussein took violent steps to ensure that he would remain in power. He carried out a bloody rampage that resulted in the deaths of an estimated five hundred people, including military officers, Baath Party officials, and even some of his close friends and associates.

Hussein used these brutal actions as a way to inspire loyalty among the Iraqi people and ensure his absolute control of the government. He recognized that Iraq faced both external threats from its neighbors and internal tension between its different ethnic and religious groups. Hussein responded to this situation by using violence to make his hold on power seem more solid and legitimate. Hussein also used propaganda (the spreading of information to further a cause) to make himself appear to be a strong leader. He placed pictures of himself all over Baghdad, for example, and ordered songs and poems to be written about him. He wanted Iraqi citizens to feel his presence in their lives and understand that there was no alternative to his rule.

Goes to war against Iran

Hussein promised the Iraqi people that the 1980s would be a "glorious decade." He planned to make Iraq the most powerful country in the Middle East and himself the recognized leader of the Arab world. The first step in Hussein's plan involved attacking Iran, Iraq's neighbor to the east. Iran was a non-Arab state that had recently been torn apart by revolution. A group of Islamic fundamentalists (people who strictly adhere to the basic principles of Islam) under a religious leader called the Ayatollah Khomeini had overthrown the government. Khomeini was a Shiite Muslim and an outspoken opponent of Hussein and his Sunni Muslim government.

Although Iran was larger than Iraq and had three times as many people, Hussein felt that his highly trained armed forces could quickly defeat his enemy. Instead, the bitter conflict lasted for eight long years. Hussein's forces used chemical weapons against Iranian troops on several occasions during the war. The two sides finally declared a cease-fire in 1988.

As soon as Hussein's troops returned home from the Iran-Iraq War, the Iraqi leader turned them against his own rebellious citizens. The non-Arab Kurds of northern Iraq had spent decades struggling to gain their independence and establish a homeland. Some Kurdish groups had supported Iran during the war. Hussein viewed the Kurds as a defiant people who posed a threat to his rule. The Iraqi army attacked Kurdish villages with chemical weapons, killing thousands of people. An estimated 250,000 Kurds fled from Iraq after the attacks and became refugees in Turkey and Iran.

Increasing tension with Kuwait

During the Iran-Iraq War, Hussein developed a tough, battle-hardened military. But the costs of the conflict left the Iraqi economy in ruins. In fact, by the time the war ended Iraq owed $80 billion to other countries. Hussein desperately needed money to help his country recover from the effects of the war.

The Iraqi leader argued that he had fought the war against Iran in order to protect the Arab world from the Islamic fundamentalists who had taken over Iran. He felt that his Arab neighbors should forgive Iraq's debts (not require repayment of loans) since Iraq fought to defend all Arab interests in the Persian Gulf region. Some countries did forgive Iraq's war debts, though Kuwait, a small but very wealthy country located to the south of Iraq, refused to do so.

Iraq's financial problems grew worse in 1990 because of a steep decline in world oil prices. Hussein accused Kuwait of pumping more oil than was allowed under international agreements. He claimed that Kuwait deliberately attempted to lower world oil prices in order to harm Iraq's economy. He considered these actions by his fellow Arab state to be an "economic war" against Iraq.

Iraq and Kuwait also were involved in long-standing disputes over ownership of land along the border between the two countries and on offshore islands in the Persian Gulf. Hussein claimed that Kuwait was trying to expand into Iraqi territory and was stealing oil from underground oil fields on the Iraqi side of the border. On July 17, 1990, Hussein made a fiery speech in which he threatened to use force against Kuwait. "The oil quota violators have stabbed Iraq with a poison dagger," he declared, as quoted in *Understanding the Crisis in the Persian Gulf.* "Iraqis will not forget the saying that cutting necks is better than cutting means of living. Oh, God Almighty, be witness that we have warned them!" Hussein also began sending military troops south to the Kuwaiti border.

Iraq invades Kuwait

Iraq launched a military invasion of Kuwait on August 2, 1990. The powerful Iraqi military successfully overran its smaller neighbor in a matter of hours. Nations around the world condemned the invasion and demanded that Iraq immediately withdraw its troops from Kuwait. The United Nations also placed economic sanctions on Iraq, meaning that Iraq was forbidden from selling its oil to other countries or buying goods from other countries. Still, Hussein refused to remove his forces and instead began threatening nearby Saudi Arabia. The United States and many other countries began sending troops into the Middle East to defend Saudi Arabia and, if necessary, force Iraq to withdraw from Kuwait.

Hussein was surprised by the strong negative response to his invasion of Kuwait. He had misread signals from U.S. government officials and convinced himself that the international community would not interfere with his plans. He never expected the countries of the world to come together against him. Hussein reacted angrily to the foreign military buildup in Saudi Arabia and to the economic sanctions imposed on Iraq by the United Nations.

Over the next six months, a number of world leaders tried to negotiate a peaceful settlement to the crisis. In the meantime, Hussein continued to provoke outrage by annexing Kuwait (formally making it a part of Iraq) and refusing to release foreign citizens who had been in Iraq or Kuwait at the time of the invasion. In November 1990 the United Nations Security Council established a deadline of January 15, 1991, for Iraq to withdraw from Kuwait or face war. Hussein declared the day of the UN deadline to be a national "day of challenge." He ordered Iraqi citizens to march through the streets of Baghdad in defiance of the U.S.-led coalition.

The 1991 Persian Gulf War

The following day the U.S.-led coalition launched a series of air strikes against military targets in Iraq. The air war lasted for nearly six weeks and caused a great deal of destruction in Iraq. But Hussein seemed unmoved by the bombing raids. He frequently appeared on Iraqi television and insisted that his troops would eventually defeat the American invaders.

A few days after the war began, Hussein ordered his forces to fire Scud missiles at Israel and Saudi Arabia. Israel is a Jewish state in the Middle East that has a long history of conflict with its Arab neighbors. Hussein wanted to provoke Israel into retaliating and joining the fight against Iraq. He believed that the Arab countries would leave the coalition, and perhaps even switch sides and support Iraq, rather than fight alongside their bitter enemy.

On February 22 U.S. President **George H. W. Bush** (see entry) established a deadline of noon the following day for Iraq to withdraw from Kuwait or face a ground assault by coalition troops. Hussein responded by saying that Iraq welcomed a ground war. He knew that his troops had prepared strong defensive positions in Kuwait over the preceding months, and he believed that they would inflict massive casualties (killed and wounded soldiers) on the coalition forces.

The coalition ground assault began on February 24. To the surprise of many military experts, the coalition forces met with very little resistance from the Iraqi troops. In fact, thousands of exhausted and hungry Iraqi soldiers surrendered to the approaching coalition forces. The ground war succeeded in liberating Kuwait from Iraqi occupation after only four days of fighting.

Iraq suffered terrible destruction during the war. Coalition bombing destroyed buildings, roads, and bridges in most major cities. The country's water, sewer, and electrical systems were destroyed as well. The total cost of rebuilding Iraq was estimated at $100 billion. The Iraqi army lost 75 percent of its tanks, and thousands of Iraqi soldiers were killed, wounded, or captured. Still, Hussein insisted that Iraq had claimed a great victory by resisting an attack by forty nations for six weeks. He viewed himself as a hero for standing alone in defiance of the United States and its allies.

But Iraq's humiliating defeat left Hussein's government in a weakened position. Some of his opponents tried to take advantage of the opportunity to remove him from power. In the days after the war ended, Shiite Muslims who lived in the southern part of Iraq launched a major revolt against Hussein's government. Kurdish rebels in the northern part of the country also launched a major uprising. The U.S. military encouraged the rebellions but did not provide any direct support. As a result, Hussein was able to use the remains of his army to crush his enemies and remain in power.

Hussein continues to defy the world

Over the next few years, Hussein did not behave like someone who had suffered a terrible military defeat. He continued to make threatening statements toward his neighbors, for example, and he plotted to assassinate former U.S. President George Bush when the American leader visited Kuwait in 1993. Hussein also refused to honor the terms of the United Nations (UN) agreement that had officially ended the war. Part of the UN agreement required Iraq to destroy or remove all of its biological, chemical, and nuclear weapons. But Hussein consistently failed to cooperate with the UN weapons inspectors sent to monitor Iraq's progress and ensure its compliance. In fact, he kicked the inspectors out of Iraq in 1998.

Hussein claimed that Iraq did not possess any weapons of mass destruction. But many experts believed that Iraq did hold such weapons. They felt that Hussein was reluctant to destroy them because it would reduce his power over his own people as well as Iraq's strength in the Middle East.

Hussein's attitude did not please the United States or other members of the international community. Since Iraq did not meet the terms of the UN agreement, the United Nations kept the economic sanctions in place against Iraq. Instead of weakening Hussein, however, the trade restrictions mostly created hardships for the Iraqi people, who suffered from malnutrition and a lack of medical care.

American and British leaders also launched bombing campaigns against Iraq on several occasions in response to Hussein's actions. Once the last of these military operations concluded in December 1998, however, the international community made little further effort to enforce the UN agreement that had ended the 1991 war.

Hussein removed from power

In September 2002 U.S. President **George W. Bush** (son of the former president who had held office during the 1991 Persian Gulf War; see entry) challenged the United Nations to take action against Iraq. He argued that the United Nations should force Iraq to honor the agreement that had ended the Persian Gulf War eleven years earlier. He claimed that the United Nations would lose its authority if it allowed Hussein to continue ignoring the agreement. Bush also told the United Nations that Iraq posed a significant threat to world security. He claimed that Hussein still possessed weapons of mass destruction and could provide such weapons to terrorists.

In November the UN Security Council unanimously passed Resolution 1441. This resolution declared Iraq to be in violation of earlier UN resolutions, authorized a new round of weapons inspections, and promised that Iraq would face serious consequences if it failed to comply. The UN inspectors returned to Iraq on November 18, 2002. Their reports over the next few months contained mixed results. Sometimes Iraqi authorities were very cooperative. At other times, however, they seemed to be hiding information from the inspectors.

Bush was not satisfied with the results of the inspections and threatened to take military action against Iraq. The Bush administration began talking about the importance of a "regime change" (removing Hussein's government from power) in Iraq and pressured the UN Security Council to authorize the use of force. Although Bush received support from Great Britain and some other countries, most other nations wanted to give the inspections more time.

Bush, however, was determined to proceed with military action despite the lack of UN support. On March 17, 2003, he gave Hussein and his sons two days to leave Iraq or face an American military invasion. But Hussein remained defiant and refused to leave Iraq. Some historians claimed that he did not believe a U.S. military invasion would succeed. Others said that power meant everything to Hussein, and that he viewed death as a better alternative than giving up his power.

On March 19 (March 20 in Iraq) the American and British forces went to war against Iraq. Some of the first missile strikes were aimed at senior Iraqi government leaders, in-

A photo of former Iraqi President Saddam Hussein after he was captured by U.S. troops on December 14, 2003, near his home town Tikrit. *Photograph by U.S. Army. Getty Images. Reproduced by permission.*

cluding Hussein. Although it appeared that Hussein survived this first round of attacks, he disappeared following later attacks and was presumed dead. American forces moved into Baghdad after only a few weeks of fighting. On May 1, 2003, President Bush declared that major combat operations were over and Iraq had been freed from Hussein's rule. American troops remained in Iraq to search for Hussein and other members of the former government, hunt for weapons of mass destruction, and help the Iraqi people rebuild the country and form a democratic government. As time passed, however, the U.S. forces came under increasingly violent attacks from angry Iraqis and foreign fighters determined to resist the occupation.

Despite a massive search, Hussein's whereabouts remained a mystery for the next nine months. He was finally captured by U.S. forces two weeks before Christmas. Responding to a tip from an informant, the Raider Brigade of the U.S. Army's Fourth Infantry Division searched a farm near the town of Adwar, about ten miles from Hussein's hometown of Tikrit. They found Hussein hiding in an eight-foot-deep "spider hole," concealed with dirt and bricks, outside a mud hut on the property. The fallen Iraqi leader, who was found with a pistol and $750,000 in cash, surrendered peacefully. He appeared shaggy and disheveled and seemed confused. The coalition released pictures of Hussein taken during a medical exam and after he was cleaned up and shaved.

U.S. civil administrator **L. Paul Bremer** (see entry) announced the capture to the world in a press conference. "Ladies and gentlemen, we got him," he stated, as quoted in *Time* magazine. "Iraq's future, your future, has never been more full of hope. The tyrant is a prisoner." Iraqi journalists attending the news conference stood up and cheered or cried. Some screamed "Kill him! Kill Saddam!" When the people of Baghdad heard the news, some of them threw candy in the streets or fired guns into the sky in celebration. But others expressed sadness or anger at seeing the longtime leader of Iraq humiliated.

President Bush was pleased at the capture of Hussein, and he hoped that it might convince former regime members to end their resistance against the U.S. occupation forces. But Bush also warned that "the capture of Saddam Hussein does not mean the end of violence in Iraq," according to the *Detroit Free Press*. "We still face terrorists who would rather go on killing the innocent than accept the rise of liberty in the heart of the Middle East." Interviews with Hussein following his capture yielded little evidence that he was involved in planning the attacks against coalition forces. Although some insurgents may have been motivated by a desire to see Hussein return to power, most seemed to be acting primarily out of hatred for the U.S. occupation of Iraq. Despite the postwar security problems, however, Iraq continued to make progress toward forming a new government.

Where to Learn More

Cipkowski, Peter. *Understanding the Crisis in the Persian Gulf.* New York: John Wiley, 1992.

Claypool, Jane. *Saddam Hussein.* Vero Beach, FL: Rourke Publications, 1993.

"Face of Defeat." *Detroit Free Press,* December 15, 2003.

Gibbs, Nancy. "Ladies and Gentlemen, We Got Him." *Time,* December 22, 2003.

Karsh, Efraim, and Inari Rautsi. *Saddam Hussein: A Political Biography.* New York: Free Press, 1991.

McGeary, Johanna. "Inside Saddam's Head." *Time,* March 31, 2003.

Miller, Judith, and Laurie Mylroie. *Saddam Hussein and the Crisis in the Gulf.* New York: Times Books, 1990.

"Saddam Hussein." *Biography Today.* Detroit: Omnigraphics, 1992.

"Saddam Hussein." *Current Leaders of Nations,* 1998. Reproduced in *Biography Resource Center.* Farmington Hills, MI: Gale Group, 2003.

"Saddam Hussein." *Encyclopedia of World Biography,* 1998. Reproduced in *Biography Resource Center.* Farmington Hills, MI: Gale Group, 2003.

Sciolino, Elaine. *The Outlaw State: Saddam Hussein's Quest for Power and the Gulf Crisis.* New York: John Wiley, 1991.

Jessica Lynch

Born 1983
Palestine, West Virginia

U.S. Army soldier who was taken prisoner
and later rescued during the 2003 Iraq War

Private First Class Jessica Lynch is one of the most famous U.S. soldiers to fight in the 2003 Iraq War. On March 23, Lynch's army unit was ambushed in the city of Nasiriyah in southern Iraq by resistance fighters. Badly injured in the fighting, Lynch was captured and taken to an Iraqi hospital. Nine days later, she was rescued in dramatic fashion by U.S. Special Forces commandos. She was widely hailed as a hero, although she later insisted that she was only a "survivor."

"For twenty years, no one knew my name. Now they want my autograph. But I'm not a hero."

Jessica Lynch in I Am a Soldier, Too: The Jessica Lynch Story.

Small-town girl joins the army

Born in 1983 in the small town of Palestine, West Virginia, Jessica Lynch was the second of three children born to Gregory Lynch, a truck driver, and his wife Deadra. She enjoyed a sheltered, rural upbringing that included riding horses and playing softball. Unlike children who grow up in the city, Lynch was in high school before she ever set foot in a shopping mall. Lynch's friendly personality won her the title of "Miss Congeniality" in a beauty pageant at a local fair. Upon graduating from Wirt County High School

Jessica Lynch. *Photograph by John Himelrick. Getty Images. Reproduced by permission.*

161

in 2001, she planned to eventually become a kindergarten teacher.

The summer after graduation, a U.S. Army recruiter came to her home. The recruiter convinced both Jessica and her older brother, Greg Jr., to enlist in the military. Lynch viewed military service as a way to earn money for college and travel around the world. After completing basic training, she was stationed at several different military bases in the United States, Mexico, and Germany. She received a promotion to Private First Class and signed up for four more years in the service shortly before the 2003 Iraq War began.

Participates in Operation Iraqi Freedom

The Iraq War grew out of long-standing disagreements between the United States and the Middle Eastern nation of Iraq. In 1990 Iraqi president **Saddam Hussein** (see entry) had invaded the neighboring country of Kuwait. Hussein argued that Iraq had a historical claim to Kuwait's territory. He also wanted to control Kuwait's oil reserves and to gain access to Kuwait's port on the Persian Gulf. This action led to the 1991 Persian Gulf War, in which a U.S.-led military coalition made up of thirty-five countries forced the Iraqi army to withdraw from Kuwait. The United Nations agreement that ended the war required Iraq to destroy all of its chemical, biological, and nuclear weapons. Over the next decade, however, Hussein consistently interfered with the UN weapons inspectors sent to monitor Iraq's progress. The international community tried a number of different approaches to convince Iraq to cooperate, but instead Hussein kicked the UN inspectors out of Iraq in 1998.

The terrorist attacks that struck the United States on September 11, 2001, led President **George W. Bush** (see entry) to adopt a more aggressive policy toward nations that he considered threats to world security, such as Iraq. He argued that Iraq possessed weapons of mass destruction and could provide such weapons to terrorist groups. Over the next year, Bush pressured the United Nations to authorize the use of military force to disarm Iraq and remove Hussein from power. Although Bush failed to generate UN support, the United States and Great Britain launched a military invasion of Iraq on March 20, 2003.

In early 2003 Lynch was stationed in Kuwait as a supply clerk with the U.S. Army's 507th Maintenance Company. Her unit consisted of mechanics, clerks, computer technicians, and other support staff. Their main job was to set up and maintain Patriot antimissile defense systems. Although Lynch and the other soldiers in her unit completed basic combat training and carried weapons, they were not equipped to fight like infantry soldiers. In fact, the maintenance company was always supposed to travel with an infantry escort to protect it. "We are supposed to enter a town after it has been secured by other combat forces," one soldier explained to ABC News. "Even when an area is completely secure, the maintenance team is still supposed to be protected. They never go anywhere alone."

Runs into an enemy ambush

When U.S. forces launched their ground invasion, thousands of tanks, armored vehicles, artillery, and personnel carriers rolled across the Kuwaiti border into southern Iraq. Lynch's maintenance company was at the tail end of a six-hundred-vehicle convoy that headed north toward Nasiriyah. On March 22 the U.S. Army's Third Infantry and V Corps came under attack by Iraqi forces that were dug in to defend the city. They responded by calling in air strikes against the enemy. After capturing a critical bridge over the Euphrates River, the American forces continued rolling across the desert toward the Iraqi capital of Baghdad.

As the convoy pushed forward, however, the Iraqi resistance grew more intense. Some of the slower-moving supply vehicles at the back of the line were left vulnerable to attack. The thirty-three soldiers in Lynch's maintenance company struggled to keep up. Their eighteen heavy trucks and other vehicles kept breaking down or becoming stuck in the sand. The water tanker that Lynch was driving broke down and had to be towed. She then rode in a crowded Humvee driven by her best friend, Private Lori Piestewa. By the early morning hours of March 23, the 507th had dropped 130 miles (209 kilometers) behind the leading edge of the U.S. invasion force.

As they neared Nasiriyah, Lynch's unit missed a turn that would have taken them around the outskirts of the city.

Instead, their convoy of vehicles crossed the Euphrates River and entered the town. At this point, Nasiriyah was not yet secure. In fact, it had been the scene of fierce fighting a few hours earlier. As the 507th passed through the city for the first time, they encountered no resistance. But they soon realized that they had made a mistake and turned around to retrace their steps. It was then that they ran into a massive ambush by Iraqi Fedayeen resistance fighters.

The maintenance company took heavy fire from Iraqi fighters in pickup trucks, on rooftops, and along the sides of the road. The Iraqis used a variety of weapons, including automatic rifles, machine guns, and rocket-propelled grenades. "They were on both sides of the street, and we were trapped in the middle, and they were hurtin' us bad," Lynch recalled in *I Am a Soldier, Too.* As various vehicles took evasive action, the U.S. Army convoy got spread out and separated. The Humvee carrying Lynch was hit by a rocket-propelled grenade and crashed into a disabled American truck. Lynch suffered serious injuries in the crash, which killed several other occupants of the vehicle, including Piestewa.

Immediately following the incident, Lynch and fourteen other soldiers from her unit were listed as missing in action (MIA). As more information became available, the U.S. Army reported that eleven soldiers from the 507th had been killed and four others captured by the Iraqis. Hussein showed the other American prisoners of war (POWs) on Iraqi television, looking battered and dazed. The incident shook the confidence of the American people and raised concerns about the Bush administration's war plan. "The ambush of the 507th suddenly came to seem like a metaphor for a war that was not going quite as smoothly as planned," Todd S. Purdum wrote in *A Time of Our Choosing.* "While it was true that the U.S. Army and the Marines were advancing swiftly toward Baghdad, and the punishing air campaign was well underway, the unexpectedly heavy fighting in Nasiriyah showed the downside of the lighter invasion force, with its long, unsecured supply lines."

Captured and rescued

Three hours after the ambush, Lynch was finally taken to a nearby hospital. She apparently suffered further injuries at the hands of angry Iraqis following the crash, but she was unconscious for much of this time and did not remember what happened. By the time she arrived at the hospital, she was in shock from serious and rapid blood loss. She suffered from compound fractures in her right arm and left leg, a crushed right foot, a spine that was fractured in two places, and a four-inch gash on her forehead. She almost certainly would have died if not for the medical treatment she received from Iraqi doctors.

Lynch was later moved to Saddam Hussein Hospital in Nasiriyah, which also served as a command center for the Fedayeen resistance fighters. The Fedayeen engaged in intense fighting with U.S. Marines during the time she was held there. In addition to treating her wounds, however, the medical staff at the hospital took steps to protect Lynch and prevent her from being moved to another location. At one point, they even loaded her in an ambulance and drove her to an American checkpoint to return her to U.S. troops. But the U.S. soldiers fired at the ambulance, forcing it to turn around.

As the days passed, U.S. Marines fighting for control of Nasiriyah heard rumors that a female American soldier was being held in the hospital. Mohammed Odeh al Rehaief, an Iraqi lawyer whose wife worked at the hospital, came forward to confirm the rumors. He later drew maps of the facility and scouted its security force in order to assist the Americans in planning a rescue. On April 1 U.S. Special Operations forces launched a dramatic mission to rescue Lynch. It was a joint operation of elite Army Rangers, Navy SEALs, marines, and air force pilots. The U.S. troops entered the hospital in full battle gear, located Lynch, and carried her out on a stretcher to a waiting helicopter. The rescue was captured on video and generated a great deal of positive media coverage. Lynch became the first American POW to be rescued since World War II (1939–45).

Lynch was transported to a U.S. Army base in Germany, where she underwent surgery and was reunited with her family. She returned to the United States a few weeks later, after U.S. troops had succeeded in capturing Baghdad and removing Hussein from power. Lynch underwent several months of physical therapy at Walter Reed Army Medical Center in Maryland. Upon her release in July she attended a

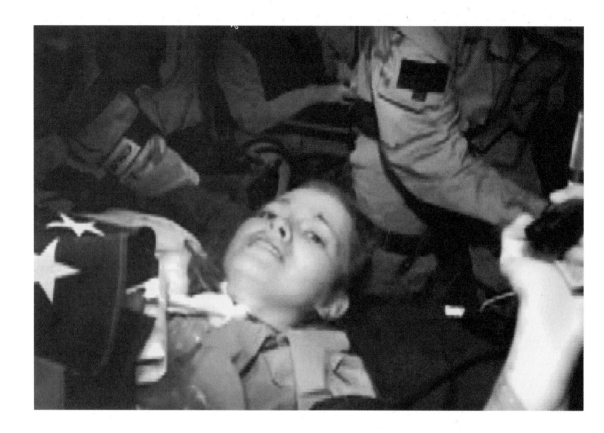

This photo from Central Command shows the rescue of POW U.S. Private First Class Jessica Lynch during an early morning raid on a hospital deep in Iraq.
Photograph by CENTCOM/Getty Images. Reproduced by permission.

ceremony to accept awards for her military service. She received the Bronze Star, Purple Heart, and Prisoner of War medals. Then Lynch finally returned home to West Virginia, where she was greeted by cheering crowds and a parade in her honor.

A hero, or merely lucky?

Lynch became a symbol of victory, courage, and hope for many Americans. Her ordeal captured the nation's attention and inspired an outpouring of gifts and financial support. For example, a company lent her family its private jet so they could travel to Germany to see her. Hundreds of people donated time and money to renovate her family's home and build a wheelchair-accessible bedroom for her. Lynch also received a number of college scholarship offers. Once she settled back in at home, she agreed to tell her story in a book and a television movie.

But some people complained that Lynch did not deserve all the attention she received. The backlash started shortly after she was rescued, when some U.S. military officials claimed that Lynch had shown great courage under fire. They said that Lynch had crawled out of her wrecked Humvee and fought fiercely to defend her fellow soldiers. The *Washington Post* quoted one army spokesman who said, "She was fighting to the death. She did not want to be taken alive." In reality, however, Lynch's gun jammed and she never fired a shot during the ambush. After the Humvee crash, she was too badly injured to put up any resistance. When the true story came out, some people criticized Lynch as a fraud, even though she had no part in spreading the false information.

Another controversy erupted over the Special Operations mission to rescue Lynch. U.S. military officials described it as a daring nighttime raid in which American soldiers fought their way into the hospital. In reality, however, the commandos who rescued Lynch encountered no resistance once they entered the hospital. The Iraqi doctors cooperated by leading the U.S. troops to Lynch's room. The *London Times* claimed that the rescue of Lynch "was not the Hollywood story told by the U.S. military, but a staged operation that terrified patients and victimized the doctors who had struggled to save her life." But U.S. military leaders stood by their characterization of the rescue mission. They noted that the commandos had to take proper precautions because all of Nasiriyah remained dangerous at that time. In addition, they pointed out that Lynch probably would have died within a few days if the mission had not succeeded.

For her part, Lynch never claimed to be a hero and expressed discomfort with all the attention she received. In late 2003 she released a book about her experiences, *I Am a Soldier, Too: The Jessica Lynch Story.* To the surprise of some readers, she came across as a humble and modest person who made no claims of heroism. "For twenty years, no one knew my name. Now they want my autograph," she wrote. "But I'm not a hero. If it makes people feel good to say that, then I'm glad. But I'm not. I'm just a survivor." Many people praised the way Lynch described her ordeal and noted that it increased their respect for her.

Where to Learn More

Bragg, Rick. *I Am a Soldier, Too: The Jessica Lynch Story.* New York: Knopf, 2003.

"Coalition Rescues U.S. Prisoner of War." *Online NewsHour,* April 2, 2003. Available online at http://www.pbs.org/newshour/extra/features/jan-june03/rescue_4-2.html (accessed on March 29, 2004).

"Jessica Lynch." *Biography Resource Center Online.* Farmington Hills, MI: Gale Group, 2003.

Purdum, Todd S., and the staff of the *New York Times. A Time of Our Choosing: America's War in Iraq.* New York: Times Books, 2003.

Rosenberg, Howard L. "Bloody Sunday: The Real Story of What Happened to Jessica Lynch's Convoy." *ABC News,* June 17, 2003. Available online at http://abcnews.go.com/sections/primetime/World/iraq_507convoy030617_pt1.html (accessed on March 29, 2004).

Colin Powell

Born April 5, 1937
Harlem, New York

Chairman of the Joint Chiefs of Staff during the 1991 Persian Gulf War and U.S. secretary of state during the 2003 Iraq War

C olin Powell served as chairman of the U.S. Joint Chiefs of Staff, the highest-ranking post in the American military, during the 1991 Persian Gulf War. As the top military advisor to President **George H. W. Bush** (see entry) and his administration, he played an important role in shaping the U.S. response to Iraq's invasion of Kuwait. He also supervised all aspects of Operation Desert Shield and Operation Desert Storm, the military operations that made up the Persian Gulf War and delivered a crushing defeat to Iraq's army. The victory over Iraq made Powell one of the United States' most popular public figures.

In 2001 Powell became U.S. secretary of state under President **George W. Bush** (see entry), son of the former president. In the weeks leading up to the 2003 Iraq War, he was responsible for presenting the Bush administration's case for war to the United Nations (UN) Security Council.

Son of Jamaican immigrants

Colin Luther Powell was born April 5, 1937, in Harlem, a neighborhood in New York City. His parents were

"We met the Iraqi army in the field and ... dealt it a crushing defeat and left less than half of what it had been"

Colin Powell in My American Journey.

Colin Powell. *AP/Wide World Photos. Reproduced by permission.*

Jamaican immigrants who worked in the city's garment district. His father, Luther Powell, worked as a shipping clerk, and his mother, Maud Ariel Powell, earned a paycheck as a seamstress. For most of his childhood, Powell's family lived in the South Bronx next to families from all sorts of ethnic backgrounds. Powell's childhood friends included boys from Irish, Jewish, Polish, Italian, and Hispanic families.

Powell grew up in a strong family environment. Surrounded by relatives who provided both security and discipline, he told *People* that "I had a great childhood. I had a close family, which provided everything I needed." Powell was a steady but unremarkable student up through his graduation from Morris High School in 1954. He then enrolled at City College of New York (CCNY), where he quickly emerged as one of the top students in CCNY's Reserve Officer's Training Corps (ROTC; ROTC programs prepare high school and college students to be officers in the U.S. Army Reserve). By the time Powell earned his bachelor's degree in geology from CCNY in 1958, he had earned the rank of cadet colonel, the top rank available to ROTC participants.

Powell treasures his ROTC experience and recognizes that it was an important first step in his successful military career. "The discipline, the structure, the camaraderie, the sense of belonging [in ROTC] were what I craved," he recalled in his 1995 autobiography, *My American Journey*. "I became a leader almost immediately. I found a selflessness within our ranks that reminded me of the caring atmosphere within my family. Race, color, background, income meant nothing. The PR (Pershing Rifles, a military society within the ROTC) would go the limit for each other and for the group. If this was what soldiering was all about, then maybe I wanted to be a soldier."

Serves in Vietnam War

After leaving CCNY, Powell joined the U.S. Army as a second lieutenant. He underwent basic training at Fort Benning, Georgia, a southern state in which segregation—a social system that limited educational, social, and economic opportunities for blacks by keeping them separate from white society—was very strong. As a black man, Powell experienced the racial bigotry of segregation nearly every day of his six-week basic training. After leaving Fort Benning, Powell spent the next four years at U.S. bases in West Germany and the United States. On August 25, 1962, he married Alma Vivian Johnson, a speech pathologist. They eventually had three children together—Michael, Linda, and Annemarie.

In 1963 Powell received orders to go to South Vietnam, a nation in Southeast Asia. His first assignment in the Vietnam War, a conflict that pitted North Vietnam against troops from South Vietnam and the United States, was to serve as a military advisor to South Vietnamese troops in a remote region of the country known as the A Shau Valley. Powell spent the next several months wondering whether he would live to see another day. "We were ambushed almost daily, usually in the morning, soon after we got under way," he recalled in *My American Journey*. "I found it maddening to be ambushed, to lose men day after day to this phantom enemy who hit and ran and hit again, with seeming impunity [without punishment], never taking a stand, never giving us anything to shoot at."

One day, Powell stepped on an enemy booby trap that drove a dirty spike through his foot. The injury was not life-threatening, but it forced his superiors to reassign him to an office position in one of South Vietnam's major cities. "It would be dishonest to say I hated to leave combat," he admitted in *My American Journey*. "But by the time I was injured, I had become the battalion commander in all but name. I had taken the same risks, slept on the same ground and eaten from the same pots as these men and had spilled my blood with them. Shared death, terror, and small triumphs in the A Shau Valley linked me closely to men with whom I could barely converse."

In 1963 Powell completed his tour of duty in Vietnam and returned to the United States. He was stationed at Fort Benning and Fort Leavenworth, Kansas, where he received advanced military training. In 1968 he was sent back to Vietnam, where the war was raging at a feverish pitch. In 1969, however, Powell was injured in a helicopter crash. Despite his injuries, Powell managed to save three soldiers trapped in the burning wreckage. But his wounds convinced the army to send Powell home. He left Vietnam for good in 1969 with numerous medals and awards, including two Purple Hearts for wounds suffered in battle, a Bronze Star for bravery, a Soldier's Medal for bravery, and the Legion of Merit.

Advances through the ranks

After returning from Vietnam, Powell remained in the army but also became more involved in politics. He earned a master's degree in business from George Washington University in 1971. The next year, he joined the White House as an assistant to Frank Carlucci, who was deputy director of the Office of Management and Budget (OMB). Powell spent the next two decades swinging back and forth between political positions and military assignments, mostly in the Department of Defense.

Powell's career advanced steadily forward throughout this period. He gained a reputation as a smart, ethical, and hard-working man who was more interested in serving his country than acquiring power and wealth for himself. For his part, Powell stated that he never felt the urge to leave the military. "I don't recall ever reaching a momentous point where I had to consciously decide whether or not I was going to continue to serve in the military," he once said, as quoted in the book *Colin Powell*. "I have always enjoyed being in the Army, and as the years went by, I continued to be challenged with each new assignment. I simply had no desire to do anything else."

Named to nation's top military post

In 1987 Powell became the first black American to serve his country as National Security Advisor. As a member of the National Security Council, an agency headed by the president of the United States that helps determine military and diplomatic decisions affecting national security, Powell became an important voice in shaping a wide variety of U.S. policies.

In 1989 President George H. W. Bush decided to name Powell to the U.S. military's top post, chairman of the Joint Chiefs of Staff (JCS). "General Powell has had a truly distinguished military career, and he's a complete soldier. He will bring leadership, insight, and wisdom to our efforts to keep the military strong," Bush declared in *Colin Powell* by Jim Haskins.

Powell thus became the youngest man and the first black in U.S. history to hold the position of chairman of the JCS.

As chairman, Powell not only served as the president's top advisor on military issues, but also supervised all four branches of the U.S. Armed Services—army, navy, air force, and marines. His first major challenge in his new job was to provide President Bush with strategies for dealing with General Manuel Noriega, the dictator of a Central American nation called Panama. American drug enforcement agents suspected that Noriega was allowing drug dealers to ship their drugs through his country on their way to the United States. Then, in December 1989, Panamanian soldiers killed a U.S. Marine and tortured an American sailor. These events prompted the U.S. government to express concern about the safety of the thirteen thousand other Americans (mostly soldiers and their families) who were living in Panama.

The tense situation with Noriega convinced President Bush to order Powell to develop plans for a surprise attack on Panama. On December 20, 1989, this plan, called Operation Just Cause, was launched. The nighttime invasion by U.S. forces destroyed Noriega's headquarters and other important military posts. On January 3, 1990, Noriega surrendered to the United States.

Later that year, Iraq's invasion of neighboring Kuwait triggered another international crisis. Iraqi leader **Saddam Hussein** (see entry) argued that Iraq had a historical claim to Kuwait's territory. He also wanted to control Kuwait's oil reserves and to gain access to Kuwait's port on the Persian Gulf. Countries around the world criticized the invasion and demanded that Hussein withdraw his troops from Kuwait. When he refused, many of these countries sent military forces to the Persian Gulf region to join a U.S.-led coalition against Iraq. The coalition eventually grew to include five hundred thousand U.S. troops and two hundred thousand soldiers from other nations.

Many of the U.S. troops sent to the Persian Gulf region were placed in Saudi Arabia, a U.S. ally that Hussein had repeatedly threatened to attack. Powell and other U.S. military and political leaders referred to the campaign to protect Saudi Arabia as Operation Desert Shield. Powell supervised all major aspects of the Desert Shield campaign. "There were many long days and nights during the Gulf War," he recalled in the book *Colin Powell*. "I talked with General [Norman] Schwarzkopf [commander of U.S. forces in the Persian Gulf] several times each day. There were lots of meetings to discuss our plans and to evaluate how well our troops were doing. It was a very stressful time with constant concern for the men and women serving so bravely and so far from home."

Throughout Operation Desert Shield, Powell gave numerous press briefings to reporters that were televised in the United States and around the world. In each of these briefings, Powell always appeared knowledgeable, confident, and calm. His manner reassured Americans who were anxious about going to war against Iraq, and led many people to hold him up as a positive role model for black and white youth alike.

Operation Desert Storm

Operation Desert Shield kept Saudi Arabia safe from the Iraqi army. But President Bush and other world leaders still wanted Hussein to end his occupation of Kuwait. In November 1990, the United Nations Security Council established a deadline of January 15, 1991, for Iraq to withdraw from Kuwait or face attack by the U.S.-led forces. When Iraq failed to withdraw its troops from Kuwait by the deadline, the coalition forces began a campaign of air strikes against Iraqi troops and military positions, including some in the capital city of Baghdad. These air strikes, known as Operation Desert Storm, blasted Iraqi military targets for thirty-eight days, leaving Iraqi forces stunned and battered. The United States then launched a massive ground offensive against Iraqi positions in Kuwait and southern Iraq on February 24, 1991. Within one hundred hours, Hussein's forces were chased out of Kuwait and sent fleeing deep into Iraq. "We met the Iraqi army in the field and … dealt it a crushing defeat and left less than half of what it had been," stated Powell in *My American Journey*.

President Bush ordered the U.S. military to end its pursuit of Iraq's battered army on February 27. This decision left Hussein in power with about half of his old military force. Powell admitted in his autobiography:

> Years from now, historians will still ask if we should not have fought longer and destroyed more of the Iraqi army. Critics argue that we should have widened our war aims to include seiz-

ing Baghdad and driving Saddam Hussein from power.... What tends to be forgotten is that while the U.S led the way [in Operation Desert Storm], we were heading an international coalition carrying out a clearly defined U.N. mission [to drive Iraq out of Kuwait]. That mission was accomplished.... I stand by my role in the President's decision to end the war when and how he did. It is an accountability I carry with pride and without apology.

Colin Powell (center) visiting troops during the Persian Gulf War. *AP/Wide World Photos. Reproduced by permission.*

A respected figure in American politics

Many observers believe that the Persian Gulf War helped the people of the United States gain a new level of confidence in their military. As one of the most visible leaders of the U.S. military campaign in that conflict, Powell became one of the most respected and well-liked figures in American society. Many people even urged him to run for political office, maybe even the presidency of the United States. But Powell resisted these suggestions, saying that he did not like the negative tone of American politics.

Powell retired from the U.S. military on September 30, 1993, after thirty-five years of service. At his retirement ceremony, President Bill Clinton awarded him one of the country's highest honors, the Presidential Medal of Freedom with Distinction, in front of thousands of guests. He wrote in *My American Journey*:

> As I looked over this spectacle of color and pageantry, I would have to be soul-dead not to marvel at the trajectory [direction] my life had followed, from an ROTC second lieutenant out of CCNY to the highest-ranking officer in the U.S. armed forces; from advising a few hundred men in the jungles of Vietnam to responsibility for over 2 million soldiers, sailors, airmen and Marines; from growing up with tough kids in the South Bronx to association with leaders from all over the world. My only regret was that I could not do it all over again.

In 1995 Powell published his autobiography, called *My American Journey*. Two years later he founded America's Promise—An Alliance for Youth, an organization that aims to help at-risk children by encouraging adults to take an active interest in their growth and development. One of the organization's highest priorities is encouraging volunteerism, which Powell sees as a key to healthy and happy communities. "Young people—like adults—usually find that when they make a real effort on behalf of others, they get back more than they contribute," he wrote in *Time* magazine. "Many youngsters report that volunteering in their communities has helped them understand people who are different from themselves, has opened up new career possibilities to them, and has enlarged their horizons."

U.S. secretary of state during the 2003 Iraq War

In 2000 Texas Governor George W. Bush, a son of the President Bush who had been in office during the 1991 Persian Gulf War, was elected to be the forty-third president of the United States. He promptly asked Powell to serve as secretary of state in his administration. Powell accepted the invitation, so when the Bush administration assumed power in January 2001, the son of poor Jamaican immigrants became the first African American secretary of state in U.S. history. As Bush's leading advisor on foreign policy issues, Powell played an important role in many administration decisions, including the decision to invade Iraq.

In September 2002 Bush challenged the United Nations to take action against Iraq. He argued that the United Nations should force Iraq to honor the agreement that had ended the Persian Gulf War eleven years earlier. He claimed that the United Nations would lose its authority if it allowed Hussein to continue ignoring the agreement. Bush also made it clear that the United States would act alone to disarm Iraq by force if necessary. As the threat of American military action increased, Iraq agreed to allow the UN weapons inspectors to return "without conditions." In November the UN Security Council responded to Bush's calls for action by unanimously passing a new resolution regarding Iraq. Resolution 1441 declared Iraq in violation of earlier UN resolutions, authorized a new round of weapons inspections, and promised that Iraq would face serious consequences if it failed to comply.

Weapons inspectors from the UN Monitoring, Verification, and Inspection Commission (UNMOVIC), led by Hans Blix of Sweden, returned to Iraq on November 18, 2002. Their reports over the next few months contained mixed results. Sometimes Iraqi authorities were very cooperative. At other times, however, they seemed to be hiding information from the inspectors. The Bush administration was dissatisfied with Blix's reports and continued to pressure the UN Security Council to authorize the use of military force to disarm Iraq and remove Hussein from power.

On February 5, 2003, Powell appeared before the UN Security Council to make the administration's case against Iraq. He presented evidence that he claimed proved that Iraq still possessed weapons of mass destruction, including chemical and biological weapons. He also argued that Hussein was determined to build nuclear weapons. "We have no indication that Saddam Hussein has ever abandoned his nuclear weapons program," Powell stated, as quoted by *Online News-Hour.* "On the contrary, we have more than a decade of proof that he remains determined to acquire nuclear weapons."

Powell presented spy photos of suspected weapons facilities in Iraq, tape recordings of intercepted telephone conversations between Iraqi officials, and statements from informants inside Hussein's government. He accused Iraq of following a policy of "evasion and deception" for a dozen years, intentionally hiding things from UN inspectors. Finally, he suggested that a link existed between Saddam Hussein and the Al Qaeda terrorist group which was responsible for the September 11, 2001, terrorist attacks on the United States. On the basis of his evidence, Powell insisted that the Security Council pass a new resolution authorizing its members to use force to disarm Iraq. "We must not shrink from whatever is ahead of us. We must not fail in our duty and our responsibility for the citizens of the countries that are represented by this body," he said in *Online NewsHour.* "Leaving Saddam Hussein in possession of weapons of mass destruction for a few more months or years is not an option, not in a post-September 11 world."

Powell needed to convince nine of the fourteen other member countries of the UN Security Council, including the four other permanent members, to vote in favor of a new resolution. But several members of the Security Council, notably France and Russia, still had doubts about the use of force against Iraq. They did not believe that Iraq posed an immediate threat and wanted to give the weapons inspectors more time to complete their work. After weeks of tense diplomatic negotiations, it became clear that France would use its veto power to block a new resolution authorizing the use of military force in Iraq. The United States and its allies decided not to seek a new resolution, instead arguing that military force was permitted under resolution 1441.

Despite the lack of UN support, the United States launched its invasion of Iraq on March 20, 2003. U.S. forces succeeded in capturing Baghdad and removing Hussein from power after just a few weeks of fighting. On May 1 Bush announced the end of major combat operations in Iraq. However, American troops remained in the country to help the Iraqi people rebuild facilities and form a democratic government. When the U.S. occupation forces faced resistance from angry Iraqis and foreign fighters, Powell continued to defend the Bush administration's policies. He acknowledged that keeping the peace in postwar Iraq was difficult, but expressed confidence that the occupation would eventually result in the creation of a free and democratic society.

Where to Learn More

America's Promise. Available at http://www.americaspromise.org (accessed on April 2, 2004).

Haskins, Jim. *Colin Powell.* Danbury, CT: Scholastic, 1997.

"Interview with Colin Powell." *Unfold,* Spring 1999.

Kunen, James S. "Colin Powell, America's Top Soldier, Has Taken His Influence from Harlem to the White House." *People,* September 10, 1990.

Powell, Colin. "Viewpoint." *Time,* December 15, 1997.

Powell, Colin, with Joseph E. Persico. *My American Journey: An Autobiography.* New York: Random House, 1995.

"Powell Presents Evidence to UN in the Case against Iraq." *Online NewsHour,* February 5, 2003. Available online at http://www.pbs.org/newshour/updates/powell_02-05-03.html (accessed on April 2, 2004).

Reef, Catherine. *Colin Powell.* Frederick, MD: Twenty-First Century Books, 1992.

"UN Members Offer Mixed Response to Powell Report." *Online NewsHour,* February 5, 2003. Available online at http://www.pbs.org/newshour/updates/reac_02-05-03.html (accessed on April 2, 2004).

Wukovits, John F. *Colin Powell.* San Diego: Lucent Books, 2000.

Condoleezza Rice

**Born November 14, 1954
Birmingham, Alabama**

U.S. national security advisor during the 2003 Iraq War

D octor Condoleezza Rice is the first woman to hold the office of U.S. national security advisor. She was appointed by President **George W. Bush** (see entry) and took office in January 2001. Rice played a key role in helping Bush draft a new American foreign policy following the terrorist attacks of September 11, 2001. She also became one of the Bush administration's leading advocates for using military force to remove **Saddam Hussein** (see entry) from power in Iraq.

Grows up in the racially charged South

Condoleezza (pronounced kahn-dah-LEE-za) Rice was born in Birmingham, Alabama, on November 14, 1954. Her father, the Reverend John W. Rice Jr., ran the Westminster Presbyterian Church, which had been founded by her grandfather. He also worked as a guidance counselor and football coach at the black high school in Birmingham where her mother, Angelena (Ray) Rice, was a teacher.

Rice's parents named her after an Italian musical term, *con dolcezza,* which means to perform "with sweetness."

"We're going to find the truth about what Saddam Hussein did with weapons of mass destruction, how he built his programs, how he concealed them."

Condoleezza Rice in an interview for National Public Radio.

Condoleezza Rice. *AP/Wide World Photos. Reproduced by permission.*

Known as Condi for short, Rice began taking piano lessons at age three. Although she once entertained hopes of becoming a concert pianist, she eventually decided that she was not good enough. "Mozart didn't have to practice," she told the *New York Times.* "I was going to have to practice and practice and practice and was never going to be extraordinary."

As her parents' only child, Rice was constantly pushed to achieve. "I grew up in a family in which my parents put me into every book club," she told the *New York Times.* "So I never developed the fine art of recreational reading." To this day, she never reads simply for pleasure, but only to learn. As a young girl, Rice was tutored in Spanish and French. She excelled in her studies and entered the eighth grade at the age of eleven. As a high-school student, she became a competitive ice skater, getting up at 4:30 AM for lessons.

Although she grew up in a middle-class black neighborhood, Rice saw her share of racial prejudice and oppression. During her childhood, Birmingham was segregated, meaning that people were divided according to their race. White people and black people had to use separate public facilities, including schools, swimming pools, and drinking fountains. This system, which was widely practiced in the South, was unfair to blacks and kept them in an inferior place in society. It also created a great deal of racial tension, which sometimes erupted into violence.

When Rice was nine years old, for example, a bomb exploded at the Sixteenth Street Baptist Church in Birmingham, only four blocks from where she was attending Sunday school. The blast killed four black girls, including one of her friends from kindergarten. Rice recalled in an essay for *Time* magazine that the "men in the community, my father among them, would go to the head of [our street] at night and sit there armed" to defend against racially motivated attacks. John Rice once organized a group of neighbors armed with shotguns to find the person who had thrown a gas bomb through another neighbor's window.

As she grew older, Rice combined the education and culture emphasized by her parents with a toughness that came from growing up in the racially charged South. "Condi was raised first and foremost to be a lady," Secretary of State

Colin Powell once told a reporter for the *New York Times*. "She was raised in a protected environment to be a person of great self-confidence in Birmingham, where there was no reason to have self-confidence because you were a tenth-class citizen and you were black."

Professor of political science and expert on the Soviet Union

At age fifteen, Rice simultaneously completed her senior year of high school and her freshman year at the University of Denver. She graduated from college in 1974, at age nineteen, with a bachelor's degree in political science. She went on to earn a master's degree in political science at the University of Notre Dame. Rice returned to the Graduate School of International Studies at the University of Denver to receive a doctorate in political science in 1981. A short time later she joined the faculty in political science at Stanford University in California.

While studying for her bachelor's degree, Rice met Doctor Joseph Korbel. Korbel, a professor and the father of future United Nations ambassador and U.S. Secretary of State Madeleine Albright (see box) became Rice's mentor and introduced her to Russian history. Rice learned to speak Russian fluently, and by 1986 she was considered an expert on Soviet arms control.

In 1995 Rice attended a lecture given by retired U.S. Army General Brent Scowcroft. During the lecture she asked Scowcroft a tough question about a government commission that he was leading. Scowcroft was impressed by her boldness as well as her thoughtful analysis. He approached her afterward and said, "I don't think anybody's ever asked me that."

Becomes the first female national security advisor

In 1988 **George H. W. Bush** (see entry) was elected president of the United States, and Scowcroft became his national security advisor. A year later Scowcroft recruited Rice to serve on the National Security Council during one of the

Madeleine Albright, First Woman to Serve as U.S. Secretary of State

Madeleine Korbel Albright served as U.S. ambassador to the United Nations (1993–97) and U.S. secretary of state (1997–2000) under President Bill Clinton. In these positions, she helped shape U.S. policy toward Iraq during the decade between the 1991 Persian Gulf War and the 2003 Iraq War.

Albright was born as Maria Jana Korbel on May 15, 1937, in Prague, Czechoslovakia. She was the daughter of Czech diplomat Josef Korbel and his wife, Anna. Her family was forced to flee Czechoslovakia when Germany invaded the country in 1938. They lived in England during World War II and later moved to the United States. They settled in Colorado, where her father became an influential professor at the University of Denver. Albright became a naturalized U.S. citizen and changed her first name to Madeleine.

Albright majored in political science at Wellesley College, graduating with honors in 1959. She then married Joseph Medill Patterson Albright. Albright initially tried to build a career as a journalist, but she quit after being the victim of sexual discrimination. During the 1960s she raised three daughters while also continuing her education. She spent more than ten years working on her doctorate in international relations at Columbia University.

After moving to Washington, D.C., in 1968, Albright became involved in Democratic politics and worked on several election campaigns. In 1977 one of her former professors, Zbigniew Brzezinski, became national security advisor to President Jimmy Carter.

Brzezinski recruited Albright to serve as a liaison between his staff and Congress.

In 1982, after separating from her husband, Albright joined the faculty of Georgetown University as a professor of international affairs. In 1992 she served as the senior foreign policy advisor for Bill Clinton's presidential campaign. Once Clinton was elected, he named Albright as U.S. ambassador to the United Nations (UN). She became only the second woman ever to fill that role and the only woman on Clinton's fifteen-member National Security Council. During her term in the United Nations, Albright earned a reputation as an effective communicator and tough negotiator.

After Clinton was reelected in 1996, he selected Albright as U.S. secretary of state. She became the first woman ever to hold that position and the highest-ranking female in U.S. government history. During her term in office, Albright became one of the key figures in an ongoing dispute between the United States and Iraq. In 1990 Iraqi leader Saddam Hussein had invaded the neighboring country of Kuwait. His actions led to the 1991 Persian Gulf War, in which a U.S.-led coalition forced the Iraqi army to withdraw from Kuwait. The UN agreement that ended the war required Iraq to destroy all of its biological, chemical, and nuclear weapons. But Hussein consistently failed to cooperate with the UN weapons inspectors sent to monitor Iraq's progress.

The United Nations used several different strategies to force Iraq to comply with

Madeleine Albright. ©*Wally McNamee/Corbis. Reproduced by permission.*

the 1991 agreement, including economic sanctions. These trade restrictions prevented Iraq from selling oil in world markets or buying many types of goods from other countries. The sanctions were originally intended to prevent Hussein from rebuilding his army after the war. Over time, however, the sanctions created severe hardships among the Iraqi people.

In 1998 the United Nations Children's Fund (UNICEF) reported that the sanctions had contributed to the deaths of five hundred thousand Iraqi children since the end of the war. Many members of the international community were appalled by such statistics and demanded that the United States lift the sanctions. But Albright and other officials in the Clinton administration insisted that the sanctions were a vital part of the United Nations' efforts to limit Hussein's power and prevent Iraq from posing a threat to world peace.

Albright became a staunch defender of the Clinton administration's policies toward Iraq. Her position created controversy following an appearance on the television news program "60 Minutes." Interviewer Lesley Stahl asked, "More than 500,000 Iraqi children are already dead as a direct result of the UN sanctions. Do you think the price is worth paying?" Albright replied, "It is a difficult question. But, yes, we think the price is worth it." Critics claimed that Albright was indifferent to the suffering of the Iraqi people. Her words provoked anger throughout the Middle East and increased feelings of sympathy for Iraq.

In late 1998 Iraq ended all cooperation with the UN weapons inspections. American and British military forces responded by launching a massive bombing campaign aimed at destroying sites that were suspected to hold Iraq's weapons of mass destruction. The bombing did not convince Hussein to cooperate. Nevertheless, the international community made little further effort to enforce the UN agreement that had ended the 1991 war. When Clinton left office in 2001, Albright returned to her teaching position at Georgetown.

Sources: Dobbs, Michael. Madeleine Albright: A Twentieth-Century Odyssey. *New York: Holt, 1999; Lippman, Thomas W.* Madeleine Albright and the New American Diplomacy. *Boulder, CO: Westview Press, 2000; "Madeleine Albright."* Contemporary Heroes and Heroines, *1998. Reproduced in* Biography Resource Center. *Farmington Hills, MI: Gale Group, 2004; "Madeleine Korbel Albright."* Encyclopedia of World Biography, *1998. Reproduced in* Biography Resource Center. *Farmington Hills, MI: Gale Group, 2004.*

most tumultuous times in world history. As director of Soviet and Eastern European Affairs and Special Assistant to the President on National Security Affairs, Rice helped forge U.S. foreign policy during the fall of communism in Eastern Europe. (Communism a system of government where the nation's leaders are selected by a single political party that controls all aspects of society. Private ownership of property is eliminated and government directs all economic production. The goods produced and accumulated wealth are, in theory, shared relatively equally by all. All religious practices are banned). During this period, the Soviet Union dissolved into a number of smaller republics and East and West Germany were reunified under a single government.

After two exhausting years in Washington, Rice left politics and returned to Stanford. In 1993 she was appointed the university's first black provost, or chief academic and budget officer. Two years later Rice went to Texas to visit former President Bush. She met his son George W. Bush, who was then in his first year as governor of Texas. The two discovered that they shared an avid enthusiasm for sports and physical fitness.

In 1998 Rice visited the Bush family home in Kennebunkport, Maine. She renewed her friendship with George W. Bush, who was then considering running for president. "Between tennis games and going out on the boat and sitting out on the back porch we would have conversations about what foreign policy challenges would face the next president," Rice recalled in the *New York Times*. Over the next two years, Rice acted as the Texas governor's foreign policy tutor.

During Bush's presidential campaign for the 2000 elections, Rice served as the candidate's foreign policy advisor. Bush won the presidency and took office in January 2001. One of his first acts was to appoint Rice as his national security advisor. This appointment made Rice the first woman in U.S. history to hold the office of national security advisor. The national security advisor is the leader of the National Security Council (NSC), which works to draft and articulate American foreign policy. Among the fifteen other members of the NSC were President George Bush, Vice President **Dick Cheney** (see entry), Secretary of State **Colin Powell** (see entry), and Secretary of Defense **Donald Rumsfeld** (see entry).

American foreign policy changes after September 11

During his campaign, Bush said little about foreign policy. His few statements on the matter suggested that he wanted to avoid becoming entangled in the affairs of other countries. For example, he claimed that America was "over-committed around the world" and "throwing its weight around." He called for a new emphasis on domestic issues and less assistance for new, struggling governments.

But Bush's position changed dramatically following the terrorist attacks against the United States that took place on September 11, 2001. It was on this day that members of a radical Islamic terrorist group called Al Qaeda hijacked four commercial airplanes and crashed them into the World Trade Center towers in New York City, the Pentagon building near Washington, D.C., and a field in Pennsylvania, killing nearly three thousand people. A short time later, Bush met with Rice and his other top advisors at Camp David, Maryland. They outlined a series of phases in a global war against terrorism. The first phase involved a military attack against the people directly responsible for the September 11 attacks, Muslim cleric (religious leader) Osama bin Laden and his Al Qaeda terrorist organization, and their protectors in Afghanistan. In the second phase, Bush planned to extend the war on terrorism to include any group or nation that possessed the ability and desire to harm the United States. Rice was one of the administration's strongest voices in favor expanding the war on terrorism to include "rogue nations."

Bush first described the new foreign policy in his State of the Union address in January 2002. In this speech, he suggested that the Cold War strategy of deterrence, maintaining a strong military in order to discourage other countries from attacking, was not effective against terrorists. He argued that the only way to defeat these new enemies was to strike first, or preemptively, to eliminate their capacity to attack American interests before they had a chance to use it. He specifically mentioned several nations that he viewed as threats to the United States, including Iraq.

Over the next several months, Rice emerged as one of the leading supporters of Bush's new foreign policy. She made a series of public statements in favor of expanding the war on terrorism to include countries that supported terrorists or could provide them with weapons of mass destruction. In one such speech, Rice claimed that Iraqi leader Saddam Hussein had ties to the Al Qaeda terrorist organization. "Saddam's regime and Al Qaeda have been orbiting each other quite a lot," she stated. "There have been contacts for quite a while. There are a number of serious Al Qaeda people who have found refuge in Iraq.... We have picked up evidence of [the Iraqis] training Al Qaeda operatives in chemical-weapons activities."

Throughout the fall of 2002, Bush pressured the United Nations (UN) to authorize the use of military force to remove Hussein from power in Iraq. Rice continued to speak out in defense of this strategy. "Saddam has used weapons of mass destruction," she told the *New Yorker,* referring to the Iraqi leader's use of poison gas against the Kurds of northern Iraq in 1988, "and continues to acquire them at an incredibly rapid pace." She also expressed concern that Hussein might be close to acquiring nuclear weapons.

Releases National Security Strategy

In September 2002 Rice's office released a document called the National Security Strategy, which articulated America's new foreign policy. It explained in greater depth the nation's reasons for wanting to invade Iraq and overthrow Hussein. The National Security Strategy asserted America's right to "dissuade [discourage] potential adversaries from pursuing a military buildup in hopes of surpassing, or equaling, the power of the United States." It also proclaimed that the United States "will not hesitate to act alone, if necessary, to exercise our right of self-defense by acting preemptively" with military force.

The right to "act preemptively" meant that the United States could attack another country without having been attacked first, as long as it perceived that nation as a threat. "It is simply not possible to ignore and isolate other powerful states that do not share [American] values," Rice explained. The National Security Strategy specifically addressed the issue of "rogue nations" like Iraq. They "reject basic human values and hate the United States and everything for which it stands," Rice told the *New Yorker.*

In the months leading up to the 2003 Iraq War, the Bush administration's new foreign policy came under criticism both within the United States and internationally. Opponents questioned the wisdom of the policy as well as its legality under international law. But Rice and other administration officials continued to defend their views and prepare for a military invasion of Iraq.

Despite a lack of UN support, the United States attacked Iraq on March 19, 2003 (March 20 in Iraq). The offensive, called Operation Iraqi Freedom, succeeded in removing Hussein from power after only a few weeks of fighting. On May 1 Bush announced the end of major combat operations in Iraq. U.S. troops remained in the country to provide security, aid in reconstruction efforts, and help the Iraqi people form a new democratic government.

Postwar problems raise doubts about policies

Over the next several months, however, the situation in Iraq raised some doubts about the Bush administration's strategy. Coalition troops struggled to maintain security in the face of Iraqi resistance and a series of terrorist attacks. A massive search failed to uncover any weapons of mass destruction or evidence linking Hussein to Al Qaeda. Critics suggested that the Bush administration should have waited to gather more reliable intelligence (information collected through spying activities) before starting a war.

Rice and other members of the Bush administration continued to claim that weapons of mass destruction would eventually be found in Iraq. But in their public statements, they also began backing away from weapons and terrorism as the main reasons for going to war. Instead, Rice and other administration officials emphasized that the war had freed the Iraqi people from a brutal dictator. "We're going to find the truth about what Saddam Hussein did with weapons of mass destruction, how he built his programs, how he concealed them," she told Tavis Smiley in an interview for National Public Radio. Rice continued:

> We didn't make this stuff up. There was intelligence. There were [foreign] intelligence services. There were UN inspectors.... But we can also say that, in addition to the threat from weapons of mass destruction, this was one of the most brutal dictators of modern times, somebody who had attacked his neighbors in the past. And the Middle East, as a region, is far better off for his removal. That, in itself, is a very important contribution.

Despite the postwar problems in Iraq, Rice continued to defend Bush's foreign policy decisions. "The people of the Middle East share the desire for freedom," she said in an October 2003 speech. "We have an opportunity—and an obligation—to help them turn this desire into reality. And we must work with others to create a world where terror is shunned and hope is the provenance of every living human. That is the strategic challenge—and moral mission—of our time."

Where to Learn More

"Condoleezza Rice." *Biography Resource Center Online.* Farmington Hills, MI: Gale Group, 2001.

"Exceeding Expectations, Rice Returns to White House in Top Job." *CNN.com,* December 17, 2000.

LeMann, Nicholas. "Without a Doubt." *New Yorker,* October 14, 2002.

Sciolino, Elaine. "Woman in the News; Compulsion to Achieve." *New York Times,* December 18, 2000.

Smiley, Tavis. "Interview: Condoleezza Rice." *NPR,* June 13, 2003. Available online at http://www.npr.org/features/feature.php?wfId=1297605 (accessed on April 1, 2004).

Zakaris, Fareed. "Bush, Rice, and the 9-11 Shift." *Newsweek,* December 16, 2002.

Donald Rumsfeld

Born July 9, 1932
Chicago, Illinois

U.S. secretary of defense who played a leading role in deciding military strategy for the 2003 Iraq War

D onald Rumsfeld served as U.S. secretary of defense during the 2003 Iraq War. In this position, he helped convince President **George W. Bush** (see entry) to invade Iraq. He also worked with U.S. military leaders to plan Operation Iraqi Freedom. The strategy crafted by Rumsfeld and other military leaders succeeded in capturing Baghdad and removing Iraqi leader **Saddam Hussein** (see entry) from power after a few short weeks of combat. But Rumsfeld faced some criticism for failing to anticipate the problems U.S. troops encountered in Iraq after the war ended.

"This is not a war against a people. It is not a war against a country, and it is most certainly not a war against a religion. It is a war against a regime."

Donald Rumsfeld at a Pentagon press briefing.

Launches career in politics

Donald Harold Rumsfeld was born in Chicago, Illinois, on July 9, 1932. His father, George Donald Rumsfeld, was a real estate broker, while his mother, Jeannette Huster Rumsfeld, was a homemaker. Rumsfeld was raised in the wealthy Chicago suburb of Winnetka. When Rumsfeld was nine years old, his father set aside his career to join the navy during World War II (1939–45). His father's decision to serve

Donald Rumsfeld.
Photograph by B. K. Bangash.
AP/Wide World Photos.
Reproduced by permission.

the country in wartime made a big impression on the young Rumsfeld.

Rumsfeld was a popular boy as well as an excellent student. He possessed endless energy and believed in the value of hard work. In fact, he held down twenty different part-time jobs during his teen years. He also was a champion wrestler at New Trier High School, where he met his future wife, Joyce Pierson. They married in 1954 and eventually had three children together.

Upon graduating from high school, Rumsfeld was accepted to Princeton University on a Reserve Officer Training Corps (ROTC) scholarship. He served as captain of the football and wrestling teams during his college years. He earned a bachelor's degree in political science in 1954. Rumsfeld spent the next three years as a pilot and flight instructor in the U.S. Navy. In 1957 he transferred to the Naval Reserves and began planning for a career in politics.

Rumsfeld spent the next three years working in Washington, D.C., as an administrative assistant to a U.S. congressman. After a brief stint as an investment banker in Chicago, he made a successful bid for a seat in the U.S. House of Representatives in 1962. The thirty-year-old congressman from Illinois joined a new generation of Republican leaders that included Bob Dole, Gerald Ford, and **George H. W. Bush** (see entry). Rumsfeld was later reelected to three additional two-year terms.

Becomes the youngest U.S. secretary of defense

In 1969 Rumsfeld resigned from Congress to accept a position in President Richard Nixon's administration. He served as director of the Office of Economic Opportunity for a year, then he was promoted to Counselor to the President and Director of the Economic Stabilization Program. In 1973 Rumsfeld was sent to Belgium as the U.S. ambassador to the North Atlantic Treaty Organization (NATO).

In 1974 Nixon resigned from office following a political scandal known as Watergate. Vice President Gerald Ford took over the presidency, and Rumsfeld returned to Washington to join the Ford administration as chief of staff. In 1975

Rumsfeld was appointed U.S. secretary of defense, the civilian head of American military operations. At forty-three, he became the youngest person ever to serve in this position. Over the next year he emerged as a major supporter of several new weapons programs, including the B-1 bomber and the Trident nuclear submarine.

When Ford lost the 1976 presidential election to Democrat Jimmy Carter, Rumsfeld decided to leave government service. His decision surprised many people. After all, Rumsfeld was a highly ambitious man who had enjoyed a rapid rise to political prominence. In fact, he had often been mentioned as a possible future presidential candidate. But he decided to put his talents to work in the world of business instead. In 1977 Rumsfeld received the Presidential Medal of Freedom, the nation's highest civilian honor, for his government service.

Upon leaving Washington Rumsfeld became president and chief executive officer (CEO) of the G.D. Searle pharmaceutical company. He helped it become a leader in its industry by introducing several new products, including the artificial sweetener NutraSweet. In 1990 Rumsfeld became CEO of General Instruments, a leading company in broadband technology. He left this position three years later but continued to serve on the boards of directors of several large corporations. Rumsfeld's successful business career helped him become a very wealthy man.

Becomes the oldest U.S. secretary of defense

Rumsfeld remained active in politics during his twenty-five-year business career. He served the U.S. government in dozens of different roles over the years. For example, he served as an envoy to the Middle East under President Ronald Reagan, and he was a member of the U.S. Trade Deficit Review Commission under President Bill Clinton. In 2000 George W. Bush (son of George H. W. Bush, the former president and Rumsfeld's old friend) won the presidency in a disputed election. Upon taking office in January 2001, Bush selected Rumsfeld to serve as U.S. secretary of defense. This time, at age sixty-eight, Rumsfeld became the oldest person ever to serve in this position.

Rumsfeld held strong opinions about the state of the U.S. military, and he immediately started pushing for significant changes. In general, Rumsfeld believed that many aspects of military weaponry and organization were out of date. He wanted to make American forces more streamlined and technologically advanced so that they could respond quickly to crises around the world. Some of his proposed changes met with opposition from military leaders and members of Congress. In addition, Rumsfeld came under criticism for his direct, uncompromising management style. Some Washington insiders believed that Rumsfeld would not last long in his job because he was creating too many powerful enemies.

But then the United States faced a national crisis. On September 11, 2001, members of a radical Islamic terrorist group called Al Qaeda hijacked four commercial airplanes and crashed them into the World Trade Center towers in New York City, the Pentagon building near Washington, D.C., and a field in Pennsylvania, killing nearly three thousand people. Rumsfeld was in his office at the Pentagon at the time of the attacks. He went to the crash site and began helping to carry injured people away from the building. His aides found him there and rushed him to a safe location, where he began planning the U.S. military response to the attacks.

In the wake of September 11, Bush announced a global war on terrorism that initially focused on the people directly responsible for the attacks, Muslim cleric (religious leader) Osama bin Laden and his Al Qaeda terrorist organization. U.S. intelligence experts (spies) quickly tracked bin Laden to Afghanistan, a country on the outskirts of the Middle East that was led by a radical Islamic government called the Taliban. The U.S. government demanded that the Taliban turn over bin Laden and members of Al Qaeda so that they could be punished for organizing the September 11 terrorist attacks. But the Taliban viewed bin Laden as a hero to the fundamentalist Islamic cause and refused to comply. (Islamic fundamentalists are people who strictly adhere to the basic principles of the Islam religion.)

In October 2001 the U.S. military launched Operation Enduring Freedom, a series of air strikes that targeted Taliban military capabilities and Al Qaeda training facilities in Afghanistan. The United States also provided military support to the Northern Alliance, an Afghan opposition group that had long fought against the Taliban. Although the U.S. troops and their Afghan allies soon succeeded in removing the Taliban from power, bin Laden managed to escape. Still, Bush administration officials claimed that they had completed the first phase in their global war against terrorism by destroying the home base of Al Qaeda.

Shifts focus to Iraq

The quick, successful end to the war in Afghanistan helped increase Rumsfeld's power and influence. He began lobbying to make Iraq the next target in the war against terrorism. Ever since Iraq had invaded Kuwait in 1990, an action which led to the 1991 Persian Gulf War, Rumsfeld had argued that Iraqi leader Saddam Hussein was dangerous. He viewed the September 11 tragedy as an opportunity to rid the world of hostile governments that possessed the ability and desire to harm the United States. His feelings were clearly expressed in notes he made in the hours following the terrorist attacks. "Go massive. Sweep it all up. Things related and not," he wrote in *Rumsfeld: A Personal Portrait* regarding the U.S. response. "Judge whether good enough hit SH [Saddam Hussein] at same time. Not only OBL [Osama bin Laden]."

In early 2002 Bush followed the advice of Rumsfeld and other administration officials. He officially expanded the fight against terrorism to include nations that he described as harboring terrorists or providing weapons, training, or financial support for their activities. Among the countries that he accused of supporting terrorists was Iraq. Although there was no clear link between Saddam Hussein's government and Al Qaeda, Bush claimed that Iraq possessed weapons of mass destruction and could provide such weapons to terrorists. He argued that Hussein posed an immediate threat to world security and should be removed from power in Iraq.

Within the Bush administration, Rumsfeld became one of the leading supporters of using military force to disarm Iraq and remove Hussein from power. He claimed that these actions were necessary in order to preserve U.S. and world security. "It is not possible to defend against terrorism in every place, at every time, against every conceivable technique. Self-defense against terrorism requires preemption, taking the battle to the terrorists wherever they are and to those who harbor them," he stated, as quoted in *Rumsfeld: A Personal Portrait.* "The link between global terrorist networks and the nations on the terrorist list that have active weapons of mass destruction capabilities is real, and poses a serious threat to the world."

In September 2002 Bush challenged the United Nations to enforce its resolutions calling for Iraq to destroy its weapons of mass destruction and submit to international weapons inspections. He also made it clear that the United States would act alone to disarm Iraq by force if necessary. Bush's threat to invade Iraq created a great deal of controversy in the international community. Some of America's longtime allies, including France and Germany, strongly opposed a U.S. invasion of Iraq.

Rumsfeld dismissed the international opposition, claiming that France and Germany were "old Europe," and not representative of world opinion. He also argued that the world had already given Iraq ample opportunity to disarm voluntarily. "We've now had 17 [UN] resolutions," he said in an interview for *Online NewsHour.* "It's been 12 years [since the 1991 Persian Gulf War]. They've tried diplomacy. The world has tried economic sanctions. The world has tried military activity in the northern and southern no-fly zones. At some point, the time runs out."

Crafts U.S. military strategy for the 2003 Iraq War

In preparation for a possible war in Iraq, Rumsfeld instituted a number of changes in U.S. military structure and rules of deployment. His strategy for the war emphasized overwhelming air power to "shock and awe" the enemy and convince them to surrender. He also planned to make extensive use of special operations forces to work with the Iraqi opposition to Hussein's government. Finally, Rumsfeld envisioned light, fast-moving ground forces pushing quickly across Iraq to capture the capital city of Baghdad.

Some people within the military complained that Rumsfeld and his inner circle of advisors took over planning functions that were usually left to military leaders. They claimed that he insisted on controlling even minor operational details, and that he bullied military leaders into going along with his plans. Some experts worried that Rumsfeld's insistence on a small ground force would create a dangerous shortage of troops and supplies. They also claimed that Rumsfeld's plan failed to anticipate potential problems and limited the troops' ability to respond to unexpected situations.

Despite a lack of UN support, the United States launched its military invasion of Iraq on March 20, 2003. Rumsfeld appeared at a Pentagon press briefing to discuss the invasion, which was assigned the code name Operation Iraqi Freedom. "This is not a war against a people. It is not a war against a country, and it is most certainly not a war against a religion. It is a war against a regime," he stated. "To the Iraqi people, let me say that the day of your liberation will soon be at hand.... Iraq belongs to the Iraqi people. And once Saddam Hussein's regime is removed, we intend to see that functional and political authority is placed in the hands of Iraqis as quickly as possible. Coalition forces will stay only as long as necessary to finish the job, and not a day longer."

Although many aspects of the U.S. invasion of Iraq proceeded according to Rumsfeld's plan, some aspects did not. For example, Rumsfeld had predicted that the Iraqi people would welcome the troops that came to free them from Hussein's rule. As it turned out, however, most Iraqis viewed the Americans with suspicion or outright hostility. While the U.S. troops encountered less resistance than anticipated from Iraqi army units, they experienced a surprising amount from paramilitary fighters and irregular forces (fighters who are not part of a formal army). Many of these attacks hit American supply lines, which were left unsecured in Rumsfeld's strategy of pushing rapidly toward Baghdad.

On March 28 the American officer in charge of the ground war, U.S. Army Lieutenant General William S. Wallace, aroused controversy with an interview he gave to the *Washington Post*. Wallace discussed the surprising intensity of resistance that coalition forces had encountered so far. He admitted that the coalition's war plan did not address some of the situations his troops had faced. When the American media picked up Wallace's comments, newspapers and television news programs were suddenly full of experts questioning the Bush administration's war plan.

General Tommy Franks, Head of U.S. Central Command during the 2003 Iraq War

As the head of U.S. Central Command during the 2003 Iraq War, General Tommy Franks directed the military effort that led to the fall of Saddam Hussein's government. Franks had first come to public attention two years earlier, as the head of the successful U.S. military invasion of Afghanistan. Although rumors circulated that the general clashed with U.S. secretary of defense Donald Rumsfeld, the men worked together to plan two successful military campaigns.

Tommy Ray Franks was born in Wynnewood, Oklahoma, on June 17, 1945. He grew up in Midland, Texas, and attended the same high school as President George W. Bush and his wife, Laura. Upon graduating in 1963, Franks studied business administration at the University of Texas at Austin. Two years later, he joined the U.S. Army to fight in the Vietnam War.

After completing military training, Franks received the rank of second lieutenant and was sent to Vietnam in 1967. He served as a forward observer in the Ninth Infantry Division and was wounded in combat three times. Upon his return to the United States in 1968, Franks was stationed at Fort Sill in Oklahoma. He married Cathryn Carley the following year.

Franks received further military training and also completed his bachelor's degree in 1971. In 1976 he was assigned to the Pentagon, where he served in the office of the army chief of staff for five years. In 1981 he was stationed in West Germany, where he commanded a battalion for the next three years. Upon returning to the United States in 1984, Franks attended the U.S. Army War College. He also earned his master's degree at Shippensburg University.

After Iraq invaded the neighboring country of Kuwait in August 1990, Franks was sent to the Persian Gulf during the military buildup known as Operation Desert Shield. He served as the assistant commander of the First Cavalry Division during Operation Desert Storm, in which the U.S.-led coalition pushed the Iraqi army out of Kuwait.

Franks continued his service to the army in a number of capacities following the 1991 Persian Gulf War. He was promoted to lieutenant general in 1997. In July 2000 Franks was named commander in chief of U.S. Central Command (CENTCOM). Headquartered in Tampa, Florida, CENTCOM was responsible for directing U.S. military operations in the Middle East. A few months later, radical Islamic terrorists launched a suicide bombing attack against the USS *Cole,* an American destroyer anchored at a port in Yemen. The attack killed seventeen U.S. Navy sailors.

The terrorists dealt the United States an even more devastating blow on September 11, 2001, when attacks on the World Trade Center towers in New York City and the Pentagon building near Washington, D.C., took the lives of nearly three thousand people. Immediately after the attacks, President George W. Bush launched a global war against terrorism. The first target of this war was Al Qaeda, the terrorist group responsible for the September 11 attacks, and its protectors in Afghanistan.

Tommy Franks. *Photograph by Scott Martin. AP/Wide World Photos. Reproduced by permission.*

As the head of CENTCOM, Franks acted as the commander of U.S. military forces during the war in Afghanistan. The war succeeded in destroying Al Qaeda training facilities and removing the Afghan government that had sheltered the terrorists. But many Al Qaeda leaders remained at large in the rugged mountains of Afghanistan. "While an awful lot has been done in Afghanistan," Franks told the Associated Press a year after the military operations there ended, "We're just going to have to stay with it for as long as it takes...."

In 2002 Bush expanded the war on terrorism to include countries that he described as threats to world security. The president claimed that Iraq possessed weapons of mass destruction and could provide such weapons to terrorist groups. He argued that military action was necessary to disarm Iraq and remove Saddam Hussein from power. As the United States moved toward war, Franks was assigned to help plan the American invasion of Iraq.

Some Pentagon officials described the planning sessions as being filled with tension between Franks and Secretary of Defense Donald Rumsfeld. They claimed that Franks resented Rumsfeld's heavy involvement in determining the military strategy. They also said that Franks resisted Rumsfeld's demands for a light, mobile invasion force that could advance rapidly toward Baghdad. But Rumsfeld insisted that Franks was responsible for drawing up the war plan. The secretary also gave Franks credit for changing the plan as needed to adjust to the actual situations the troops encountered.

The 2003 Iraq War succeeded in capturing Baghdad and removing Hussein from power after only a few weeks of fighting. Franks received a great deal of praise for the successful U.S. strategy, which kept American casualties to a minimum. In May 2003, just a few weeks after major combat operations ended, Franks announced his intention to retire from active military service. Rumsfeld offered him the position of army chief of staff, the highest position in the army, but Franks declined. The general later signed a contract with HarperCollins to write his memoirs.

Sources: "Profile: General Tommy Franks." BBC News, May 22, 2003. Available online at http://news.bbc. co.uk/1/hi/world/americas/ 1647358.stm (accessed on April 2, 2004); "Tommy Franks." Newsmakers, Issue 1. Reproduced in Biography Resource Center. Farmington Hills, MI: Gale Group, 2004.

Postwar problems lead to more questions

But the U.S. military soon managed to overcome the Iraqi resistance. They succeeded in capturing Baghdad on April 9, after only three weeks of fighting. Rumsfeld received widespread praise for planning the impressive military victory. On May 1 Bush announced the end of major combat operations in Iraq. The U.S. troops remained in Iraq to maintain security, rebuild the country, and help the Iraqi people form a democratic government.

As the reconstruction of Iraq got underway, however, security became a problem. Looting and unrest broke out in Baghdad and several other cities. Iraqi insurgents (people who fight against an occupying power) and foreign fighters launched a series of attacks against American troops and Iraqis who seemed to be cooperating with the occupation. The Bush administration drew heavy criticism for failing to anticipate this possibility. Rumsfeld downplayed the postwar problems by comparing them to the everyday violence that occurs in cities across the United States and around the world.

But some experts placed the blame for the postwar difficulties on Rumsfeld's war plan. They claimed that the light ground forces he favored were no longer sufficient during the military occupation of Iraq. "Rumsfeld may understand modern combat but doesn't seem attuned to the more complex, difficult, and political challenges of nation-building, peacekeeping, and occupation missions," Marcus Corbin wrote in *Newsday.* "The occupation of Iraq suggests that military transformation now needs to be thought of as better preparation for peacekeeping and security-building missions, for unconventional wars, and for the important political dimensions of modern conflicts. To do otherwise will mean our armed forces will be ready for the wars of the 20th century, not the 21st."

Rumsfeld has acknowledged that keeping the peace in postwar Iraq has been a difficult task. But he continued to express confidence that the occupation of Iraq will eventually result in the development of a free and democratic society in the country.

Where to Learn More

Corbin, Marcus. "Rumsfeld's Strategy: Fine for the War; Now What about the Peace?" *Newsday,* April 14, 2003. Available online at http://www.

cdi.org/document/search/displaydoc.cfm?DocumentID=1008&Start
Row=1&ListRows=10 (accessed on April 2, 2004).

Decter, Midge. *Rumsfeld: A Personal Portrait.* New York: HarperCollins, 2003.

"Donald Harold Rumsfeld." *Encyclopedia of World Biography,* vol. 23. Reprinted in *Biography Resource Center.* Farmington Hills, MI: Gale Group, 2003.

"Donald Rumsfeld." *Newsmakers,* Issue 1. Reprinted in *Biography Resource Center.* Farmington Hills, MI: Gale Group, 2004.

Hersh, Seymour M. "Offense and Defense: The Battle between Donald Rumsfeld and the Pentagon." *New Yorker,* April 7, 2003. Available online at http://www.newyorker.com/fact/content/?030407fa_fact1 (accessed on April 2, 2004).

Krames, Jeffrey A. *The Rumsfeld Way.* New York: McGraw-Hill, 2002.

"Operation Iraqi Freedom: U.S. Defense Secretary Donald H. Rumsfeld, Pentagon Briefing." U.S. Department of Defense, March 20, 2003. Available online at http://www.defendamerica.mil/iraq/iraqifreedom. html (accessed on April 2, 2004).

"Prepared for War." *Online NewsHour,* February 20, 2003. Available online at http://www.pbs.org/newshour/bb/middle_east/jan-june03/ rumsfeld_2-20.html (accessed on April 2, 2004).

Tyler, Raven. "Player Profile: Donald Rumsfeld." *Online NewsHour,* undated. Available online at http://www.pbs.org/newshour/bb/middle_ east/iraq/postwar/player_5.html (accessed on April 2, 2004).

Jabir al-Ahmad al-Jabir al-Sabah

Born June 29, 1926
Kuwait City, Kuwait

Ruler of Kuwait during the Persian Gulf War

The small but wealthy Middle Eastern nation of Kuwait was the main focus of the Persian Gulf War when Iraq invaded its neighbor to the south in August 1990. The emir (ruler) of Kuwait at this time was Jabir al-Ahmad al-Jabir al-Sabah. Jabir and his royal family barely escaped the country as the Iraqi military forces approached. In exile in Saudi Arabia, the emir made numerous appeals to the world community to help liberate his country from Iraq's brutal occupation. In January 1991 the U.S.-led coalition made up of thirty-five countries went to war to force the Iraqi army to withdraw from Kuwait.

"I came here to tell you of the horrors and suffering we are enduring both inside and outside our occupied homeland.... Now, the fate of a people, of a nation, is in your hands."

Jabir al-Ahmad al-Jabir al-Sabah in a speech before the UN Security Council.

Born into the ruling Sabah family

Jabir al-Ahmad al-Jabir al-Sabah was born on June 29, 1926, in Kuwait City, the capital of the Middle Eastern nation of Kuwait. He was born into the powerful Sabah family, which had ruled the area along the Persian Gulf that eventually became Kuwait since the 1800s. In the late 1800s Kuwait became part of the Ottoman Empire. The Ottomans were

Jabir al-Ahmad al-Jabir al-Sabah. *AP/Wide World Photos. Reproduced by permission.*

non-Arab Turks who controlled much of the Middle East at that time. Under Ottoman rule, Kuwait was added to the Basra province, which later became part of modern Iraq.

In 1899 the Sabah family gained Kuwait's independence from Ottoman rule by negotiating a treaty to become a protectorate (dependent political unit) of Great Britain. Following the fall of the Ottoman Empire in 1918, Great Britain gained control over even greater areas of former Ottoman territory. In 1921 British authorities formed new countries in the areas under their control. They established the modern borders of Kuwait, Iraq, and Saudi Arabia at this time. They also installed leaders in these new countries that would be loyal to Great Britain and support British interests. The leader chosen for Kuwait was Jabir's father, Sheikh Ahmad al-Jabir.

Jabir was born five years later. As the third son of the ruler of Kuwait, he enjoyed a privileged upbringing. He was educated at Kuwait's first school, Mubarakiya School, and by private tutors. He also was exposed to politics and groomed to become emir of Kuwait someday. Jabir began his career in 1949 as the head of public security in the Ahmadi oil-producing region of Kuwait. In 1959 he became the head of the finance department in Kuwait's national government. In this position he helped establish budgets for all government departments. In 1960 he was involved in the international negotiations that led to the formation of the Organization of Petroleum Exporting Countries (OPEC), of which Kuwait became a member.

In 1961 Kuwait gained its full independence from Great Britain. As the government was reorganized, the finance department was elevated to a ministry, which made it cabinet-level, and Jabir gained the title of minister for finance and economy. Over the next few years he earned a reputation as a competent administrator. In 1963 Jabir was named deputy prime minister, and two years later he became prime minister. In 1966 he was designated crown prince, which meant that he was next in line to become the emir of Kuwait. Jabir gradually gained responsibility over the next decade as his predecessor, Emir Sabah al-Salim, suffered from poor health.

Becomes emir of Kuwait

Upon the death of his predecessor, Jabir became the thirteenth emir of Kuwait on December 31, 1977. He thus took control of one of the wealthiest countries in the world. Although Kuwait had a small land area, it contained the third-largest underground oil reserves of any nation. It also had a relatively small population, so its oil wealth provided the Kuwaiti people with a generous average income.

Jabir faced the first challenge of his rule in 1979, when Shiite Muslim fundamentalists (people who strictly adhere to the basic principles of the Islam religion) overthrew the government of the neighboring country of Iran. Although the Sabah family and the majority of Kuwaiti citizens were Sunni Muslims who were concerned about Shiites taking over Iran, about 30 percent of Kuwait's population was Shiite and supported the Iranian revolution.

In 1980 Iran and Iraq became involved in a bitter, eight-year war. Like many other Arab nations, Kuwait provided financial assistance to Iraq during its war against non-Arab Iran. Jabir's decision to support Iraq created anger and hostility among Kuwait's Shiite population, which launched a series of terrorist attacks within Kuwait. One of these attacks was an assassination attempt against Jabir in 1985. During the Iran-Iraq War (1980–88), Kuwait worried that the conflict might threaten shipping in the Persian Gulf. Jabir asked the United States to help protect commercial traffic in the Gulf. The U.S. government responded by sending American warships to the Gulf and flying American flags over Kuwaiti oil tankers. Jabir's decision to seek U.S. assistance also was unpopular with some Kuwaitis.

In 1986 the Sabah family became involved in a financial scandal. The Kuwaiti stock market suffered a disastrous fall and lost much of its value. Afterward, some people claimed that the Sabah family used public funds to pay its private debts. Facing vocal opposition in the national assembly, Jabir dissolved the elected body, suspended the nation's constitution, and placed restrictions on the media. These actions angered many Kuwaiti citizens, who effectively lost their right to participate in the country's government.

Tension grows between Kuwait and Iraq

When the Iran-Iraq War ended in 1988, Iraqi leader **Saddam Hussein** (see entry) found his economy in terrible shape. He had borrowed billions of dollars from Kuwait and other Arab countries to finance the war, and he desperately needed money to rebuild Iraq. Arguing that Iraq had fought the war to protect the interests of all Arab nations, Hussein asked his neighbors to forgive his debts (not require repayment of the loans). Several Arab countries agreed to this request, but Kuwait refused.

Iraq and Kuwait had been involved in disputes over territory since the British established the border between the two countries in 1921. Because Kuwait had been part of the Basra province when the region was controlled by the Ottoman Empire, many Iraqis believed that Kuwait should have been part of Iraq. They felt that the British government had taken away land that lawfully belonged to them. The Iraqi interest in Kuwait was increased by the fact that Kuwait possessed a Persian Gulf coastline that stretched 120 miles (193 kilometers), while Iraq had only a very small point of access to the Gulf. These disputes had caused Iraq to threaten to take over Kuwait on several occasions over the years.

The tension between the two countries escalated quickly in 1990. Hussein accused Kuwait of pumping more oil than was allowed under Organization of the Petroleum Exporting Countries (OPEC) agreements. He claimed that Kuwait's actions caused worldwide oil prices to fall and harmed the Iraqi economy further. Hussein also accused Kuwait of stealing oil from the Iraqi side of oil fields that straddled the border between the two countries. In July 1990 thousands of Iraqi troops massed along the Kuwaiti border. World leaders tried frantically to negotiate a peaceful settlement of the conflict, but these efforts failed.

Iraq invades Kuwait

On August 2, 1990, to the shock of many people in the Middle East and around the world, Iraq launched a military invasion of Kuwait. The emir learned about the invasion a short time before the Iraqi troops reached Kuwait City. He and many other members of the ruling family managed to escape the country by boat. They fled to Saudi Arabia, where they spent the next eight months in relative safety.

Countries around the world condemned the invasion and demanded that Hussein immediately withdraw his troops from Kuwait. Many of these countries then began sending military forces to the Persian Gulf region as part of a U.S.-led coalition against Iraq. In the meantime, the Iraqi armed forces that occupied Kuwait treated its residents terribly. Iraqi soldiers randomly took civilians off the streets of Kuwait City and held them for questioning. Many witnesses reported that the Iraqi forces set up "torture centers" to intimidate and extract information from the Kuwaiti people. The Iraqi troops also did a great deal of physical damage to Kuwaiti homes and businesses during the occupation. In the face of such terror and destruction, more than 1.5 million people fled the region during the months leading up to the Persian Gulf War.

In September 1990 Jabir made a speech before the United Nations Security Council. He made a strong appeal for the countries of the world to help liberate Kuwait from Iraq's brutal occupation. "I came here to tell you of the horrors and suffering we are enduring both inside and outside our occupied homeland, and to put before you our case. Now, the fate of a people, of a nation, is in your hands," he stated. "We trust that you will not waver in deciding on the measures needed to compel the invading aggressors to restore the legitimate authority and to put an end to their barbaric acts."

In November 1990 the Security Council established a deadline of January 15, 1991, for Iraq to withdraw from Kuwait or face war. When Hussein failed to meet the deadline, the U.S.-led coalition launched a series of air strikes against military targets in Iraq. The air war went on for nearly six weeks and caused major damage to Iraq's military capability. On February 24 the coalition launched a dramatic ground assault to force the Iraqi troops out of Kuwait. It met with little resistance from Hussein's army, which had been devastated by the air strikes. The Persian Gulf War ended on February 27, when coalition forces succeeded in liberating Kuwait from Iraqi occupation.

Emir struggles to rebuild his country

Jabir returned to Kuwait on March 14. He found that his country had suffered terrible destruction during the Iraqi occupation and the Persian Gulf War. Most Kuwaiti citizens found themselves without electricity or phone service, for ex-

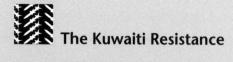

The Kuwaiti Resistance

Immediately after Iraq invaded Kuwait in August 1990, some Kuwaiti citizens formed a secret resistance movement to fight against the Iraqi occupation. The Kuwaiti resistance took a number of different forms. Some people resisted the Iraqis through civil disobedience. They displayed anti-Iraqi signs and graffiti, for example, or stayed away from work even when the Iraqi forces ordered them to return to their jobs. Other resistance members helped maintain the morale of their fellow citizens by securing food, water, medical supplies, and other necessities.

Another area of Kuwaiti resistance involved sabotaging Iraqi efforts to destroy the country's oil-production facilities. The Iraqi forces set explosive devices to blow up all of Kuwait's one thousand oil wells. But the resistance was able to disarm some of the devices and save three hundred wells from destruction. The Kuwaiti resistance also featured some military operations. Resistance fighters acquired guns and ammunition from police and Kuwaiti military sources and used them against the Iraqi forces. One of the best-known resistance attacks involved a car bomb that went off outside the Kuwait International Hotel, where a number of high-ranking Iraqi military leaders were meeting. Kuwaiti resistance members also collected information about Iraqi troop strength and movements and gave it to coalition leaders.

Women played a key role in the Kuwaiti resistance. Since they were less likely to be suspected and searched than men, they often carried weapons and documents through Iraqi checkpoints. The most famous female resistance leader was Asrar al-Qabandi, a thirty-one-year-old Kuwaiti who had

ample, and food and other necessities were in short supply. Unexploded land mines littered the beaches and highways, while the wreckage of Iraqi tanks was scattered across the desert. In addition to the damage caused by coalition bombing campaigns, Kuwait had to repair or replace hundreds of homes and office buildings that had been destroyed or vandalized by the Iraqi occupying forces. Some experts estimated that it would cost at least $50 billion to repair Kuwait's roads, cities, and oil facilities.

Perhaps the most pressing concern was the damage the fleeing Iraqi troops had done to Kuwait's oil-production facilities. Hussein's forces had set fire to six hundred of studied in the United States. In the first days of the Iraqi occupation, she helped members of Kuwait's ruling family, including fifteen Sabah children, to leave the country safely. She also forged driver's licenses with fake nationalities to protect American and British citizens living in Kuwait. Qabandi was captured by Iraqi secret police in November 1990. She suffered daily torture as the Iraqis tried to get information from her. In mid-January, as the war to liberate Kuwait began, the Iraqis killed Qabandi. The pieces of her dismembered body were placed in a plastic bag and dumped outside her family's abandoned home.

The Iraqis were initially surprised by the resistance they encountered from Kuwaiti citizens. The Iraqi soldiers who invaded Kuwait had been led to believe that they were liberating Kuwait from the Sabah family's rule. The resistance had its greatest effect during the first six weeks of the Iraqi occupation. After that, the capture of several key resistance leaders and the brutal response from the Iraqi troops reduced its effectiveness. In fact, some people claimed that the resistance only made the Iraqi occupying forces behave more violently toward Kuwaiti citizens. About three hundred Kuwaitis died during the invasion and occupation, and around six thousand others were arrested by the Iraqis. As of 2003, more than six hundred Kuwaitis remained missing and were believed to be held as prisoners of war in Iraq.

Sources: Levins, John M. "The Kuwaiti Resistance." Middle East Quarterly, *March 1995. Available online at http://www.meforum.org/pf.php?id=238 (accessed on March 27, 2004); Levins, John M. "The Secret War of Asrar Qabandi."* Arab Times, *January 13–14, 1994; "The Plight of Kuwait's POWs."* Kuwait Information Office. *Available online at http://www.kuwait-info.org/POWs/plight_of_ kuwaits_pows.html (accessed on March 27, 2004).*

Kuwait's one thousand oil wells during the war. These enormous blazes created thick, toxic, black smoke that dimmed the sun across the Middle East. Putting out the fires was very difficult, dangerous, and expensive. In fact, the process of capping the burning wells took several months and cost up to $10 million per well. The last fire was finally extinguished in November 1991. By this time, the fires had destroyed an estimated ten billion barrels of valuable oil, reducing Kuwait's total oil reserves by between 10 and 15 percent.

Kuwait also struggled to repair its government and society after the war ended. The citizens who remained in Kuwait during the Iraqi occupation and the war, and especially those who joined the resistance movement against the Iraqis, were shaped by the violence they experienced. They felt a great deal of bitterness toward the emir and other leaders who fled the country and spent those months in relative safety.

Some members of the resistance openly criticized the emir and demanded a greater say in the government. They angrily pointed out, for example, that only around 10 percent of Kuwait's population had been allowed to vote before the war. The fight for greater democracy (a form of government in which the people direct the country's activities through elected representatives) in Kuwait eventually died down as people focused on the task of rebuilding the country. But in 1992 Jabir did follow through on a wartime promise to reestablish Kuwait's elected national assembly.

Where to Learn More

"Jaber Al-Ahmad Al-Jaber Al-Sabah." *Encyclopedia of World Biography,* 1998. Reproduced in *Biography Resource Center.* Farmington Hills, MI: Gale Group, 2003.

"Jabir III, Amir of Kuwait." *Current Leaders of Nations,* 1998. Reproduced in *Biography Resource Center.* Farmington Hills, MI: Gale Group, 2003.

Sabah, Jabir al-Ahmad al-. "A Gulf War Retrospective: The 1990 Amiri Address to the UN." *Kuwait Information Office.* Available online at http://www.kuwait-info.org/Gulf_War/gulf_war_retrospective.html (accessed on March 27, 2004).

Mohammed Said al-Sahhaf

Born 1940
Hilla, Iraq

Iraqi information minister known for his defiant and overly optimistic statements during the 2003 Iraq War

A s Iraq's Information Minister, Mohammed Said al-Sahhaf was the main public spokesman for Saddam Hussein's government during the 2003 Iraq War. He became known for the vast array of colorful insults he used to describe the American and British troops that were invading his country. As the U.S.-led coalition of more than thirty-five countries closed in on Baghdad, al-Sahhaf repeatedly insisted that Iraq's army was on the verge of a major victory. Journalists gave him the nicknames "Baghdad Bob" and "Comical Ali" because of his defiant and overly optimistic statements to the media.

"I reassure you Baghdad is safe. There is no presence of the American columns in the city of Baghdad. None at all."

Mohammed Said al-Sahhaf quoted in War on Baghdad.

Rises through the ranks of Iraq's Baathist government

Mohammed Said al-Sahhaf was born in 1940 in Hilla, Iraq. His hometown is located south of Baghdad, near the city of Karbala. Like the majority of Iraq's citizens, al-Sahhaf was raised in the Shiite branch of the Islamic religion. He studied journalism at the University of Baghdad and initially planned to become an English teacher. But his career plans changed in

Mohammed Said al-Sahhaf.
Photograph by Jamal Nasrallah. AFP/Getty Images. Reproduced by permission.

1963, when he became interested in politics and joined the Iraqi Baath Party.

Baathism is a radical political movement founded in the 1940s with the goal of uniting the Arab world to create one powerful Arab state. Baath means "rebirth" or "renaissance" in Arabic. The Baath Party succeeded in overthrowing the Iraqi government in 1963. The Baathists held power for less than a year before being ousted in a military coup (a sudden and violent overthrowing of the government), but they regained control of Iraq in 1968. One of the most influential figures in the Baathist government was its head of security, **Saddam Hussein** (see entry), who controlled the forces of violence and terror that helped the party maintain power.

Once the Baath Party returned to power in 1968, al-Sahhaf entered government service. He served as director of the Baghdad Broadcasting and Television agency for the next six years. In 1974 he was appointed as Iraq's ambassador to India. He later served as the Iraqi ambassador to Nepal and Myanmar (Burma). In 1977 he became Iraq's ambassador to the United Nations (UN).

When Hussein became president of Iraq in 1979, al-Sahhaf became one of the few Shiite members of his Sunni Muslim government. (Sunni and Shiite are the two main branches of the Islamic religion. Shiite Muslims make up about 60 percent of Iraq's population, but this majority was repressed under Hussein's Sunni-dominated regime.) He was also one of a small number of high-ranking Iraqi officials who did not come from Hussein's hometown of Tikrit in northern Iraq. Despite these differences, al-Sahhaf gradually rose through the ranks of Iraq's Ministry of Foreign Affairs. He became deputy minister in 1983, and he also served as his country's ambassador to Italy and Sweden.

Becomes Iraq's foreign minister following the 1991 Persian Gulf War

In August 1990 the Iraqi army invaded Kuwait. Hussein argued that Iraq had a historical claim to Kuwait's territory. He also wanted to control Kuwait's oil reserves and to gain access to Kuwait's port on the Persian Gulf. The invasion set in motion a series of events that ultimately led to the 1991 Persian Gulf War. Countries around the world condemned the invasion and demanded that Hussein immediately withdraw his troops from Kuwait. Many of these countries then began sending military forces to the Persian Gulf region as part of a U.S.-led coalition against Iraq. When Iraq failed to withdraw its troops from Kuwait by the UN deadline of January 15, 1991, the coalition forces launched a war. The war succeeded in liberating Kuwait from Iraqi occupation on February 27.

As part of the agreement that officially ended the war, Iraq agreed to destroy all of its biological, chemical, and nuclear weapons. Hussein also agreed to allow UN weapons inspectors to enter the country in order to monitor its progress. As the years passed, however, Iraq consistently failed to cooperate with the UN weapons inspectors. The international community tried several different approaches to get Iraq to comply with the terms of the peace agreement, including military strikes and economic sanctions (trade restrictions intended to punish a country for violating international law), but none were effective.

In 1993, two years after the war ended, al-Sahhaf was appointed as Iraq's foreign minister. He thus became his country's top diplomat and main representative in international affairs. In this position, he faced the difficult task of explaining Iraq's refusal to cooperate with UN weapons inspections. He also tried to convince the United Nations to lift the economic sanctions that were taking a toll on Iraq's economy.

In 2001 al-Sahhaf was removed from his post as foreign minister. His performance had come under increasing criticism over the years, and he was often compared unfavorably to his predecessor, Tariq Aziz. Some foreign leaders complained that al-Sahhaf was too combative. They also noted that he did not appear to have the authority to make decisions on behalf of Hussein's government. Within Iraq, rumors circulated that Hussein's oldest son, Uday Hussein, had forced al-Sahhaf out of office. The rumors said that Uday was angry because al-Sahhaf had failed to win the support of other Arab nations for lifting the UN sanctions against Iraq.

Becomes Iraq's information minister during the 2003 Iraq War

The terrorist attacks that struck the United States on September 11, 2001, led President **George W. Bush** (see entry) to adopt a more aggressive policy toward nations that he considered threats to world security, such as Iraq. He argued that Iraq possessed weapons of mass destruction and could provide such weapons to terrorist groups. Although Iraq allowed the UN weapons inspectors to return in late 2002, Bush was not satisfied and threatened to take military action to disarm Iraq and remove Hussein from power.

As the ongoing disagreements between Iraq and the United States escalated toward war, al-Sahhaf was appointed as Iraq's minister of information. Since Hussein limited his public appearances out of concern for his own safety, al-Sahhaf often served as main spokesman for the Iraqi regime. But al-Sahhaf was still viewed as an outsider within the top levels of Hussein's government during this time. In fact, some Iraqis claimed that his appointment as information minister reflected Hussein's indifference about al-Sahhaf's life and future.

In any case, al-Sahhaf became the face of the Iraqi government in the weeks leading up to the 2003 Iraq War. He seemed to enjoy his role. He appeared at daily press conferences in Baghdad wearing a military uniform, complete with black beret and pistol. Using strong, defiant language, he repeatedly denied that Iraq possessed weapons of mass destruction or had ties to terrorist groups. He also used colorful insults to describe Bush and British Prime Minister **Tony Blair** (see entry) for threatening to invade Iraq.

Descriptions of war attract a worldwide TV audience

Despite a lack of UN support, U.S. and British military forces invaded Iraq on March 20, 2003 (March 19 in the United States). Once the war began, al-Sahhaf continued his daily press conferences, which attracted a worldwide audience on both Arab and Western television networks. The Iraqi information minister became a source of amusement, and sometimes confusion, for journalists in Baghdad and viewers around the world. He consistently presented a view of the conflict that was skewed in Iraq's favor. As the war continued, his statements became increasingly fantastic and more obviously at odds with the reality of the situation. Some analysts claimed that al-Sahhaf presented an upbeat assessment of the war because he felt it was his job to raise the spirits of the Iraqi people and encourage them to fight the invaders.

Even though the information al-Sahhaf presented was rarely accurate, journalists attended his press conferences because he provided them with interesting "sound bites." Shortly after the war began, for example, he led reporters on a tour of a palace that had been destroyed by coalition bombs. He said that the site clearly contradicted U.S. Secretary of Defense **Donald Rumsfeld**'s (see entry) claims that only military targets were hit in the coalition bombing campaign. According to the Internet site called "We Love the Iraqi Information Minister," Al-Sahhaf then described the coalition leaders as a "gang of international rascals" that "deserve only to be beaten by shoes."

Al-Sahhaf often claimed that the Iraqi army was successfully resisting the invasion. At one point he urged the U.S. troops to surrender, saying that their situation was hopeless. "It is better for you this way because if you do not we will cut your heads off, all of you," he declared as quoted on "We Love the Iraqi Information Minister." When international news organizations aired footage of U.S. troops advancing toward Baghdad, al-Sahhaf claimed that the footage came from a Hollywood movie. After the coalition captured Saddam International Airport outside Baghdad, al-Sahhaf insisted that Iraqi forces had successfully defended the airport. "We have fed them a sour taste, a poison yesterday, all this by the brave forces of Saddam Hussein," he stated on "We Love the Iraqi Information Minister."

Even as battles raged in the streets of Baghdad, just a few hundred yards from his location, the information minister told reporters that there were no American troops within 100 miles (161 kilometers) of the city. "I reassure you Baghdad is safe," he said defiantly, as quoted in *War on Saddam*. "There is no presence of the American columns in the city of Baghdad. None at all." Instead, al-Sahhaf proclaimed that Iraq was on the verge of winning the war. "[The enemy forces] are beginning to commit suicide at the gates of Baghdad and I'd encourage them to commit more suicide," he declared.

Becomes a cult favorite

As the war progressed, al-Sahhaf attracted a worldwide following. Millions of people watched his daily press

A photo dated March 22, 2003, showing Iraqi Information Minister Mohammed Said al-Sahhaf heading to a press conference in Baghdad. Al-Sahhaf became a cult favorite because of the ridiculous descriptions of the 2003 Gulf War that he provided. *Karim Sahib/AFP/Getty Images. Reproduced by permission.*

conferences to see what he would say next. Millions of others tracked his statements on an Internet site called "We Love the Iraqi Information Minister." The site featured sound bites and pictures of al-Sahhaf in various dangerous situations proclaiming, "Everything is just fine." His likeness appeared on T-shirts and mugs and in countless political cartoons. The American media gave him the nickname "Baghdad Bob," while the British press dubbed him "Comical Ali" (a reference to "Chemical Ali," the alias of Ali Hassan al-Majid, an Iraqi general who allegedly ordered the use of chemical weapons against the Kurdish people of northern Iraq).

But not everyone viewed al-Sahhaf as a ridiculous figure. His descriptions of the war were well received by some Iraqis, who felt that he expressed their feelings of anger over the U.S.-led invasion. When he gave statements in Arabic, al-Sahhaf often used long-forgotten expressions that sent many viewers to their dictionaries. One example is "uluj," an insulting term that scholars explained could mean anything from "blood-sucking worm" to "mad donkey." Surprisingly, al-Sahhaf was the only source of information available in some parts of the Arab world. For viewers who heard nothing but his account of events, the fall of Baghdad to coalition forces on April 9 came as a surprise.

Al-Sahhaf held his last official press conference on April 8, the day before the fall of Baghdad. After that, his whereabouts remained unknown for more than two months. Some people believed that he had been killed in the fighting, while others claimed that he had gone into hiding. In late June he resurfaced to give two brief interviews on Arab television. In comparison to his demeanor during the war, al-Sahhaf seemed withdrawn and uncommunicative. He said that he had surrendered to U.S. forces, undergone several weeks of questioning, and then was released. He also discussed his plans to write a book. As of 2004, he was believed to be living in the United Arab Emirates.

Where to Learn More
"Mohammed Saeed al-Sahaf." *Wikipedia: The Free Encyclopedia,* undated. Available online at http://en.wikipedia.org/wiki/Mohammed_Saeed_al-Sahaf (accessed on March 29, 2004).

"Muhammad Said al-Sahhaf." *Biography Resource Center Online.* Farmington Hills, MI: Gale Group, 2003.

"Profile: Mohammed Saeed al-Sahhaf." *BBC News,* June 27, 2003. Available online at http://news.bbc.co.uk/1/hi/world/middle_east/2927031.stm (accessed on March 29, 2004).

Rooney, Ben. *The Daily Telegraph War on Saddam: The Complete Story of the Iraq Campaign.* London: Robinson, 2003.

"We Love the Iraqi Foreign Minister." Available online at http://www.welovetheiraqiinformationminister.com/ (accessed on April 9, 2004).

H. Norman Schwarzkopf

**Born August 22, 1934
Trenton, New Jersey**

**American General who commanded victorious
Allied forces in the Persian Gulf War**

General H. Norman Schwarzkopf led U.S. military forces through the Persian Gulf War. Iraq's swift and decisive defeat at the hands of the U.S.-led Allied forces, combined with Schwarzkopf's charismatic personality and fierce loyalty to his troops, made him an American military hero.

Son of a famous military father

Norman Schwarzkopf was born in Trenton, New Jersey, on August 22, 1934. His parents were Ruth (Bowman) Schwarzkopf and Herbert Norman Schwarzkopf, a World War I general who went on to become the founding commander of the New Jersey State Police. Schwarzkopf was his parents' only son, but they also had two daughters.

Throughout his childhood, Schwarzkopf idolized his father. "My father was a very honorable man," he told *Insight on the News*. "He epitomized [represented] the best West Point graduate of his day that's totally committed to a sense of duty, totally committed to a sense of honor, totally dedicated to his country, and a selfless servant."

"Any soldier worth his salt should be antiwar. And still there are things worth fighting for."

*H. Norman Schwarzkopf in
U.S. News and World Report.*

H. Norman Schwarzkopf.
*AP/Wide World Photos.
Reproduced by permission.*

219

Schwarzkopf's father returned to active duty in the U.S. Army in 1942, when the United States entered World War II (1939–45). His absence left young Schwarzkopf the only male in a house full of females. Looking back, he believes that this period of his life as he recalled in *Insight on the News:*

> I wasn't your normal, tough, macho young boy. Maybe it was the influence of my mother and my sisters, the fact that I had this responsibility on my shoulders. I can remember being pushed around a lot. I can't really say why. I learned to hate the bully. I learned to hate the playground group that went around pushing other people around. I never ran with that bunch as a young boy.

After World War II ended in 1945, Schwarzkopf's father remained in the military. He served at a variety of posts all across the Middle East and Europe, including Iran, Italy, Germany, and Switzerland, before returning to the United States in 1951. His son accompanied him on many of these assignments. This exposure to different cultures taught Schwarzkopf "that you judge a person as an individual," he told *Insight on the News.* "I also learned that the American way is great, but it's not the only way. There are a lot of other ways things are done that are just as good, and some of them are better."

Following in his father's footsteps

Schwarzkopf earned his high school diploma at Trenton's Bordentown Military Institute in 1952. He then entered the U.S. Army's West Point Military Academy, from which he graduated in 1956. After leaving West Point, he joined the army as a second lieutenant in the infantry. He spent the next nine years serving the country in positions all around the United States and Germany. He also continued his education, graduating from a master's program in guided missile engineering in June 1964.

Served in Vietnam

In June 1965 Schwarzkopf entered the Vietnam War (1954–75), a bloody conflict that pitted North Vietnam against troops from South Vietnam and the United States. During this first tour of duty, he served as an advisor to a

South Vietnamese Airborne brigade. "When they slept on the ground, I slept on the ground; what they ate, I ate. It was truly serving a cause I believed in," he recalled in *U.S. News and World Report*. When Schwarzkopf completed his tour in 1966 he returned to the United States and spent the next three years working in Washington, D.C. From there he returned to West Point, where he worked as an instructor.

In December 1969 Schwarzkopf shipped over to Vietnam for a second tour of duty as a battalion commander. When he arrived, he was stunned by the battalion's poor morale and leadership. "When I took over the battalion it was totally unprepared for battle yet it had been in battle; all they were doing was taking casualties, [not] inflicting them," he told *U.S. News and World Report*. "It was a nightmare."

Schwarzkopf labored mightily to improve the battalion's performance, and he repeatedly showed his bravery in combat. He earned three Silver Stars for Heroism and two Purple Heart medals for wounds suffered in battle during this tour. But most of his memories from this period of his life are of dying soldiers and ineffective military strategies. When he returned home in late 1970, he was angry and frustrated about the war. "We all carry scars from Vietnam, and those scars will never go away," he wrote in his autobiography *It Doesn't Take a Hero*.

After returning to the United States, Schwarzkopf worked in Washington, D.C., until October 1974, when he was made deputy commander of the 172nd infantry brigade in Fort Richardson, Alaska. This proved to be one of his favorite assignments, as he was able to spend much of his time outdoors with his troops. In addition, the wilds of Alaska gave him many opportunities to pursue his love for hunting and fishing. In 1975 he was promoted to full colonel and reassigned to Fort Lewis, Washington, where he stayed for about two years before taking a post in Hawaii. His family accompanied him on each of these new postings, and Schwarzkopf later estimated that his military career required at least sixteen different relocations for his wife and children.

In 1980 Schwarzkopf was made a general. He spent most of the next decade in various posts in Europe and the United States, including a two-year stint (1985–87) as commanding general of the Fort Lewis army base in Georgia. In

1987 he returned to Washington, D.C., and a year later he was appointed a full general and given the reins of the U.S. Central Command. Thirty-one years after first joining the U.S. military, Schwarzkopf had become the leader of the entire U.S. Army.

Preparing for a Persian Gulf showdown

As commander of U.S. Central Command, Schwarzkopf paid special attention to the Middle East, an unstable region of the world that simmered with the potential for violence. In fact, he began planning a variety of U.S. military strategies just in case American forces were ordered into the region.

Schwarzkopf received a chance to use some of his plans when Iraqi leader **Saddam Hussein** (see entry) had ordered his military forces to invade the neighboring country of Kuwait on August 2, 2001. Hussein argued that Iraq had a historical claim to Kuwait's territory. He also wanted to control Kuwait's oil reserves and to gain access to Kuwait's port on the Persian Gulf. Countries around the world criticized the invasion and demanded that Hussein withdraw his troops from Kuwait. When he refused, many of these countries sent military forces to the Persian Gulf region to join a U.S.-led coalition against Iraq. Schwarzkopf supervised this military build-up, which eventually grew to include more than four hundred thousand U.S. troops and thousands of soldiers from other nations. During this period, he gained an international reputation for blunt talk (he once described Hussein and his generals as nothing more than "a bunch of thugs") and fierce devotion to the men and women under his command. Indeed, Schwarzkopf's obvious concern for his soldiers and his warm personality made him enormously popular with the troops. "He's a legend over here," one air force sergeant told *People* magazine. "All the guys in the field love him."

Meanwhile, men and women who had worked with Schwarzkopf over the years assured the American people that he was a great choice to lead the coalition forces. For example, one former West Point classmate noted in *U.S. News and World Report* that he had a son in the military who could be ordered any day to go to the Persian Gulf. "I feel really good that if he goes, Schwarzkopf is running things," the father said. "They'll fight like hell, but lives aren't going to be wasted. I just know that, as a father."

For his part, Schwarzkopf told *U.S News and World Report* that he hated war, but knew that it was sometimes necessary.

> A professional soldier understands that war means killing people, war means maiming people, war means families left without fathers and mothers.... All you have to do is hold your first soldier who is dying in your arms, and have that terribly futile feeling that I can't do anything about it; that the life is literally flowing out of this young man and I can't do anything about it. Then you understand the horror of war. Any soldier worth his salt should be antiwar. And still there are things worth fighting for.

Operation Desert Storm

In November 1990, the United Nations (UN) Security Council established a deadline of January 15, 1991, for Iraq to withdraw from Kuwait or face attack by the U.S.-led forces. When Iraq failed to withdraw its troops from Kuwait by the UN deadline, the coalition forces launched a campaign of air strikes against Iraqi troops and military positions, including some in the capital city of Baghdad. These air strikes, known as Operation Desert Storm, blasted Iraqi military targets for thirty-eight days, leaving Iraqi forces stunned and battered. Schwarzkopf then ordered a massive ground offensive against Iraqi positions in Kuwait and southern Iraq on February 24, 1991.

As U.S. and coalition military forces poured into Kuwait and southern Iraq, many Iraqi military units surrendered or fled. Other Iraqi troops resisted, but they were quickly crushed. In the space of only one hundred hours, Schwarzkopf's forces freed Kuwait and chased the tattered remains of Hussein's army nearly to Iraq's capital city of Baghdad. At that point, President **George H. W. Bush** (see entry) called off the attack.

The triumph of coalition forces in the 1991 Persian Gulf War has been described by some military historians as one of the most brilliant and decisive in history. Schwarzkopf was delighted by the success of the mission, and he took particular pride in the fact that U.S. and allied forces suffered only light casualties in the war. He also heaped scorn on Hus-

Norman Schwarzkopf (right) and Colin Powell (left) at a briefing during the Persian Gulf War. Schwarzkopf was delighted by the success of Operation Desert Storm. *Photograph by John Gaps. AP/Wide World Photos. Reproduced by permission.*

sein, who had led his country into the disastrous confrontation. In one news conference, cited in Richard Pyle's book *Schwarzkopf: In His Own Words,* the general declared that Hussein was "neither a strategist, nor is he schooled in the operational art, nor is he a tactician, nor is he a general , nor is he a soldier." He then paused and added sarcastically, "Other than that he is a great military man." But Schwarzkopf had little time to bask in the glow of victory, for the next several weeks required him to oversee countless postwar issues, from securing the release of prisoners of war (POWs) to helping Kuwait return to a more normal existence.

In March 1991 U.S. forces began to return home. Schwarzkopf personally addressed many of these troops before their departure to express his appreciation for their performance. As recalled in *Schwarzkopf: In His Own Words,* on March 8, 1991, he told departing troops:

> It's a great day to be a soldier! Big Red One, First Team, Old Ironsides, Spear Head, Hell on Wheels platoon, Jay Hawk

patrol, today you're going home. You're going home to Fort Riley, Kansas, you're going home to Fort Hood, Texas, you're going home to locations all over Germany. Your country, your countrymen, your wives, your children, and your loved ones are all there waiting for you.... It's hard for me to put into words how proud I am of you. How proud I have been to be the commander of this war. I'm proud of you, your countries are proud of you, and the world's proud of you. God bless you, God's speed for your trip home, and God bless America.

After the war

Schwarzkopf retired from active military service in July 1991, five months after the greatest triumph of his long and distinguished career. In honor of his role in the Persian Gulf War, he received numerous prestigious awards in the months and years following his retirement, including the Congressional Gold Medal of Honor, the Presidential Medal of Freedom, and the Order of Kuwait with Sash of Most Excellent Order. In 1992 he joined with writer Peter Petre to publish his autobiography, *It Doesn't Take a Hero*. The book covered his entire life, from childhood through the Vietnam War to the Persian Gulf War. It was widely praised by reviewers as a candid and fascinating account of the life of America's newest military hero.

Since that time, Schwarzkopf has remained interested in military issues. For example, he has followed research into "Gulf War Syndrome," a term used to describe a variety of mysterious illnesses suffered by many U.S. Gulf War veterans, with great interest. But he has spent most of his retirement with his family, wife Brenda (Holsinger) Schwarzkopf, whom he married in 1968, and their three children, Jessica, Christian, and Cynthia, and pursuing his love for outdoor activities such as fishing and hunting.

Where to Learn More

Eisenhower, John. "It Doesn't Take a Hero." *New York Times Book Review,* October 18, 1992.

Galloway, Joseph L. "The Bear: General H. Norman Schwarzkopf Knows Soldiers and Loves Them, Knows War and Hates It." *U.S. News and World Report,* February 11, 1991.

Mackenzie, Richard. "Fierce Loyalty and Affection for His Troops." *Insight on the News,* March 18, 1991.

Pyle, Richard. *Schwarzkopf: In His Own Words*. New York: Penguin Books, 1991.

Schwarzkopf, H. Norman, with Peter Petre. *It Doesn't Take a Hero*. New York: Bantam, 1992.

"Stormin' Norman: Born to Win." *People,* March 11, 1991.

Yitzhak Shamir

Born 1915
Ruzinoy, Poland

Prime Minister of Israel during the 1991
Persian Gulf War

As the prime minister of Israel during the Persian Gulf War, Yitzhak Shamir faced a difficult decision about whether or not to enter the war. Shortly after the fighting started, Iraq began firing Scud missiles at Israeli cities. Iraqi leader **Saddam Hussein** (see entry) apparently wanted to draw Israel into the war in hopes of breaking up the U.S.-led coalition. Hussein believed that the Arab members of the coalition would leave it, and perhaps even switch sides and support Iraq, rather than fight alongside Israel, their longtime enemy. But Shamir responded to U.S. pressure and followed a policy of restraint in the face of the Iraqi attacks. Israel stayed on the sidelines of the conflict, while the coalition remained intact and defeated Iraq.

Fights for a Jewish homeland

Yitzhak Shamir was born Yitzhak Yizernitzky in 1915 in the village of Ruzinoy in eastern Poland. He changed his last name to Shamir, which means "hard substance" or "sharp thorn" in Hebrew, around 1940. Shamir was the son of

> "The populace will come to understand ... that everything the PLO stands for will produce only disasters."
>
> *Yitzhak Shamir quoted in the New York Times.*

Yitzhak Shamir. *Photograph by David Rubinger. Time Life Pictures/Getty Images. Reproduced by permission.*

227

prosperous Jewish parents, Shlomo and Penina Yizernitzky, and he enjoyed a happy childhood. He graduated from the Hebrew Gymnasium in Bialystok, Poland, and attended Warsaw University Law School. During his student years, Shamir became a strong supporter of the idea of forming a permanent homeland for the world's Jews in the ancient region of Palestine in the Middle East.

After the Nazi Party came to power in Germany in 1933, anti-Semitism (discrimination and hostility toward Jews) began to spread across Eastern Europe. The changing political climate convinced Shamir to immigrate to Palestine in 1935. At this time, Palestine was controlled by British authorities. The British were supposed to supervise the formation of a Jewish state in the region, but they moved slowly because of opposition to the plan from surrounding Arab nations. In 1939, when European Jews were trying to escape the Holocaust (the systematic extermination of six million European Jews by Germany during World War II), the British government restricted Jewish immigration to Palestine. Shamir's parents remained in Poland after he left, and they were eventually killed in the Holocaust.

Once he arrived in Palestine, Shamir attended Hebrew University of Jerusalem. He married Shulamith Levy and the couple had a son, Yair, and a daughter, Gil'ada. Shamir also joined a Jewish underground military organization called Irgun Zvai Leumi. This group opposed British rule in Palestine and sponsored violent attacks aimed at forcing the British to form a Jewish state. In 1940 Shamir helped create another underground military group called Lehi (Lohamei Eretz Yisrael, or Fighters for the Freedom of Israel). He was involved in a number of Lehi attacks against the British government and in retaliation for Arab violence toward Jews. In his autobiography, *Summing Up,* Shamir admitted that he gave orders resulting in at least five deaths. He justified his actions as a necessary part of the fight for a Jewish homeland, and said that he recalled them "without apology or regret."

The creation of Israel

In 1946 Shamir was captured by the British and sent to a prison camp in Eritrea. He escaped to France the following year. Shamir returned to the Middle East in 1948, when the United Nations created the nation of Israel as a homeland for all Jewish people. The newly created state covered most of the region of Palestine, which Jews regarded as their historic holy land. But Palestine was also home to an Arab people known as the Palestinians, whose ancestors had lived in the region since ancient times. When Israel took over this territory, about five hundred thousand Palestinians fled and became refugees in neighboring countries.

Some of the displaced Palestinians formed a group called the Palestine Liberation Organization (PLO). The purpose of the PLO was to fight to reclaim lost territory and establish an independent Palestinian state. The PLO often resorted to acts of violence and terrorism in its dispute with Israel. It gained the support of many Arab nations, however, and it was eventually recognized by the United Nations as the legitimate government of Palestine.

The creation of Israel and displacement of the Palestinians angered many Arabs. In fact, five Arab countries—Egypt, Syria, Jordan, Lebanon, and Iraq—went to war against Israel shortly after it was formed. The Arab-Israeli War lasted for nine months before Israel defeated the Arab armies in early 1949. Over the next few years Shamir worked in the construction business, though he maintained a strong interest in politics. In 1955 he took a job as a secret security officer for Mossad, the Israeli intelligence agency.

In 1967 the tension between Israel and its Arab neighbors once again erupted into war. Israel quickly prevailed in this conflict, which became known as the Six-Day War. Israeli forces crushed the combined armies of Egypt, Syria, and Jordan, and took control over large areas of enemy territory. They captured the Sinai Peninsula and Gaza Strip from Egypt, the strategic Golan Heights from Syria, and the West Bank of the Jordan River from Jordan. Israel's military occupation of these Arab territories became another area of dispute between the Jewish state and its neighbors.

Becomes prime minister of Israel

In 1973 Shamir was elected to the Knesset (the 120-member Israeli parliament). He was elected speaker of the

Knesset four years later. In 1980 Shamir served as foreign minister under Prime Minister Menachem Begin. In this position he helped improve relations between Israel and the Soviet Union, France, and several Latin American and African countries. When Begin resigned from office in 1983, Shamir took over and served one year as the temporary prime minister.

The results of the 1984 elections failed to give any political party a majority in the Israeli government. Shamir and his Likud party negotiated with the Labor party to form a coalition government. Under this arrangement, the two parties divided the prime minister's term between their two candidates. Shimon Peres served as prime minister for two years, while Shamir served as deputy prime minister and foreign minister. In 1986 the two men switched positions and Shamir became prime minister.

In 1987 Palestinians living in the West Bank and Gaza launched a series of uprisings against Israeli occupation of these lands. The uprisings, which often included violence against Israeli troops and civilians, became known as the Intifada, which means "throwing off" in Arabic. As prime minister, Shamir took a hard line against the Intifada. He argued that the Palestinians were determined to destroy Israel and that he had a responsibility to defend it. He sent Israeli troops into the occupied territories and authorized them to use force to put down the rebellions. Some Israelis wanted to negotiate a political settlement, but Shamir rejected this idea. "The populace will come to understand from the bitter experience of the Intifada violence that this struggle will lead nowhere and that everything the PLO stands for will produce only disasters," he was quoted as saying in an October 1989 *New York Times* article.

Shamir won a full four-year term as prime minister in the 1988 elections. One of the biggest challenges of this term involved finding a way for Israel to absorb hundreds of thousands of Jewish immigrants from the Soviet Union. Helping the Soviet Jews to find homes and jobs placed a great deal of stress on Israel's economy. In fact, Israel depended on billions of dollars in aid from the United States to help it deal with the situation.

Shows restraint during the Persian Gulf War

In August 1990 the Middle Eastern nation of Iraq invaded its smaller neighbor, Kuwait. Iraqi leader Saddam Hussein had ordered his military forces to invade the neighboring country because he argued that Iraq had a historical claim to Kuwait's territory. Hussein also wanted to control Kuwait's oil reserves and to gain access to Kuwait's port on the Persian Gulf. Countries around the world condemned the invasion and demanded that Hussein immediately withdraw his troops from Kuwait. Many of these countries then began sending military forces to the Persian Gulf region as part of a U.S.-led coalition against Iraq. As the military buildup continued, a number of world leaders tried to negotiate a peaceful resolution to the crisis. During these negotiations, Hussein repeatedly tried to link Iraq's withdrawal from Kuwait with Israel's withdrawal from the occupied territories. But Shamir insisted that the two issues were not related and refused to consider giving up any land.

In November 1990 the United Nations (UN) Security Council established a deadline of January 15, 1991, for Iraq to withdraw from Kuwait or face war. When Hussein failed to meet the deadline, the U.S.-led coalition launched a series of air strikes against military targets in Iraq. A few days after the war began, Hussein ordered his forces to fire Scud missiles at Israel and Saudi Arabia. Hussein chose to attack Israel, even though Israel was not involved in the war, because he wanted to provoke Israel into retaliating. He believed that the Arab countries would break up the U.S.-led coalition rather than fight alongside their bitter enemy.

Deciding whether or not to strike back against Iraq's attacks was very difficult for Shamir. He ultimately gave in to strong pressure from the United States and agreed not to retaliate unless Iraq used chemical weapons. Still, he admitted in his autobiography, *Summing Up: An Autobiography,* that the decision went against his personal feelings. "I can think of nothing that went more against my grain," he stated. Shamir earned international praise for his restraint and calm leadership in the face of forty Scud missile attacks against the Israeli cities of Tel Aviv and Haifa. Many of the Scuds were intercepted and destroyed by American Patriot missiles before they reached their targets. The Scuds that did land in Israel destroyed thousands of homes and apartments but caused only one death.

The coalition air strikes went on for nearly six weeks and caused major damage to Iraq's military capability. On February 24 the coalition launched a dramatic ground assault to force the

President George H. W.
Bush shakes hands with
Israeli Prime Minister
Yitzhak Shamir at the 1991
Middle East Peace
Conference in Madrid,
Spain. *©Peter Turnley/Corbis.
Reproduced by permission.*

Iraqi troops out of Kuwait. It met with little resistance from Hussein's army, which had been devastated by the air strikes. The Persian Gulf War ended on February 27, when coalition forces succeeded in liberating Kuwait from Iraqi occupation.

Takes a hard line in peace talks

Once the Persian Gulf War ended, the U.S. government turned its attention to establishing lasting peace in the Middle East. Knowing that Israel needed their financial help, American leaders placed a great deal of pressure on Shamir to grant self-rule to the Palestinians in the occupied territories. Shamir participated in the Middle East Peace Conference in Madrid, Spain, in October 1991. This conference marked the first direct negotiations between Israel and neighboring Arab states.

The peace talks failed to produce an agreement, however. Shamir believed in permanent Israeli control of the occupied territories and was reluctant to exchange land for peaceful relations with the Arab countries. In fact, he encouraged Jewish immigrants to build settlements in the occupied territories in order to strengthen Israel's hold on them. But this policy displaced Arab residents and triggered more violence from angry Palestinians.

Shamir's policies strained relations with the United States and drew criticism from many people in Israel. In *Summing Up: An Autobiography,* Shamir characterized his constant struggle with his political opponents as a "dispute between those who believed in immediate gain and were … willing to settle for the least and those who believed that they were responsible for future generations and bound … to hold out for the most."

Shamir was defeated in the 1992 elections by Yitzhak Rabin, who spent a great deal of time and energy seeking a peace agreement with the PLO. Although he was no longer prime minister, Shamir continued to influence Israel's government by holding a seat in the Knesset. Shamir criticized Rabin's efforts to make peace with the Palestinians in *Summing Up: An Autobiography.* He claimed that Israel became "a nation led by men who made peace paramount, like a golden calf, to be worshiped at the expense of the values and aspirations that made Israel unique." In 1996 Shamir retired from the Knesset and left public life.

Where to Learn More

Diehl, Jackson. "Israel's Moment of Truth: Restraint or Retaliation? As Scuds Fell, Shamir Faced Tough Choices." *Washington Post,* March 19, 1991.

Hull, Jon D. "Angling for the Postwar Edge: Fearing Pressure to Compromise with the Palestinians, Yitzhak Shamir Carefully Plots His Strategy." *Time,* February 18, 1991.

Shamir, Yitzhak. *Summing Up: An Autobiography.* Boston: Little, Brown, 1994.

"Yitzhak Shamir." *Current Leaders of Nations,* 1998. Reproduced in *Biography Resource Center.* Farmington Hills, MI: Gale Group, 2003.

"Yitzhak Shamir." *Encyclopedia of World Biography,* 1998. Reproduced in *Biography Resource Center.* Farmington Hills, MI: Gale Group, 2003.

"Yitzhak Shamir." *Israel Ministry of Foreign Affairs.* Available online at http://www.israel-mfa.gov.il/mfa/go.asp?MFAH00gb0 (accessed on March 27, 2004).

Bob Simon

Born May 29, 1941
Bronx, New York

**American journalist who was held as a prisoner
of war in Iraq during the Persian Gulf War**

CBS News correspondent Bob Simon is one of the most honored journalists in international reporting. Instead of simply reporting on the Persian Gulf War, however, Simon made news when he and his news team disappeared along the border between Saudi Arabia and Iraqi-occupied Kuwait. Simon and his crew were captured by Iraqi soldiers and held as prisoners of war for nearly six weeks. They endured interrogations, beatings, hunger, and the constant fear that they would be executed as spies. The world did not learn what happened to them until they were released after the war ended.

"At first we didn't realize how serious our situation was."

Bob Simon in People.

Talented reporter joins CBS News

Bob Simon was born on May 29, 1941, in the Bronx section of New York City. He earned a bachelor's degree in history at Brandeis University in 1962. He also studied in France on a Fulbright scholarship, where he met his wife, Francoise. They eventually had one daughter, Tanya. In 1964 Simon became an officer in the American Foreign Service. Three years later he accepted a job as a reporter with CBS News.

Bob Simon. *Photograph by Jim Cooper. AP/Wide World Photos. Reproduced by permission.*

235

Simon quickly impressed his bosses with his talent and ambition. Within a period of four years, he progressed from a cub reporter in New York City to a foreign correspondent covering the Vietnam War in the South Vietnamese capital of Saigon. Simon reported on the final years of American military involvement in South Vietnam and the capture of Saigon by North Vietnamese Communist forces in 1975. The young reporter won an Overseas Press Club Award and two Emmy Awards for his Vietnam coverage.

Over the next few years Simon was assigned to CBS News bureaus in London, England, and Tel Aviv, Israel. In 1981 he spent a year based in Washington, D.C., as the network's U.S. State Department correspondent. From 1982 to 1987 he was CBS's national correspondent based in New York City. In 1987 he was named the CBS News chief correspondent for the Middle East. He moved his family back to Tel Aviv, where he was based when the region became embroiled in a conflict that would eventually lead to the Persian Gulf War.

Captured by Iraqi soldiers

On August 2, 1990, Iraqi leader **Saddam Hussein** (see entry) had ordered his military forces to invade the neighboring country of Kuwait. Hussein argued that Iraq had a historical claim to Kuwait's territory. He also wanted to control Kuwait's oil reserves and to gain access to Kuwait's port on the Persian Gulf. Countries around the world condemned the invasion and demanded that Hussein immediately withdraw his troops from Kuwait. Many of these countries then began sending military forces to the Persian Gulf region as part of a U.S.-led coalition against Iraq. The United States sent more than four hundred thousand troops to the Persian Gulf over the next six months. Simon went to Saudi Arabia in mid-August to cover the military buildup.

In November 1990 the United Nations (UN) Security Council established a deadline of January 15, 1991, for Iraq to withdraw from Kuwait or face war. Simon left Saudi Arabia in mid-December to spend a few weeks with his family in Israel and returned in early January to cover the start of the war. When Hussein failed to meet the deadline, the U.S.-led coalition launched a series of air strikes against military targets in Iraq on January 17.

Once the war began, U.S. military leaders placed tight restrictions on the activities of the media. Most reporters were forced to remain far away from the action and rely on periodic briefings from military officials as their main source of information. Like many other experienced war correspondents, Simon found these restrictions very frustrating. He understood the need for some strategic information to remain secret in order to protect the troops from unnecessary risk. But he also knew that the development of satellite communications had enabled television networks to air live combat footage for the first time in history. He wanted to take full advantage of this technology for the benefit of CBS viewers.

Within a few days, Simon and his news team, producer Peter Bluff; soundman Juan Caldera; and photographer Roberto Alvarez, started making unauthorized trips into the Saudi desert looking for stories. On January 21, 1991, they drove to a remote area of northeastern Saudi Arabia. "We weren't expecting to find anything monumental when we left our hotel in Dhahran, 250 miles [402 kilometers] south of the border, early Sunday morning," Simon explained in his memoir *Forty Days*. "We weren't combing the desert for scoops, revelations, or prizes. We just wanted to break away from the pack because it was becoming clear that the Pentagon [headquarters of the U.S. Department of Defense] was not planning to lead the pack anywhere anything was happening."

When Simon and his crew came to the border of Iraqi-occupied Kuwait, they stopped their car and walked a few hundred yards into Kuwaiti territory. Simon made some comments on camera, then they turned and began walking back to their vehicle. Before they recrossed the border into Saudi Arabia, however, they were captured by Iraqi soldiers. Their abandoned car, which still contained cash, camera equipment, and other possessions, was found by Saudi troops on January 24.

Spends forty days as a prisoner of war in Iraq

Simon's wife was the first person to suspect that something bad had happened to the CBS team. "Three days running, Bob was not on the news," she recalled in *People* magazine. "My intuition told me that something was terribly wrong." When the crew's vehicle was discovered at the border, their mysterious disappearance became a hot topic in the news. But no one knew what had happened to Simon and his crew for several weeks. On January 28 one news agency reported that an Iraqi deserter told them that the CBS crew were alive. On February 11 another Iraqi deserter told U.S. military officials that they were being held as prisoners of war (POWs) in Kuwait. But the Iraqi government consistently refused to acknowledge that they were holding any civilian (nonmilitary) prisoners.

Throughout the war, CBS and Simon's wife tried frantically to find out what happened. They enlisted the help of world leaders like Soviet President Mikhail Gorbachev and **King Hussein** (see entry) of Jordan to pressure the Iraqi government for information. Their concern was increased by the fact that Saddam Hussein's government had a history of mistreating foreign journalists. In 1990 Iraq had executed Farzad Bazoft, an accredited journalist reporting for the *London Observer,* after accusing him of being a spy. Some people were particularly worried about Simon's safety, because he was Jewish and based in Israel. Like many Arab nations, Iraq is primarily Muslim and has a long history of conflict with the Jewish state of Israel. In an attempt to protect Simon, the world media did not mention his religion in stories about the missing CBS crew.

In the meantime, Simon and his crew were taken to a detention facility in Basra in southern Iraq. "At first we didn't realize how serious our situation was," Simon recalled in *People.* "What worried me most was that they grabbed my cigarette lighter, which shows how long it takes for reality to sink in." Over the next six weeks, they were frequently questioned by Iraqi authorities and routinely beaten by guards. They were held in filthy cells and given little food or water. "The really unbearable thing was the hunger," Simon noted in *People.* He continued:

> One does not get used to it. It gets worse, in fact—we were actually starving. We got two pieces of bread a day and maybe two glasses of water. Sometimes they gave us a bit of thin soup. One tries to prolong the process of eating, but that simply doesn't work; you swallow that tiny ration of food in a minute. I really went crazy with hunger and knew that in the future I would never again casually say, 'I'm hungry.'

At one point coalition air strikes hit and seriously damaged the complex in Basra where Simon was being held.

Simon and his crew were then taken on a terrifying journey on the dangerous road to Baghdad, which was the target of nearly constant air strikes. "Every time a bomb exploded, we were thrown backwards, the cuffs cutting into our swollen and bleeding wrists," he remembered in *People*. "The couple of times I asked them to loosen the handcuffs, they beat me. I never asked for anything again."

Over the course of six weeks, the coalition air strikes caused major damage to Iraq's military capability. On February 24 the U.S.-led coalition launched a dramatic ground assault to push the Iraqi forces out of Kuwait. Coalition ground forces met with little resistance from the Iraqi army and succeeded in liberating Kuwait from Iraqi occupation after only four days of fighting. On March 2 the Iraqi government released Simon and his crew as a "goodwill gesture" during cease-fire negotiations. They were taken to the Al Rasheed Hotel in Baghdad, where they were greeted by CBS News officials. They were later driven across the border to Jordan and

Bob Simon and his crew are greeted by the press after being released from their Iraqi captors during the Persian Gulf War. Simon and his crew were held as prisoners for forty days. *©Francoise de Mulder/Corbis. Reproduced by permission.*

then flown to London. Doctors found the four men thin and weak but in generally good health.

Continues his award-winning international reporting

Upon returning to his home in Tel Aviv, Simon found more than one thousand letters from viewers and fellow reporters waiting for him. He took some time off to recover from his ordeal and respond to his mail. Two months later, however, he returned to Baghdad to film an hour-long documentary called *Bob Simon: Back to Baghdad.* He went back again on several other occasions over the years. In 1992 Simon published a book about his experiences as a prisoner in Iraq called *Forty Days.* In 1996 he joined the CBS news program "60 Minutes." Three years later he expanded his reporting duties to include the spin-off show "60 Minutes II."

By the turn of the century Simon was one of the most honored journalists in international reporting. He covered virtually every major foreign news story that occurred during his thirty-five-year career. He covered civil unrest and revolutions in Eastern Europe, Central America, and Africa. He also reported on the American military interventions in Grenada, Somalia, and Haiti. He covered the activities of many major international figures, from Pope John Paul II to Nelson Mandela, and landed a number of exclusive interviews.

Simon won dozens of prestigious awards for his work. He received a Peabody Award for his reporting on the violent student protests at Tiananmen Square in Beijing, China. He claimed two Emmys, a Peabody, and two Overseas Press Club awards for his coverage of the assassination of Israeli Prime Minister Yitzhak Rabin. He earned another Overseas Press Club Award for his coverage of the Persian Gulf War.

Where to Learn More

"Bob Simon." *CBSNews.com.* Available online at http://www.cbsnews.com/stories/1999/01/04/60II/printable26916.shtml (accessed on March 27, 2004).

"Bob Simon." *The Complete Marquis Who's Who,* 2003. Reproduced in *Biography Resource Center.* Farmington Hills, MI: Gale Group, 2003.

"Bob Simon." *People,* Special Issue, Summer 1991.

Hewitt, Bill. "Hunting a Dangerous Story in Kuwait, CBS's Bob Simon Goes MIA." *People,* February 11, 1991.

Kurtz, Howard. "The 40-Day Ordeal." *Washington Post,* March 4, 1991.

Simon, Bob. *Forty Days.* New York: Putnam, 1992.

"Simon, Bob." *POW Network.* Available online at http://www.pownetwork. org/gulf/sd026.htm (last accessed on March 27, 2004).

Margaret Thatcher

Born October 13, 1925
Grantham, England

Prime minister of Great Britain when Iraq staged 1990 Invasion of Kuwait

The first female prime minister of Great Britain, Margaret Thatcher was an early supporter of using military force against Iraq after it seized control of Kuwait. She firmly believed that Iraq and its president, Saddam Hussein, needed to be harshly punished for invading Kuwait. As the Persian Gulf crisis unfolded, she worked closely with U.S. President **George H. W. Bush** (see entry) to establish a military force capable of defending other vulnerable Middle Eastern nations from Hussein. In addition, Thatcher helped build international support for a military assault on Iraqi forces in Kuwait and Iraq.

A small-town upbringing

Margaret Hilda Roberts Thatcher was born October 13, 1925, in the small town of Grantham, England. Her parents were Beatrice and Alfred Roberts, and she had one older sister, Muriel. Thatcher's family was well known throughout Grantham. Her parents owned and operated one of the town's most successful grocery stores, and her father was a

"Aggression must be stopped. That is the lesson of this century."

Margaret Thatcher as quoted on "Frontline."

Margaret Thatcher. *AP/Wide World Photos. Reproduced by permission.*

243

leader in the community. One of the most prominent members of the local Methodist church, he also served as a town councilman and spent several years as Grantham's mayor. He had an enormous influence on Thatcher, who credits him with giving her confidence, shaping her political views, and molding her overall outlook on life.

As a youth, Thatcher's parents ensured that she went to the finest schools in the area. At age ten, she enrolled at Kesteven and Grantham Girls' School, where she achieved top grades in chemistry, biology, and mathematics. She also showed strong leadership qualities at an early age. A captain of her school's field hockey team, she took leadership positions in various extracurricular school clubs.

Encouraged by her father, Thatcher became interested in politics at an unusually young age. In fact, by the time she was a young teenager she had declared that she wanted to be an MP, a member of British Parliament, when she grew up. When she entered Oxford University's Somerville College in 1943, she initially pursued a degree in chemistry. But she also devoted much of her spare time to the Oxford University Conservative Association, a group of students that supported Great Britain's Conservative Party. By her junior year, Thatcher was president of the association, and she led the group during her senior year as well.

Early career in politics

In 1947 Thatcher graduated from Somerville with a chemistry degree, and she spent the next four years supporting herself as a research chemist. In the early 1950s she studied to become a barrister (a lawyer). She also remained heavily involved in England's Conservative Party, and was named a party candidate in two Parliamentary elections, but she lost both of these campaigns, in 1950 and 1951. On December 13, 1951, she married businessman Denis Thatcher, and in August 1953 they became the parents of twins, Mark and Carol.

In 1959 Thatcher finally achieved her childhood dream of becoming a MP when she won a seat in the House of Commons. At age thirty-four, she was the youngest woman in the House of Commons, but she did not let that stop her from speaking out on all sorts of issues. In fact, the outspoken Conservative emerged as one of her party's most visible members during the 1960s. She also gained the respect of other lawmakers, who recognized her as one of the country's hardest-working members of Parliament. She rose rapidly through the party ranks, and in 1970 she was named secretary of state for education and science to Prime Minister Ted Heath, the leader of Britain's Conservative Party.

In early 1975 Thatcher registered a stunning upset victory over Heath in party elections to claim the top post in the Conservative Party. As leader of the Conservatives in the House of Commons, she battled the ruling Labour Party on a wide array of issues, from education and economic policies to foreign affairs. By the late 1970s Thatcher's tough, blunt, and uncompromising personality had earned her the nickname "Iron Lady" in England and within international diplomatic circles.

Elected prime minister of Great Britain

Thatcher became prime minister of Great Britain in May 1979, when her Conservative Party won the majority of seats in Parliamentary elections. She held the position for the next eleven years, leading the Conservatives to victory in three straight general election victories during that time. Thatcher's eleven-year-run as prime minister was the longest in England since the 1820s.

During Thatcher's run as prime minister, she successfully introduced many Conservative policy goals, from dramatic reductions in government spending to transfer of water and telephone utilities and various industries (including British Airways) from government to private control. She also supervised major changes in the country's education and health care systems and strongly opposed any European treaties that she felt weakened British independence. In addition, she established a warm and friendly relationship with U.S. President Ronald Reagan. The two leaders held many of the same conservative views on government, business, and social issues, and they worked together on many foreign policy issues.

Thatcher's popularity with the British public reached its peak in 1982, when Great Britain defeated Argentina in the Falklands War. The Falkland Islands are a cluster of islands located in the South Atlantic that had been under British control since 1833. Argentina has long claimed that it was the rightful owner of the islands, however, and in 1982 Argentina's army seized the islands by force. The invasion enraged Thatcher, who ordered a British military force headed by the Royal Navy to take back the islands. The British counterattack battered the Argentine army, and on June 14, 1982, Argentina surrendered and removed its remaining military forces from the Falklands.

During the mid-1980s, strong economic growth kept Thatcher and her Conservative Party in power. But in the late 1980s, Thatcher's popularity in England declined. A downturn in the economy was partly to blame for this. Concerned by high rates of inflation, high interest rates on loans, and high unemployment levels, many people in Great Britain came to believe that a change in leadership might be in order. In addition, many British strongly opposed changes to the tax structure being proposed by Thatcher. Finally, critics complained that Thatcher's policies had produced a decline in the quality of education, health care, and other social services. But despite her declining popularity, Thatcher never changed her style, and when the Persian Gulf Crisis erupted in the summer of 1990, she responded in her usual bold and decisive manner.

Showdown in the Persian Gulf

On August 2, 1990, Iraqi leader **Saddam Hussein** (see entry) had ordered his military forces to invade the neighboring country of Kuwait. Hussein argued that Iraq had a historical claim to Kuwait's territory. He also wanted to control Kuwait's oil reserves and to gain access to Kuwait's port on the Persian Gulf. The international community reacted strongly to Iraq's attack, with many nations issuing demands that Hussein give up his claim on Kuwait. When he refused, the United States organized a military coalition against Iraq that eventually grew to include more than four hundred thousand U.S. troops and thousands of soldiers from other nations. In addition, the Bush administration successfully lobbied the United Nations to pass a tough resolution approving the use of military force to free Kuwait from Iraq's army.

As the Persian Gulf crisis unfolded, Great Britain quickly emerged as the United States' strongest ally. Thatcher repeatedly warned Hussein that he and his army would pay a steep price if Iraq did not withdraw from Kuwait. When Hussein ignored these threats, she approved a major transfer of British firepower—including elements of the country's army, air force, and navy—to Saudi Arabia, where they joined coalition forces from the United States and other nations.

Thatcher believed that if Hussein was not punished for his actions, the world would become a much more unstable and dangerous place. "Aggression must be stopped," she later told the PBS program "Frontline." "That is the lesson of this century. And if an aggressor gets away with it, others will want to get away with it too, so he must be stopped, and turned back. You cannot gain from your aggression." In addition, she pointed out that if Iraq was not stopped, it would be in a position to seize control of many of the world's oil reserves. "Oil is vital to the economy of the world," she said. Thatcher continued:

> If you didn't stop [Hussein], and didn't turn him back, he would have gone over the border to Saudi Arabia, over to Bahrain, to Dubai … and right down the west side of the Gulf and in fact could have got access and control to 65 percent of the world's oil reserves, from which he could have blackmailed every nation. So there were two things, aggressors must be stopped and turned back, and he must not get control of this enormously powerful economic weapon.

As the weeks passed, Thatcher urged President Bush and other coalition members to maintain their tough stance toward Iraq. "Don't forget I'd had all the experience of the Falklands [War] and so I had no doubt what you had to do to deal with an aggressor," she told "Frontline." With each passing day, she became more convinced that the best way to deal with the crisis was to attack Iraq's military and crush it, removing Hussein from power in the process.

In November 1990, however, Thatcher's political difficulties at home convinced her to resign from office. With popular support within her own Conservative Party in decline, she gave up the prime minister post to another party leader, John Major. As a result, she watched the rest of the Persian Gulf War from the political sidelines.

Questions U.S. strategy at end of war

On January 16, 1991, President Bush approved the launch of Operation Desert Storm, a major bombing cam-

John Major, British Prime Minister, 1990–97

John Major succeeded Margaret Thatcher as British prime minister in November 1990, during a period of rising tensions between Iraq and the coalition countries led by the United States and Great Britain. Upon taking office, Major voiced firm support for the coalition's demand that Iraq withdraw from Kuwait, and he confirmed that England was ready to go to war. A few months later, the coalition's offensive, known as Operation Desert Storm, swept Iraq out of Kuwait, handing Iraqi President Saddam Hussein a decisive defeat.

John Roy Major was born on March 29, 1943, in London, England. His parents were Gwendolyn and Thomas Major. The elder Major supported his family with a career that included years as a circus acrobat, mercenary soldier, and manufacturer of garden ornaments. During Major's youth, his family suffered a number of severe financial setbacks, and he developed an intense dislike for school. He dropped out of school at age fifteen, taking a series of jobs. By the early 1960s he had found a career in the banking industry, but he left England in the mid-1960s for several years of community work in the impoverished African country of Nigeria.

When Major returned to England, he decided to dive into the world of politics. Beginning as a local councilman in 1968, he became a Conservative member of Parliament in 1979. In 1970 he married Norma Johnson, with whom he eventually had two children.

During the 1980s, Major steadily rose through the ranks of the Conservative Party's leadership. He attracted the notice of Thatcher, who appreciated his calm and self-confident style as well as his con-

paign against Iraqi military positions in Kuwait and Iraq. The American-led bombing campaign lasted for thirty-eight days before giving way to a ground assault on Iraqi positions in Kuwait and southern Iraq. This ground attack pounded Iraq's remaining military forces in less than one hundred hours. As Iraq's battered forces retreated to Baghdad, Iraq's capital city, Bush decided to call off the attack. A short time later, Iraq agreed to all of the coalition demands, including its claim to Kuwait.

But while the Persian Gulf War forced Hussein to withdraw from Kuwait and badly damaged Iraq's military, Thatcher believes that the United States ended the war too quickly. In her "Frontline" interview, she explained:

servative views on economic issues. In July 1989 Thatcher appointed him foreign secretary, one of the top positions in the British government. Major admitted that the promotion "totally astonished" him, but he had little opportunity to acquaint himself with his new responsibilities. In October 1989 Thatcher made Major chancellor of the exchequer, a position that gave him significant authority over England's economy.

In November 1990 Thatcher resigned as prime minister when it became clear that she no longer had the full support of her own Conservative Party. Major quickly mounted a campaign to succeed her as leader of the party and Britain's new prime minister. His bid was supported by Thatcher as well as many other Conservatives who hailed his expertise on economic issues. He won the Conservative Party's leadership election on November 27, 1990, and became prime minister one day later.

As prime minister, Major quickly declared his belief that if Iraq did not voluntarily leave Kuwait, it should be removed by force. He thus offered strong support to the United States throughout the Persian Gulf crisis, and he expressed delight when the U.S.-led coalition forces defeated Iraq in February 1991. Major served as prime minister of Great Britain until 1997, when his Conservative Party was defeated by the Labour Party and its leader, Tony Blair, who became the new prime minister.

Sources: "John Major." In Encyclopedia of World Biography, 1998. Reproduced in Biography Resource Center, Farmington Hills, MI: Gale Group, 2003; Major, John. John Major: The Autobiography. New York: HarperCollins, 1999; Pearce, Edward. The Quiet Rise of John Major. London: Weidenfeld and Nicolson, 1991.

It's not enough just to reverse the invasion. You've got to destroy their army. We couldn't bring down Saddam Hussein. What I thought it was our job to do, was to make it quite clear to the world and particularly the people who'd been wronged, that he'd been totally and utterly defeated and his army had been totally and utterly defeated.... And it didn't seem to me that that part of it was fully achieved.

Thatcher admitted that she was surprised when Bush called an end to the assaults on Iraq's fleeing army. She also believes that if Iraq's army had been totally destroyed, Hussein probably would not have been able to retain power. "These people [Iraq's army] should have been seen to have been defeated, they should have surrendered their equipment and their armed forces," she told "Frontline." "I just didn't under-

Former British Prime Minister Margaret Thatcher meets with Kuwaiti Minister of the Royal Court Sheikh Nasser Mohammed al-Sabah in February 2001 for a two-day celebration to mark a decade of Kuwait's liberation from Iraq.
©AFP/Corbis. Reproduced by permission.

stand it, this is how we'd done it in the Falklands.... So the people of Iraq never saw this dictator, humiliated and beaten."

Thatcher retires from political office

On March 7, 1991, Thatcher received the U.S. Medal of Freedom, one of the highest honors bestowed by the United States, in recognition of the strong friendship she had established with the United States during her long tenure as prime minister of Great Britain. A few months later, on June 28, 1991, she announced that she would not attempt to retain her seat in the House of Commons in the next election, which was to be held the following year. In July 1992 she formally brought her remarkable thirty-two-year career in British politics to a close.

Even after leaving Parliament, however, Thatcher remained keenly interested in British politics and world affairs.

She spent much of the 1990s giving lectures and writing columns on various issues. In addition, she wrote two volumes of memoirs detailing her life in politics, *The Downing Street Years* (1993) and *The Path to Power* (1995).

Where to Learn More

Bierman, John. "The Forging of the Iron Lady." *Maclean's,* May 8, 1989.

Dale, Iain, ed. *Memories of Maggie: A Portrait of Margaret Thatcher.* London: Politico's Publishing, 2000.

"Interview with Margaret Thatcher." *Frontline: The Gulf War.* Available online at http://www.pbs.org/wgbh/pages/frontline/gulf/oral/thatcher/1.html (accessed on March 30, 2004).

Lewis, Russell. *Margaret Thatcher: A Personal and Political Biography.* London and Boston: Routledge & Kegan Paul, 1984.

"Margaret Thatcher." *Current Biography,* November 1989.

"Margaret Thatcher." *Encyclopedia of World Biography,* 1998. Reproduced in *Biography Resource Center,* Farmington Hills, MI: Gale Group, 2003.

"Margaret Thatcher." *Historic World Leaders,* 1994. Reproduced in *Biography Resource Center,* Farmington Hills, MI: Gale Group, 2003.

Thatcher, Margaret. "Don't Go Wobbly." *Wall Street Journal,* June 17, 2002.

Thatcher, Margaret. *The Downing Street Years.* New York: HarperCollins, 1993.

Thatcher, Margaret. *The Path to Power.* New York: HarperCollins, 1995.

Joseph Wilson

Born 1949
California

Former U.S. ambassador who questioned the Bush administration's reasons for invading Iraq in 2003

In February 2002 former U.S. Ambassador Joseph Wilson went to Africa on a mission for the Central Intelligence Agency (CIA). He was sent to investigate claims that Iraq had tried to acquire uranium, a rare, radioactive element that can be used to create nuclear weapons, from the African nation of Niger. Wilson determined that the claims were false and reported his findings to the CIA and the Bush administration.

In the months leading up to the 2003 Iraq War, however, White House officials repeatedly mentioned the uranium story in public statements as they tried to drum up international support for the use of military force to disarm Iraq. The Bush administration's belief that Iraq was on the verge of acquiring nuclear weapons was one of the main justifications for the U.S.-led invasion that took place in March 2003. Two months after the war ended, Wilson came forward and accused the White House of exaggerating the threat of Iraq's weapons of mass destruction in order to make its case for war.

"The problem really is a war which has us invading, conquering, and then subsequently occupying Iraq may not achieve that liberation that we're talking about."

Joseph Wilson in an interview with Bill Moyers.

Joseph Wilson. *Photograph by Alex Wong. Getty Images. Reproduced by permission.*

Career diplomat specializing in Africa and the Middle East

Joseph C. Wilson IV was born around 1949 in California. He graduated from the University of California at Santa Barbara in 1972, and four years later he joined the U.S. Diplomatic Service. Wilson served the U.S. government in various capacities for the next twenty-three years. His earliest diplomatic assignments were in the African nations of Niger, Togo, and South Africa, but he also spent many years stationed in the Middle East.

In 1982 Wilson was appointed deputy chief of mission (top assistant to the U.S. ambassador) to Burundi. He returned to the United States in 1985 to serve as an American Political Science Association Congressional Fellow in the offices of U.S. Senator Al Gore and U.S. Representative Thomas Foley. The following year he returned to Africa as the deputy chief of mission in Congo.

In 1988 Wilson received a new assignment as deputy chief of mission at the U.S. Embassy in Baghdad, Iraq. He served as the top assistant to U.S. Ambassador **April Glaspie** (see entry). In 1990 Glaspie came under criticism for giving Iraqi leader **Saddam Hussein** (see entry) the impression that the U.S. government would not interfere if Iraq invaded the neighboring country of Kuwait. When Hussein later sent his army into Kuwait, Glaspie was relieved of her duties and Wilson became the acting U.S. ambassador to Iraq.

Meets with Saddam Hussein

Four days after the invasion of Kuwait on August 2, Wilson was invited to meet with Hussein. The Iraqi leader rarely met with foreign diplomats stationed in Baghdad, so Wilson realized that the request was unusual. He later came to believe that Hussein called the meeting, the last one to take place between the Iraqi leader and an American official before the 1991 Persian Gulf War, because he wanted to make sure that the United Nations (UN) would control the response to Iraq's invasion of Kuwait. Hussein knew that the United Nations had passed resolutions calling for Israel to end its occupation of Palestinian territory in the 1960s but never enforced them. "He concludes from that that if he goes into the

United Nations system, he's got 25 or 30 years to occupy Kuwait," Wilson noted in an interview with Bill Moyers for PBS, "during which time he can flag Kuwait City with Iraqis, pump all their oil, steal all their money, and then submit it to a referendum [vote] in which he would have stacked the odds for his victory."

The United Nations passed a resolution calling for Iraq to withdraw its troops from Kuwait. To Hussein's surprise, however, it also backed up the resolution by sending military troops from a coalition of nations to the Middle East. The military buildup received the code name Operation Desert Shield. Wilson remained in Baghdad as acting U.S. ambassador during this time. Angry about the international military buildup, Hussein announced that he would use foreign citizens as "human shields" to defend strategic Iraqi sites from attack. The Iraqi leader also threatened to execute anyone caught protecting these foreign citizens. Wilson defied Hussein by sheltering more than one hundred U.S. citizens at the American embassy in Baghdad and in the homes of American diplomats. According to *BBC News,* he appeared at a press conference wearing a hangman's noose around his neck and told the Iraqi leader that "If you want to execute me, I'll bring my own rope." Thanks in part to Wilson's efforts, all the foreign citizens were allowed to leave Iraq.

In early 1991 Operation Desert Shield turned into Operation Desert Storm, as the U.S.-led coalition launched a military offensive to force Iraqi troops to withdraw from Kuwait. The conflict, which became known as the Persian Gulf War, ended in a dramatic victory for the coalition after six weeks of fighting.

In 1992 Wilson completed a seminar in international affairs offered by the U.S. government. Immediately afterward he was named U.S. ambassador to the nations of Gabon and São Tomé and Príncipe in West Africa. Three years later Wilson became the political advisor to the commander in chief of U.S. Armed Forces in Europe. In 1997 he served as senior director for African Affairs in the National Security Council under President Bill Clinton. In this position, he was responsible for coordinating U.S. foreign policy toward the forty-eight nations of sub-Saharan Africa. He also organized Clinton's trip to Africa in 1998.

Later that year, Wilson retired from government service. He received a number of awards and honors for distinguished service from the Department of Defense and Department of State. He also earned the William R. Rivkin Award from the American Foreign Service Association. Following his retirement, Wilson entered the private sector. He became chief executive officer of the international business consulting firm JCWilson International Ventures and a professor at the Middle East Institute in Washington, D.C.

Investigates intelligence reports about Iraq's weapons programs

The UN agreement that ended the 1991 Persian Gulf War required Iraq to destroy all of its biological, chemical, and nuclear weapons. Over the next several years, however, Hussein repeatedly interfered with the UN inspectors sent to verify that Iraq had abandoned its weapons programs. The international community tried a number of different approaches to force Hussein to cooperate with UN weapons inspectors, but none of them proved effective. In fact, Hussein kicked the inspectors out of Iraq in 1998.

On September 11, 2001, members of a radical Islamic terrorist group known as Al Qaeda hijacked four commercial planes and crashed them into the World Trade Center in New York City, the Pentagon building near Washington, D.C., and a field in Pennsylvania, killing nearly three thousand people. Immediately after these attacks against the United States, President **George W. Bush** (see entry) announced a global war on terrorism that initially focused on Al Qaeda and other known terrorist organizations. Bush eventually expanded the war on terrorism to include enemy nations that he described as supporters of terrorist activities, such as Iraq. The president claimed that Iraq possessed weapons of mass destruction and could provide these weapons to terrorist groups.

In February 2002 the U.S. Central Intelligence Agency (CIA) sent Wilson to Africa. His mission was to investigate a British report that Hussein had tried to buy uranium in Niger so that Iraq could build nuclear weapons. Wilson determined that the reports were false. "I traveled out there, spent eight days out there, and concluded that it was impossible that this sort of transaction could be done clandestinely [secretly]," he told CNN. "It seemed that this information was inaccurate. That view was shared by the ambassador out there and largely shared in Washington even before I went out there."

Upon completing his mission, Wilson reported his findings to the U.S. ambassador to Niger, the CIA, and the State Department. He believed that his investigation had put an end to the question of whether Iraq had tried to acquire uranium from Africa. Over the next year, however, the Bush administration repeatedly referred to the story as it tried to drum up international support for the use of military force to disarm Iraq.

In January 2003 President Bush mentioned the allegations in his State of the Union address. "The British government has learned that Saddam Hussein recently sought significant quantities of uranium from Africa," he stated. In early March the head of the International Atomic Energy Agency, Mohamed El Baradei, confirmed Wilson's findings. He said the reports claiming that Iraq tried to buy uranium from Niger were "not authentic" and "unfounded." But a week later Vice President **Dick Cheney** (see entry) contradicted El Baradei on national television and claimed that Iraq was reconstituting its nuclear arms program.

Makes public statements opposing the invasion of Iraq

By this time it was clear that the United States was preparing to launch a military invasion of Iraq. Wilson opposed the war because he believed that the stated purpose of disarming Iraq could be achieved in other ways. But he also recognized that the Bush administration had broader goals for the war than simply Iraq's disarmament. As time passed Bush had expanded his rationale for war to include alleged links between Hussein and Islamic terrorists, freeing the Iraqi people from Hussein's brutal government, and installing a democratic government in Iraq to help increase political stability in the Middle East.

"I'm not against the use of force for the purposes of achieving the objective that has been agreed upon by the United Nations and the international community—disarmament," Wilson told Moyers. Wilson went on to say:

But I think disarmament is only one of the objectives. And the president has touched repeatedly and more openly on the other objectives in recent speeches, including this idea of liberating Iraq and liberating its people from a brutal dictator.... The problem really is a war which has us invading, conquering, and then subsequently occupying Iraq may not achieve that liberation that we're talking about.

Accuses the Bush administration of exaggerating the Iraq threat

The United States launched its invasion of Iraq on March 20, 2003 (March 19 in the United States). The war succeeded in removing Hussein from power after only a few weeks of fighting. On May 1, 2003, Bush announced the end of major combat operations in Iraq. Over the next few months, however, U.S. military forces struggled to maintain security in the face of Iraqi resistance and a series of terrorist attacks. In addition, a massive search failed to uncover any evidence that Iraq possessed weapons of mass destruction. The Bush administration came under increasing criticism for the intelligence (information gained through spying operations) it used to justify the war.

Wilson added fuel to this controversy in July 2003. In an article for the *New York Times,* he discussed his mission to Niger and its findings about the alleged uranium sales to Iraq. He said that the Bush administration ignored his reports and continued to claim that Iraq was trying to acquire uranium to build nuclear weapons. "Based on my experience with the [Bush] administration in the months leading up to the war, I have little choice but to conclude that some of the intelligence related to Iraq's nuclear weapons program was twisted to exaggerate the Iraqi threat," he wrote. "Either the administration has information that it has not shared with the public or ... there was selective use of facts and intelligence to bolster a decision that had already been made to go to war."

In its response to Wilson's article, the Bush administration admitted that the uranium claim should not have appeared in the president's State of the Union address. White House officials suggested that the CIA was responsible for the mistake, since it had cleared the information in the speech. A few days later CIA Director George Tenet formally accepted responsibility, stating that "These 16 words should never have been included in the text written for the president." But Tenet also claimed that members of Bush's National Security Council had pushed to include the statement.

Wife exposed as a CIA agent

As they struggled to defend themselves against Wilson's accusations, Bush administration officials also attacked Wilson's credibility. They raised questions about his political leanings, his opposition to the war, and the manner in which he was selected for the mission to Niger. A week after Wilson's article appeared, a reporter named Robert Novak published a column about the controversy. Novak reported that Wilson may have been given the Niger mission because his wife, CIA agent Valerie Plame, recommended him for it. Plame was an undercover operative working to track weapons of mass destruction. Novak said that two White House insiders had informed him of Plame's identity as an American spy.

Revealing the identity of an active CIA operative is a crime under U.S. law. In addition to endangering the agent's life and ending his or her career, uncovering an agent also can sabotage other spy operations. When they learn the identity of an American operative, foreign governments often retrace the spy's steps and become suspicious of anyone with whom he or she had contact. Nevertheless, the *Washington Post* noted that the two top White House officials had called at least six different reporters with the information about Plame. Some critics claimed that the Bush administration leaked Plame's identity on purpose in order to take revenge against Wilson.

The leak received little public attention until September 2003, when the CIA requested an official Justice Department investigation into the matter. Bush said that he welcomed the investigation and wanted the person who had leaked the information to be punished. But the incident still created a rift between the Bush administration and the CIA. As time passed and U.S. forces found no evidence of weapons of mass destruction in Iraq, the White House claimed that it had received faulty intelligence about Hussein's weapons programs. But the Wilson incident enabled the CIA to argue that Bush had ignored its warnings in his determination to go to war in Iraq.

Since that time, Wilson has continued to run his consulting business. He also has presented lectures about the war in Iraq and the difficult postwar task of forming a democratic government there. "[The Iraqi people] have tribal and ethnic cleavages [differences] that are difficult for outsiders to understand but which make up the fabric of politics and make it a very, very difficult place to govern, as history has shown," he explained to Moyers. "Coming up with a democratic system that is pluralistic [represents all segments of society], functioning, and ... not inclined to make war on other democracies, is going to be extraordinarily difficult."

Where to Learn More

"Ambassador Joseph C. Wilson IV." Interdisciplinary Humanities Center, University of California, Santa Barbara, January 2003. Available online at http://www.ihc.ucsb.edu/events/past/winter03/wilson/ (accessed on March 29, 2004).

Duffy, Michael. "Leaking with a Vengeance." *Time,* October 13, 2003.

"Evolving Untruths: How Did False Evidence Make It to the President?" *ABC News,* July 14, 2003. Available online at http://abcnews.go.com/sections/world/US/uranium030714_timeline.html (accessed on March 29, 2004).

"Ex-Envoy: Uranium Claim Unfounded." *CNN.com,* July 8, 2003. Available online at http://www.cnn.com/2003/US/07/07/cnna.wilson (accessed on March 29, 2004).

Moyers, Bill. "Bill Moyers Talks with Joseph C. Wilson IV." *PBS,* 2003. Available online at http://www.pbs.org/now/printable/transcript_wilson_print.html (accessed on March 29, 2004).

"Profile: Joseph Wilson." *BBC News,* October 1, 2003. Available online at http://news.bbc.co.uk/go/pr/fr/-/2/hi/americas/3156166.stm (accessed on March 29, 2004).

"U.S. Diplomat Raises Dossier Doubts." *BBC News,* July 7, 2003. Available online at http://news.bbc.co.uk/go/pr/fr/-/2/hi/uk_news/politics/3049894.stm (accessed on March 29, 2004).

Jeffrey Zaun

Born c. 1963
Cherry Hill, New Jersey

U.S. Navy officer captured by the Iraqis and forced to make a televised statement against the war

U.S. Navy Lieutenant Jeffrey Zaun was the navigator on an American warplane that was shot down over Iraq in the early days of the Persian Gulf War. After ejecting from the plane, he was captured by Iraqi soldiers. The Iraqis forced Zaun to appear on television and make a statement against the war. The video was broadcast around the world on CNN. Zaun's battered face created outrage at Iraq's mistreatment of coalition prisoners of war (POWs) and generated support for the war effort.

Sent to the Persian Gulf with the U.S. Navy

Jeffrey Norton Zaun was born around 1963 in Cherry Hill, New Jersey. He attended Cherry Hill High School West, where he was a member of the Reserve Officer Training Corps (ROTC) and competed on the gymnastics team. After completing high school he entered the U.S. Naval Academy in Annapolis, Maryland, graduating in 1984.

Zaun completed flight training in the navy but his poor eyesight prevented him from reaching his goal of be-

Jeffrey Zaun. ©Les Stone/Corbis Sygma. Reproduced by permission.

coming a pilot. Still hoping to fly, he trained as a weapons systems operator in the A6E Intruder fighter/bomber. The A6E is a two-man, low-altitude attack plane. Its advanced navigation and weapons systems allow it to operate at night and in all kinds of weather. It specializes in locating and attacking small targets with precision. Upon qualifying as a navigator and bombardier in the A6E, Zaun was assigned to Oceana Naval Air Station in Virginia Beach, Virginia.

On August 2, 1990, Iraqi leader **Saddam Hussein** (see entry) had ordered his military forces to invade the neighboring country of Kuwait. Hussein argued that Iraq had a historical claim to Kuwait's territory. He also wanted to control Kuwait's oil reserves and to gain access to Kuwait's port on the Persian Gulf. Countries around the world condemned the invasion and demanded that Hussein immediately withdraw his troops from Kuwait. Many of these countries then began sending military forces to the Persian Gulf region as part of a U.S.-led coalition against Iraq. The United States sent more than four hundred thousand troops to the Persian Gulf over the next six months. Zaun's squadron, Attack Squadron 35, was shipped out on the aircraft carrier USS *Saratoga* during this time. They were stationed in the Red Sea (a large body of water that runs along the west coast of Saudi Arabia).

In November 1990 the United Nations (UN) Security Council established a deadline of January 15, 1991, for Iraq to withdraw from Kuwait or face war. When Hussein failed to meet the deadline, the U.S.-led coalition launched a series of air strikes against military targets in Iraq. Zaun's squadron took part in the first wave of coalition air strikes. On January 18 Zaun flew in the backseat of an A6E piloted by Lieutenant Robert Wetzel. Their mission was to bomb the H3 Airfield in southwestern Iraq. But their plane was hit by anti-aircraft fire, and they were forced to eject over the desert. Zaun was captured by Iraqi forces and transported to Baghdad as a prisoner of war.

Forced to appear on Iraqi television

Like many other coalition POWs, Zaun was held in a dark, unsanitary cell in the basement of the Iraqi secret police headquarters. He was kept blindfolded and handcuffed for

British Royal Air Force Pilot John Peters

British Royal Air Force (RAF) pilot John Peters was another prisoner of war (POW) who was forced to appear on Iraqi television. Peters was the pilot of a Tornado GR1 fighter/bomber that was shot down on January 16, 1991, the first day of coalition air strikes against Iraq. Peters and his navigator, John Nicols, ejected from their aircraft and were captured by Iraqi troops.

After enduring four days of mental and physical torture, Peters was forced to appear on Iraqi television. Iraqi leader Saddam Hussein apparently felt that displaying coalition POWs would demonstrate his power and raise the morale of his people. In his videotape, Peters made a short statement against the war. He tried to emphasize his injuries and make it clear that he was acting against his will. "I knew I looked bad, so I deliberately put my head down and I deliberately made sure that my bad eye was towards the film," he recalled in an interview for "Frontline." Peters's video was broadcast all over the world on CNN. His bruised and battered face became a symbol of Saddam Hussein's cruelty and ruthlessness.

Peters was released on March 3, 1991. He returned to his wife, Helen, and their two sons in England. He teamed up with Nicols to write a book about their experience, *Tornado Down*, which became a best-seller. He also took part in a documentary film by the same name, which won the Independent Documentary of the Year Award for 1992.

After the war ended, Peters became a flight instructor for the RAF. In this position he instituted a cultural change program that won the 1999 Flight International Aerospace Industry Award for Training and Safety. Peters then left the RAF to attend graduate school, earning a master's degree in business administration from Leicester University.

Peters formed his own corporate development company, which specialized in helping large companies improve their teamwork, leadership, and communication skills. He became a successful motivational speaker and gave presentations around the world. His presentations provide a dramatic account of his experiences as a POW in order to inspire people to overcome their own obstacles. The audiences for his speeches have included the Queen of England, South African President Nelson Mandela, and a number of other international figures.

Sources: "Frontline Interview: John Peters." PBS. Available online at http://www.pbs.org/wgbh/pages/frontline/gulf/war/4.html (accessed on March 30, 2004); "Leadership and Motivational Speakers: John Peters." London Speaker Bureau. Available online at http://www.londonspeakerbureau.co.uk/speakers/viewSpeaker.aspx?speakerid=83 (accessed on April 9, 2004); "Peters, John G." POW Network. Available online at http://www.pownetwork.org/gulf/pd023.htm (accessed on March 30, 2004); Peters, John, with John Nicols. Tornado Down: The Horrifying True Story of Their Gulf War Ordeal. 1992.

much of his time there. He faced interrogations, severe beatings, death threats, and starvation.

On January 20 Zaun and six other coalition POWs were paraded through the streets of Baghdad. They were taken to an Iraqi television station, where they were forced to make videotaped statements against the war. In Zaun's case, an Iraqi guard pointed a gun at him and threatened to kill him if he did not do as he was told. Zaun turned his bruised and swollen face toward the camera and said, "Our leaders and our people have wrongly attacked the peaceful people of Iraq." He spoke very slowly and deliberately to make it clear that he was acting against his will.

Zaun felt guilty about making the televised statement. He admitted that the Iraqi torture broke his will, and he expressed regret that he was not as strong as some of the other coalition POWs. "I'll remember the rest of my life, a guy with a nickel-plated pistol to my head, made me make a video," he told the *New York Daily News.* "It's the worst thing I'd ever do, and I thought they'd kill me after I made the film. I don't have to tell you how mentally disturbed I was about, you know, having been on TV," he added on *ABCNews.com.*

The Iraqi video footage of the coalition POWs was broadcast around the world on CNN. Zaun's picture also appeared in countless newspapers and magazines. In fact, his battered image became known as "the face of the Persian Gulf War." Most people assumed that his cuts, bruises, and broken nose were the result of Iraqi beatings (though Zaun later admitted that some of them had been caused by ejecting from his aircraft). This created feelings of anger toward Hussein and helped increase support for the war effort. Iraq's brutal mistreatment of the POWs was a direct violation of the Geneva Conventions, a set of international rules guiding the humane treatment of military prisoners and civilians in times of warfare.

The coalition air strikes went on for nearly six weeks and caused major damage to Iraq's military capability. On February 24 the coalition launched a dramatic ground assault to force the Iraqi troops out of Kuwait. It met with little resistance from Hussein's army, which had been devastated by the air strikes. The Persian Gulf War ended on February 27, when coalition forces succeeded in liberating Kuwait from Iraqi occupation. Shortly before the end of the war, the Iraqi secret

police headquarters was destroyed by coalition bombs. U.S. military leaders were not aware that Zaun and other coalition prisoners were being held inside. "That night turned out to be pretty good because the secret police lost custody of us," Zaun remembered on *ABCNews.com*.

After being released former prisoner of war Jeffrey Zaun is greeted by Chairman of the Joint Chiefs of Staff Colin Powell and his wife, Alma. Zaun was held in captivity for forty-six days by the Iraqis during the Persian Gulf War.
Photograph by Ron Edmonds. AP/Wide World Photos. Reproduced by permission.

Regains his freedom and returns home

Zaun was released on March 4, 1991, after forty-six days in captivity. The Iraqis turned him over to the International Red Cross in Baghdad, and from there he was flown to freedom. Until that time, no one knew what had happened to his pilot, Robert Wetzel. But Wetzel was released on the same day. Zaun lost thirty pounds during his time as a POW, but his facial injuries healed and he was otherwise found healthy.

Zaun returned home to a hero's welcome. His hometown held a parade in his honor, and he told his story over and over again in the media. Zaun insisted that his ordeal was not nearly as bad as the problems faced by some other people. "To my mind, what I went through was not as emotionally troubling as losing a kid or going through a divorce. It wasn't as emotionally troubling as the problems faced by thousands of soldiers who fought in the war and are eating out of straws because of Gulf War syndrome [a collection of mysterious and often serious ailments affecting more than one hundred thousand American veterans]," he stated in the *Philadelphia Inquirer*. "I went through a severe month and a half, but I'm safe at home. I think about the Iraqis who died during the war and how they are dying like weeds because of this guy [Saddam Hussein]."

Zaun received several awards for his wartime service, including the Prisoner of War Medal and the Distinguished Flying Cross. He retired from the navy in 1998 and entered graduate school. He earned a master's degree in business administration from the Wharton School of the University of Pennsylvania in 2000. Zaun worked as an investment banker in New York City for a while. When he was laid off, he returned home to Cherry Hill to conduct his job search. "I'm famous for being shot down and, hey, I got shot down again, but I will survive that, too," he told the *Philadelphia Inquirer*.

In 2002 Zaun joined a group of sixteen other Gulf War POWs and their families in filing a lawsuit against Saddam Hussein and the government of Iraq. They asked for $910 million in compensation for the unlawful mistreatment they suffered during the war. The group hoped to claim their settlement from the $1.7 billion in Iraqi assets that remained frozen in American banks. "I never got to my target in the Gulf War," Zaun said in the *All POW-MIA InterNetwork*. "I'd really like to get a piece of him [Saddam Hussein]."

As it appeared likely that the U.S. military would launch another war against Iraq in 2003, Zaun expressed support for the idea of removing Hussein from power and bringing democracy to Iraq. After all, he had experienced the brutality of Hussein's government firsthand. "There's a sinking feeling that it's the least bad alternative to have to fight over there again," he noted in the *New York Daily News*. "It's an ugly place; the people are suffering there."

Where to Learn More

Colimore, Edward. "Gulf War Hero Is Broke, and Back at Home." *Philadelphia Inquirer,* January 26, 2003. Available online at http://www.philly.com/mld/inquirer/5033103.htm (accessed on March 30, 2004).

"Ex-POWs Demanding Millions from Iraq." *AII POW-MIA InterNetwork.* Available online at http://www.aiipowmia.com/inter23/in032403suit.html (accessed on March 30, 2004).

O'Shaughnessy, Patrice. "Payback from POWs Savaged by Saddam." *New York Daily News,* February 16, 2003. Available online at http://www.nydailynews.com/front/story/60173p-56204c.html (accessed on March 30, 2004).

"Saddam's Wrath: Gulf War POWs Tell of Horrors Troops Could Face." *ABCNews.com,* March 14, 2003. Available online at http://abcnews.go.com/sections/2020/world/2020_gulfpows030314.html (accessed on March 30, 2004).

"Zaun, Jeffrey Norton." *POW Network.* Available online at http://www.pownetwork.org/gulf/zd020.htm (accessed on March 30, 2004).

Where to Learn More

The following list focuses on works written for readers of middle school or high school age. Books aimed at adult readers have been included when they are especially important in providing information or analysis that would otherwise be unavailable.

Books

Al-Khalil, Samir. *Republic of Fear: The Inside Story of Saddam's Iraq.* Berkeley: University of California Press, 1989.

Al-Radi, Nuha. *Baghdad Diaries: A Woman's Chronicle of War and Exile.* New York: Vintage, 2003.

Alterman, Eric, and Mark J. Green. *The Book on Bush: How George W. (Mis)leads America.* New York: Viking, 2004.

Atkinson, Rick. *In the Company of Soldiers: A Chronicle of Combat.* New York: Holt, 2003.

Boyne, Walter J. *Operation Iraqi Freedom: What Went Right, What Went Wrong, and Why.* New York: Forge, 2003.

Cipkowski, Peter. *Understanding the Crisis in the Persian Gulf.* New York: John Wiley, 1992.

Cronkite, Walter. *LIFE: The War in Iraq.* New York: Time Life Books, 2003.

Editors of *Time* Magazine. *21 Days to Baghdad: Photos and Dispatches from the Battlefield.* New York: Time Life Books, 2003.

Foster, Leila M. *The Story of the Persian Gulf War.* Chicago: Children's Press, 1991.

Frum, David. *The Right Man: The Surprise Presidency of George W. Bush.* New York: Random House, 2003.

Garrels, Anne. *Naked in Baghdad: The Iraq War as Seen by NPR's Correspondent.* New York: Farrar, Straus, and Giroux, 2003.

Goldschmidt, Arthur. *A Concise History of the Middle East.* Boulder, CO: Westview Press, 1989.

Haskins, James. *Colin Powell: A Biography.* New York: Scholastic, 1992.

Katovsky, Bill, and Timothy Carlson. *Embedded: The Media at War in Iraq.* Guilford, CT: Lyons Press, 2003.

Kent, Zachary. *George Bush.* Chicago: Children's Press, 1993.

Kent, Zachary. *The Persian Gulf War: The Mother of All Battles.* Hillside, NJ: Enslow, 1994.

King, John. *The Gulf War.* New York: Dillon Press, 1991.

Lehr, Heather. *The Kurds.* Philadelphia: Chelsea House, 2003.

Miller, Judith, and Laurie Mylroie. *Saddam Hussein and the Crisis in the Gulf.* New York: Times Books, 1990.

Moore, Robin. *Hunting down Saddam: The Inside Story of the Search and Capture.* New York: St. Martin's, 2004.

NBC Enterprises. *Operation Iraqi Freedom: The Inside Story.* New York: NBC, 2003.

Pax, Salam. *Salam Pax: The Clandestine Diary of an Ordinary Iraqi.* New York: Grove Press, 2003.

Pimlott, John. *Middle East: A Background to the Conflicts.* New York: Franklin Watts, 1991.

Purdum, Todd S., and the staff of the *New York Times.* *A Time of Our Choosing: America's War in Iraq.* New York: Times Books, 2003.

Rai, Milan. *War Plan Iraq.* London: Verso, 2002.

Renfrew, Nita. *Saddam Hussein.* New York: Chelsea House, 1992.

Richie, Jason. *Iraq and the Fall of Saddam Hussein.* Minneapolis: Oliver Press, 2003.

Ridgeway, James. *The March to War.* New York: Four Walls Eight Windows, 1991.

Rivera, Sheila. *Operation Iraqi Freedom.* Edina, MN: Abdo, 2004.

Rivera, Sheila. *Rebuilding Iraq.* Edina, MN: Abdo, 2003.

Rooney, Ben. *The Daily Telegraph War on Saddam: The Complete Story of the Iraq Campaign.* London: Robinson, 2003.

Ryan, Mike. *Baghdad or Bust: The Inside Story of Gulf War II.* Yorkshire, UK: Leo Cooper, 2003.

Salzman, Marian, and Anne O'Reilly. *War and Peace in the Persian Gulf: What Teenagers Want to Know.* Princeton, NJ: Petersen's Guides, 1991.

Sasson, Jean P. *The Rape of Kuwait: The True Story of Iraq's Atrocities against a Civilian People.* New York: Knightsbridge, 1991.

Scheer, Christopher. *The Five Biggest Lies Bush Told about Iraq.* New York: Akashic Books, 2003.

Sciolino, Elaine. *The Outlaw State: Saddam Hussein's Quest for Power and the Gulf Crisis.* New York: John Wiley, 1991.

Sifry, Micah L., and Christopher Serf, eds. *The Iraq War Reader.* New York: Simon and Schuster, 2003.

Steloff, Rebecca. *Norman Schwarzkopf.* New York: Chelsea House, 1992.

White, Thomas E., et al. *Reconstructing Eden: A Comprehensive Plan for the Postwar Political and Economic Development of Iraq.* Houston: Country Watch, 2003.

Videos and DVDs

CNN Presents: The War in Iraq—The Road to Baghdad. Wea Corp, 2003.

National Geographic: 21 Days to Baghdad. Warner Home Video, 2003.

Nightline: War against Iraq Begins. Mpi Home Video, 2001.

21st Century Guide to Operation Iraqi Freedom. U.S. Department of Defense, 2003.

War in the Desert. Red Distribution, Inc., 2003.

Web Sites

"Fog of War." *Washington Post.* Available at http://www.washington-post.com/wp-srv/inatl/longterm/fogofwar/fogofwar.htm (last accessed on May 13, 2004).

Frontline: The Gulf War. Available at http://www.pbs.org/wgbh/pages/frontline/gulf (last accessed on May 13, 2004).

Gulf Hello. Available at http://www.persiangulf.com (last accessed on May 13, 2004).

Gulf War.com. Available at http://www.gulfwar.com (last accessed on May 13, 2004).

Gulf War Index. Available at http://www.britains-smallwars.com/gulf/index.html (last accessed on May 7, 2003).

"The New Iraq." PBS *Online NewsHour.* Available at http://www.pbs.org/newshour/bb/middle_east/iraq/index.html (last accessed on May 13, 2004).

"War in Iraq." *CNN.com.* Available at http://www.cnn.com/SPECIALS/2003/iraq/index.html (last accessed on May 13, 2004).

Index

Bold type indicates main
entries and their page
numbers. Illustrations are
marked by (ill.)

H

Heath, Ted 245

Holliman, John 21, 25

Hussein ibn Talal 9, **141–48**, 141 (ill.), 146 (ill.), 238

Hussein, Qusay 151

Hussein, Saddam 16 (ill.), 24, 27–28, 32–34, 38, 41, 49, 52, 56, 67, 69, 73, 78, 80, 96, 98, 146 (ill.), **149–59**, 149 (ill.), 158 (ill.), 188, 191, 195, 212, 222, 236, 266

as a military leader 224

capture of 61, 158–59

decision to invade Kuwait 135–38, 153–54, 205-06

Iraqi opposition to 85

meeting with U.S. Ambassador April Glaspie 137–39, 254

meeting with U.S. Ambassador Joseph Wilson 254–55

popularity among Palestinians 15, 145–46

Hussein, Uday 151, 213

I

I Am a Soldier, Too: The Jessica Lynch Story 167

IGC

   See Iraq Governing Council (IGC)

INC

   See Iraqi National Congress

Intifada 14, 230

Iran 2, 205

Iran-Iraq War 34, 136, 145, 152, 205

Iraq

   1991 uprisings in 155–56

   postwar reconstruction of 57–61, 81, 106, 200, 260

   postwar security problems in 52, 57–61, 81, 189, 200, 258

   resistance to U.S. occupation 60, 81, 158, 189, 200, 258

   treatment of coalition prisoners of war 238–39, 262–64, 266

   treatment of Kuwaiti citizens during occupation of Kuwait 207, 209

   United Nations economic sanctions against 156, 185, 213

   United Nations weapons inspections in 37, 50, 79, 156–57, 177, 213

   use of chemical weapons against Kurdish population 153

   use of foreign citizens as "human shields" 255

   weapons of mass destruction in 37, 50–52, 98, 156–57, 177, 188–89, 195, 253, 258–59

Iraq Governing Council (IGC) 60, 87, 90

Iraqi National Congress (INC) 83, 85

Islam 126

Israel 12, 14, 142, 147, 155, 227, 229

   decision not to enter the 1991 Persian Gulf War 231

Israeli-Palestinian conflict 12–14, 18–19, 142–43, 229–30

It Doesn't Take a Hero 225

J

John Paul II, Pope 37

Jordan

   history of 142–44

   Palestinian population of 144

   support of Iraq during 1991 Persian Gulf War 145–46

K

Kent, Arthur 6–7

Khomeini, Ayatollah Ruhollah 2, 34, 152

King Hussein of Jordan

   See Hussein ibn Talal

Kurdish refugee crisis 5

Kurds 5, 153, 156

Kuwait 35, 137, 153

   damage from 1991 Persian Gulf War 207–09

   history of 203–04

   Palestinian population of 15